Obama's Political Saga

Obama's Political Saga

From Battling History, Racialized Rhetoric, and GOP Obstructionism to Re-Election

Mary L. Rucker

LEXINGTON BOOKS
Lanham • Boulder • New York • Toronto • Plymouth, UK

Published by Lexington Books
A wholly owned subsidiary of The Rowman & Littlefield Publishing Group, Inc.
4501 Forbes Boulevard, Suite 200, Lanham, Maryland 20706
www.rowman.com

10 Thornbury Road, Plymouth PL6 7PP, United Kingdom

British Library Cataloguing in Publication Information Available

Library of Congress Cataloging-in-Publication Data

Rucker, Mary L.
Obama's political saga : from battling history, racialized rhetoric, and GOP obstructionism to re-
election / Mary L. Rucker.
pages cm
Includes bibliographical references and index.
ISBN 978-0-7391-8290-1 (cloth : alk. paper) — ISBN 978-0-7391-8291-8 (electronic)
1. Obama, Barack. 2. Obama, Barack—Political and social views. 3. United States—Politics and
government—2009– 4. Politics, Practical—United States—History—21st century. 5. Political culture—United States—History—21st century. I. Title.
E908.3.R84 2013
973.932092—dc23
2013016657

Printed in the United States of America

This book is dedicated to my heavenly Father,
in the name of my Lord and Savior Jesus Christ
to whom I give the glory, honor, and praise.

Contents

List of Tables   ix

Foreword   xi

Preface   xiii

Acknowledgments   xix

1 Battling History: Obama, Systemic Racism, and Colorism   1

2 The Obama Presidency: A Backlash of Racism and
       Conservative Radicalism   47

3 The Media: Transmitters of Eliminationist and Racialized
       Rhetoric   79

4 American "Exceptionalism": Roots, Racism, and Obama   105

5 The Re-Election of Barack Obama: "The People Spoke"   133

Bibliography   153

Index   165

About the Author   173

List of Tables

Table 2.1   Repatriation in 2004.   51

Table 2.2   What Some Top U.S. Companies Pay in Taxes.   52

Table 2.3   Where Americans Favor and Oppose Cuts.   61

Table 3.1   Approval of U.S. in 16 Foreign Countries.   82

Table 3.2   GOP Eliminationist Rhetoric.   89

Foreword

I was honored when Dr. Mary Rucker first approached me about writing the foreword for this book. Dr. Rucker is both an educator and prolific writer with a passion for scholarship. In *Obama's Political Saga: From Battling History, Racialized Rhetoric, and GOP Obstructionism to Re-Election*, Dr. Rucker dissects the communication process then uses the theoretical microscope to scrutinize the inner workings of the phenomena that helped to catapult Barack Obama from obscurity to presidency to re-election.

In this book, Dr. Rucker uses systemic racism to provide the reader with the tools needed to delve below the surface of what is presented as reality in our sound bite culture to analyze the messages that shape the American electorate's perception of Obama and the racialized rhetoric he has endured. The thrust behind this book is to emancipate the disenfranchised, as well as the middle class, from the cultural and ideological dominance of the political and media elite so as to create a new self-awareness that serves to liberate them from limiting ideologies.

No doubt, this book will challenge the reader to examine the assumptions that have influenced how one views the world of politics and the media. So you'll have to closely follow Dr. Rucker's exposition of the historical framework she used to analyze Obama's experience as the first African American president, the current state of politics, and the media and the role each plays in the oppression of members of society.

Dr. Rucker moves beyond merely pointing out the problem of the subjugation of the less powerful members of society. She demonstrates that Barack Obama's rise to the presidency has provided a ray of hope for those who have lacked a champion for their cause. As Mary Engelbreit so aptly put it, "If you don't like something change it; if you can't change it, change the way you think about it."

Roosevelt Quick II

Preface

Naturally, Americans of color, more specifically the African American electorate, were excited about the election and re-election of Barack Obama and were enthusiastic to witness history in the making. The whole world was tuned in to the television when Obama won the 2008 election. And again, America and the rest of the world stood by to witness whether President Obama would win or lose his bid for re-election in 2012 — they witnessed the electorate giving Barack Hussein Obama a second term to lead this nation.

It was a very emotional time for those who had waited for this day to happen. After slavery, the Jim Crow era, and outright discrimination that prompted the civil rights movement, many white Americans and Americans of color were pleased with the outcome of the election. It must be noted that the African American community was under no illusion that Barack Obama could do away with centuries of racism following the election.

W .E. B. DuBois had warned that race and color would still plague this society in the twentieth century. DuBois was correct in his assessment, but the problem of race and color has been carried into the twenty-first century. Even though racism had gone underground, it raised its ugly head with the election of Obama, emerged from underground, and began launching vitriol attacks and retribution on the first African American president. However, overt racism goes underground when everything is skewed in favor of white America and re-emerges when white America feels threatened, for example, when they perceive that Americans of color are benefitting from the limited resources, as a result of the election of a black President. In spite of Obama's rise to the presidency, racism is still a problem in twenty-first-century America and remains a recurring problem for Americans of color.

As American society moved from liberalism to conservatism and universalism to particularism, racist partisan narratives began construing Obama as America's number one enemy, refusing to acknowledge his U.S. citizenship, and remaining silent about his numerous accomplishments in his first term. Conservative radicals claimed that Obama was advancing a socialist agenda, immersing himself in African American radicalism, and pushing big-goverment liberal policies. These dialogues "peddled division and discord"[1] among the American electorate and turned the attention of the American people away from the real problems of the country, namely self-serving politics and the power and greed that "trump trust and benevolence."[2] Looking at the deep-seated racism toward Americans of color and the first black president, *Obama's Political Saga: From Battling History, Racialized Rhetoric, and GOP Obstructionism to Re-Election* is a counterpoint to the anti-narratives that have paralyzed this nation and interfered with Obama's ability to get things done.

Barack Hussein Obama's presidency initially provided an avenue of hope for the voiceless and the oppressed. But some scholars believe that since then Obama's politics of hope has been transformed into the politics of accommodation and compromise.[3] Although Obama's politics of difference provided a ray of hope to the oppressed and their dissatisfaction with a depressed economy, his politics have been constrained by the very democratic institutions that made it possible for him to rise to the presidency.[4] Consequently, Obama has been at the receiving end of hatred, where radical conservative ideologues, systemic racism, and eliminationist and racialized rhetoric, have contaminated the public's perception about his ability to lead as a black man.

As a political force in demand for social change, Obama was made for a new era. His victories in both national and international spaces reveal his increasing inability to exercise the most fundamental power of the presidency, the power to restore the people's confidence in American democracy. To restore this confidence fully, Obama needs to make more radical change on behalf of the American people. Radical in this case does not mean Tea Party radicalism that operates outside the mainstream, the kind of radicalism that drives the Tea Party adamantine to impose economic austerity measures on limited government.[5] If we follow Obama's demonstrated desire for "bipartisanship, we can have productive debates" about what he desires to accomplish for the American people.[6]

FOCUS OF THE BOOK

Through a systemic racism lens, this book examines the many ways systems of oppression have shaped the lives of Americans of color and how the system of oppression has affected the presidency of Barack Obama. I focus on the enactment of systemic racism and how this has been perpetuated against the Obama presidency, relying on extant literature about the African American experience. I also use examples of blatant racism against Obama in the form of attacks. The research used in this book is drawn from diverse sources: academic research, the media (major newspapers, online sources), and recent articles (conservative and progressive) written about Obama. In contrast to the majority of the books about Obama, which are written about his campaign and more often than not by journalists, this book focuses on his still evolving presidency, from a more or less academic perspective.

In this book, I hope to accomplish four goals. First, I desire to extend the political communication literature to include the political experiences of the first black president of America, including how racism constrained his presidency in his first term and details of the theoretical tools used to develop this. Second, I bring a systemic racism lens to the exploration of how racism in the form of strident, eliminationist, and racialized rhetoric has contributed to the rise of radicalism and retribution against the Obama administration. Third, it is not my intent to inform Americans of color, more specifically African Americans, that the election of a black president mean we live in a post-racial society, nor can his election eliminate economic, political, and social inequality and injustice among minority racial groups. Fourth, I hope this book contributes to the literature on Americans of color, with an aim to show how the heightened disrespect for the first African American president, in general, can help Americans rethink their experiences about systemic racism and the notion that Americans need to demand social change.

The target audience for this book includes academics, specifically students and professors of communication, political science, and sociology. In the field of communication, this book can be used in organizational communication; race, class and gender, political communication, and special topics in communication courses. In political science, this book can be used in political life, American national government, political parties, modern political ideologies, American presidency, American politics, and American public policy analysis courses. In sociology, this book can be used in political sociology and courses in selected studies, such as social change. Finally, this book can be read by a general audience of people concerned about the political future of this country.

DEFINITIONS AND TERMINOLOGY

Following is a brief introduction to certain concepts used throughout this book. "African American" and "black" are used interchangeably.

Systemic racism is an oppressive system designed by the white elite to exclude African Americans and other Americans of color from participating in the economic, social, and political life of the United States. From the time slavery was instituted in America, racism became systemic in American society. After African Americans were nationally emancipated from slavery, they have continually fought for racial equality and justice, and the fight still consumes their lives today.

Radicalism is an effort to uproot, dismantle, or reform established laws. An example would be the bill passed by the Arizona House in response to the birther debate over Obama's citizenship that would require presidential candidates to show their birth certificates should they want their names placed on the state's ballot. I call this "white radicalism" because whites have the power to change or reform laws. Beyond this, radicalism is also used in connection with certain states to suppress voter rights and politicize women's bodies by denying them their constitutional rights to make their own decisions about their bodies.

Retribution means to punish Obama, Americans of color, and women for daring to fight for their constitutional rights. This retribution is exacted in the form of physical abuse and threatening language for what whites perceive as a violation of racist laws. When African Americans insisted on their rights during the Civil Rights movement, the force of violence was used to stop them from achieving their rights and also to stop them from expanding their participation in American society. Many of them were beaten and murdered for challenging both the status quo and the racist institutions of this country. Martin Luther King's non-violent resistance strategy minimized the use of harsh physical force by white citizens and by officers of the law against movement members.

Obstructionism means to deliberately interfere with the progress of the president in making changes to the infrastructure of the country that would benefit all Americans, and not just a few.

Eliminationist and racialized rhetoric means mean-spirited political discourse or rhetoric that suggests an opponent is illegitimate and should be eliminated. David Neiwert explains that eliminationist rhetoric "advocates the excision and extermination of enemies by violent, civil, [and political] means."[7]

OVERVIEW OF THE BOOK

Chapter 1, "Battling History: Obama, Systemic Racism, and Colorism," provides an overview of systemic racism and overt white retribution against African Americans during the pre- and post-civil rights era, and details on how this marred Obama's presidency. This chapter suggests that Obama is viewed through a different lens, the white racial frame, when compared to his predecessors and that in this context he is a subject of vicious racist attacks. This chapter also examines colorism, the role it plays in society, and how it affects Obama as an African American. Colorism is the rejection of dark-complexioned blacks by light complexioned people, a system of oppression that started in the era of slavery and continues today.

Chapter 2, "The Obama Presidency: A Backlash of Racism and Conservative Radicalism," examines the problems the Obama administration had inherited from earlier administrations, and the partisan politics and obstructionist tactics of the conservative right that suppressed Obama's ability to resurrect this country from the ashes of a depressed economy caused by the policies of George W. Bush and Congressional Republicans. I examine the effects of special interests, reified politics, ideological hegemony, and how these corrupt democracy, magnified by systemic racism and sexism. In essence, we have a black man being constrained by the power elite in his attempts to make the country a better place for all working class Americans and Americans of color, and this constraint by the conservative right has been relentless.

Chapter 3, "The Media: Transmitters of Eliminationist and Racialized Rhetoric," examines the media, specifically conservative media outlets like Fox News, that serve as an incubator for eliminationist and racialized rhetoric to influence the opinions and perceptions of the American electorate against Obama and his policies. I also examine how media coverage lends itself to sectional interests, frames political discourse, and creates and perpetuates ideological hegemony that obscures and obstructs the political process. Using the Wisconsin and Ohio union busting protests as examples, I discuss how the media is used as a positive force of change as Americans today are beginning to organize, protest, and challenge a broken political system in order to reclaim democracy.

Chapter 4, "American 'Exceptionalism': Roots, Racism, and Obama," defines American exceptionalism, traces its historical roots (including the related concept of manifest destiny) and modern interpretations of it. I examine the big government versus small government debate and how these terms are used and misused in the ideological battle between the two major political parties. I also explore Obama's commitment to American democracy and American exceptionalism. Because Obama's political initiatives have received little attention amidst eliminationist and racialized rhetoric and there are claims that he is anti-American, I examine the economic crisis that resulted directly from policies of deregulation that were put in place during the preceding two decades by Obama's predecessors Bill Clinton and George W. Bush. Yet, some Americans that held Obama himself responsible for failing to restore prosperity, and criticized the steps he took including the stimulus package and bank bailout, which most observers agree in fact helped prevent an even deeper crisis saw that he was not responsible for this crisis. So incoherent is the American public debate on this that Obama's critics simultaneously blamed him for an economic situation he did nothing to cause and also opposed larger infusions of money into the economy through much greater government spending, which is the only option that might directly address the problem and keep the economy away from a free fall.

Chapter 5, "The Re-Election of Barack Obama: 'The People Spoke'" redresses issues discussed in the previous chapters. The American electorate spoke and made the decision to re-elect Barack Obama for a second term, in spite of the GOP's efforts to make him a one-term president through obstructionist behavior, the use of racialized rhetoric, and the use of voter suppression to defeat him at the ballot box. This chapter goes on to discuss how changing demographics and the voices of women and

Americans of color are demanding to be part of the national conversation concerning the issues that concern them most. Finally, this chapter offers emancipatory ways (understanding, critique, and education) that the American electorate can use to equip themselves with the necessary political knowledge, to demand change, and to help Obama re-write his political saga in his second term.

NOTES

1. Will Bunch, *The Backlash: Right-wing Radicals, High-Def Hucksters, and Paranoid Politics in the Age of Obama*, cover flap (New York: HarperCollins, 2010).

2. Ibid.

3. Henry A. Giroux, *Politics After Hope: Obama and the Crisis of Youth, Race and Democracy* (Boulder, CO: Paradigm Publishers, 2010), 15.

4. James T. Kloppenberg, *Reading Obama: Dreams, Hope and the American Political Tradition* (Princeton, NJ: Princeton University Press, 2010), X.

5. Robert Kuttner, *Obama's Challenge: America's Economic Crisis and the Power of a Transformative Presidency* (White River Junction, VT: Chelsea Green Publishing Company, 2008), Kindle Electronic Edition, Paragraph 2, Location 110 of 3263.

6. Roy L. Brooks, *Racial Justice in the Age of Obama* (Princeton, NJ: Princeton University Press), xvi.

7. David Neiwert, *The Eliminationists: How Hate Talk Radicalized the American Right* (Sausalito, CA: PolitiPointPress, 2009), 12.

Acknowledgments

My interest in writing about President Barack Hussein Obama started long after he entered the presidential race. He was relatively unknown to me, and I allowed a racist culture make me believe that a black man could never become president, at least no time soon. It was my department chair, Dr. Melissa Spirek of Wright State University, to whom I extend my deepest gratitude who sparked my interest in lecturing on and writing about Obama. Dr. Spirek hosted a panel for the 2008 presidential race, and together with Dr. Donna Schlagheck, chair of the Political Science department, hosted a special session for the 2012 presidential race that shaped the outcome of the final chapter in this book.

Other scholars have helped to shape the arguments in this book. To Ella C. McFadden and Professor Joe R. Feagin at Texas A&M University, I owe my deepest gratitude for reading the first three chapters of the initial draft of this book. Professor Feagin pushed me to clarity, suggested I use systemic racism to undergird my arguments, and advised me to write about the unprecedented attacks on President Obama. I thank my good friend and colleague Professor Theresa Myadze for being my sounding board. She and I have written journal articles about the obstructionist relationship between Obama and Congressional Republicans and how this relationship has heightened our awareness of what it means to be black in America. I also thank my long-time good friend Elder George D. Johnson for his prayers and the any hours we spent on the phone discussing the political saga of the first African American president. Our discussions were lively and informative and his calm patience is much appreciated. To my Interim Pastor, Supt. H. Douglas McMahon, Sr., I thank him for his prayers and encouragement. He had no doubt the book would get published.

I also thank Justin Race, a positive, patient, and encouraging editor with whom I have had a fruitful relationship, and his assistant, Alissa Parra, for easing me through the process of producing this book. Justin's encouragement from the outset has been remarkable.

ONE

Battling History

Obama, Systemic Racism, and Colorism

"[T]he path to a more perfect union means acknowledging that what ails the African-American community does not just exist in the minds of black people; that the legacy of discrimination—and current incidents of discrimination, while less overt than in the past—are real and must be addressed." —Senator Barack Obama, "A More Perfect Union" Speech, Philadelphia (March 18, 2008)

The election of Barack Hussein Obama was a historic one, bringing to the forefront the intersection of race, class, gender, and welcoming the changing demographics that catapulted him to the presidency. As the first African American elected to the most coveted and powerful office of the United States, Obama signaled the end of an era that the presidency is no longer limited to white males only. When Obama was elected president in 2008, "enthusiasm swept over the world," and close to two million people attended his inauguration, a number unmatched by any of his predecessors, making him a unique historic figure.[1] The participants in the second inauguration parade represented the changing demographics of participants, including Native Americans, which also lent itself to the uniqueness of this historic event. From the start, history and U.S. society placed a different set of expectations and standards on Obama, far more than those placed on any of his predecessors.[2] This is not an atypical expectation for the first African American president. Historically, more stringent higher expectations and standards have been placed on African Americans than whites. No matter how well African Americans perform or how intellectually astute they are, they are typically treated as "*The Other*." Grounded in a racist history, African Americans will never be viewed on the same level as whites or recognized for their achieve-

1

ments, unless these achievements are in the sports area. Could Obama's overwhelming victory mean that America feels a need to be cleansed from its racist past, where many white Americans have consciously and/ or unconsciously served as the purveyors of racism? Some social theorists believe in this notion and suggest in their scholarship that the election of Obama has somewhat redeemed America of its racist past, thus creating a post-racial era.[3]

Despite its auspicious start, the Obama presidency has been marred by conspicuous overtones of racism, retribution, and radicalism. As will be discussed later in this chapter, Obama has been the constant subject of blatant racist attacks, racialized rhetoric, and Republican (GOP) obstructionism. Consequently, the GOP has undermined and prevented him from exercising the necessary leadership to address the country's most pressing challenge, the unemployment problem. It was noted in *The New York Times* that "The truth, rarely heard [during the GOP National Convention] in Tampa, Florida, is that the Republicans charted a course of denial and obstruction from the day Mr. Obama was elected, determined to deny him a second term by denying him any achievement, no matter the cost to the economy or American security." Here, former House Speaker Newt Gingrich, Majority Leader Eric Cantor, Majority Whip Kevin McCarthy, U.S. Representative and vice presidential candidate Paul Ryan, and other Obama haters conspired to obstruct Obama's success and used Fox News to persuade a large number of low-information Americans that Obama's economic policies would fail them. These men agreed to "show a united and unyielding opposition to the President's economic policies. . . . [As a result, then] Minority Whip Cantor would hold the House Republicans to a unanimous 'No' [vote] against Obama's economic plan. They agreed to begin attacking vulnerable Democrats on the airwaves and run attack ads. Win the spear point of the House in 2010. Jab Obama relentlessly in 2011. Win the White House and the Senate in 2012."[4] The problem Obama faced as president was the unresolved problem in this country's history, the unresolved problem of race and racial oppression against African Americans in particular.

So why have racism and conservative radicalism dominated our intellectual life and undermined the great ideals that gave America its strength and character? Why is the Obama presidency inflicted with the hucksterism of the radical right that demonizes him? Have these hucksters been designated as what Ishmael Reed calls "the nigger breakers"?[5] To answer these questions, we must appreciate the relationship between ideological hegemony, ideological warfare, and ideological power that developed in America and the racism on which America was founded. This chapter goes on to examine a brief history of systemic racism in this country, the effects of colorism on African Americans, a divisive phenomenon of pitting lighter-skinned and darker-skinned African

Americans against each other, which has its beginnings in slavery and has modern-day implications for Obama.

A BRIEF HISTORY OF SYSTEMIC RACISM

While it is not the intent of this book to provide a discussion about slavery in 1619, when the first ship of Africans was forced into involuntary labor in the North American British colonies, this is where systemic racism begins for African Americans. From the time of slavery and throughout the history of America, systemic racism has affected all institutions in every realm—politics, economics, the arts, religion, and so forth.

At the time the Declaration of Independence was being drafted by the founding fathers who also owned slaves, the U.S. economy relied heavily on slave labor to build this nation. Americans have been ill-informed about the history of this nation, and few Americans are aware that slaves built the White House and the U.S. Capitol and most mainstream historians have given little attention to the contributions that slaves made in building these architectural structures.[6] While the founding fathers wrote that all men are created equal, are endowed by God with the same rights, and are entitled to the pursuit of happiness without any interference, they were depriving African Americans of "all privileges of humanity—of their historic memories, of something as fundamental as the family, and of their language and customs without, however, having acquired any claim to European privileges."[7] By doing so, they laid the foundation for systemic racism to pervade every institution for generations to come. Racism has affected some consciously and others unconsciously, and lives deep within our psyche, whether we are the victims or the victors.

The institution of American slavery was about the oppression and degradation of people of African descent.[8] It has its roots in the theological ideas that justified slavery and past and present racism, but the roots of racism trace back much further than slavery in the South. It can be traced to the racist attitudes of the Puritans in the North. White northerners had used theological ideas to justify slavery and racism before they turned on their southern counterpart to claim that slavery was evil.[9] The seeds of racism were deliberately planted in U.S. institutional structures, and a hybridization of ideas, including Christian-supported ideas that gave birth to white supremacy, fostered the idea that God consigned African Americans to an inferior status who were not fit to commune with the rest of humanity, specifically white humanity.[10] White clergy legitimated racism and gave white America their blessings and the moral justification to practice conscious and/or unconscious racism against African Americans and other Americans of color. Here lies the problem. Since racism has been morally and legally justified, that makes it difficult for African Americans to fight their cause even before the U.S. Supreme Court. It is easier for other racial groups to fight discrimination before the high court than it is for African Americans. From a Eurocentric perspective, God, Bible themes, and the arts were portrayed in the image of whites that contributed to white superiority and Americans of color inferiority.[11] Consequently, whites can easily take white privilege and racism for granted.

In 1861, Congress passed the Confiscation Act, officially entitling the government to confiscate any property, including slaves as property, used in confederate insurrections against the government.[12] This law, among others, made African Americans inferior to whites and justified social institutions and laws that privileged whites. These laws created a mentality of hatred and violence in many white Americans that were justified by laws deeming African Americans as inferior beings to be demonized as evil, unfit lowly beings who were cursed by God and worthy of white oppression, a similar justification Nazi Germany used to mistreat the Jews between 1933 and 1945, before exterminating six million of them.

After the Civil War, white men of power continued to create an America that privileged whites and marginalized African Americans, thus creating an "unjust, deeply institutionalized, ongoing intergenerational reproduction of white wealth, power, and privilege," while simultaneously creating an unjust system of intergenerational transmission of poverty among African Americans.[13] Despite the end of slavery by constitutional amendment in 1865, many states passed laws that systematically discriminated against African Americans in areas from housing to politics, and the power elite wanted to transform American society into a homogenous white one.[14] In 1868, the Fourteenth Amendment gave African Americans the right to citizenship, but these rights were scaled back during the Jim Crow era in the South. While the Mississippi Black Code of 1865 gave free blacks the rights and responsibilities of citizenship, the ruling elite limited those rights to advantage whites over blacks in order to maintain the antebellum order. A free black, for example, was prohibited from breaking a labor contract with a white person, even if the white cheated the black in his wages. From a black perspective, this illusory law was clearly designed to ensure that former slaves stayed under the oppressive and exploitative control of whites, which fueled ignorance and poverty among African Americans for generations to come.[15] Other rights, such as the right to marry, were truncated and sharply defined for African Americans. As the Mississippi Code reads, "it shall not be lawful for any freedman, free Negro, or mulatto to intermarry with any white person."[16] Though the same code prohibited whites from marrying African Americans, the intent was to keep the white race pure from inferior black blood, commonly known as the "one-drop rule." The one-drop rule posits that anyone born with even one drop of black blood in his or her veins is considered black. In reverse, this rule suggests that the whole of white blood is less potent than even one strain of black blood. What African Americans experienced in American society under the Jim Crow laws is similar to what European Jewry experienced under Nazi tyranny. This one-drop rule is discussed in connection with colorism.

As late as 1896, nearly fifty years after the Civil War, the U.S. Supreme Court handed down its decision in *Plessy v. Ferguson*. At issue was a Louisiana law that mandated "separate but equal" accommodations for blacks and whites. Under this law, southern states pretended to provide blacks with equal accommodations, but these accommodations were inferior to the accommodations that whites enjoyed. Basically, this law paved the way for the segregation of public facilities until the Civil Rights Movement of the 1960s. Social and economic advancement of African Americans was stalled by limiting their educational opportunities. Many of these injustices that created opportunities for whites have not been resolved for more than seventy-five years, and inequality still prevails in the United States. Obama has tried to make it possible for all Americans to have equal access to opportunity, which the power elite resists and part of a misinformed electorate denies.

When African Americans attempted to take their self-determination— economic situation—into their own hands, it was met with white hostile resistance. In the early 1900s, blacks formed prosperous communities in Rosewood, Florida; and Tulsa, Oklahoma. Since these African Americans like many others were denied access to white doctors, local hospitals, dentists, and food chains, they created and became the granary of their own economic vitality. However, these prosperous black communities angered local whites because blacks would not have to rely on white handouts and would destroy whites' negative view of them. And if this negative view is destroyed, then whites could not use blacks as a scapegoat for their own economic woes. With the blessings of the power elite, white mobs destroyed these prosperous communities under the pretext of the black rapist myth, where white women's bodies and the black male phallus were politicized for destructive purposes. This was the only way whites could falsely justify their unrighteous indignation against a people that wanted to determine their own destiny apart from a system whites used to keep blacks oppressed.

The white mob could not accept that African Americans could build prosperous lives independent of whites and live as well as or better than poorer whites in segregated southern towns. Although these towns were in the South, northern towns were equally exclusionary. They "simply chose not to let blacks live among them: they violently drove them out of their communities en masse and forbade them to return thereafter."[17] Perhaps this is one reason some states, such as Montana, Utah, North Dakota, and Wyoming have a low black population and embrace the conservative ideology. As a consequence, "there has never been an adequate accounting of the long-term effects of the widespread exclusion of African Americans and the resulting demographic segregation enforced by whites nationally. And thus the unsettled legacy of racism, in the South and elsewhere, continues to be a wound in the national psyche that refuses to heal."[18]

In 1955, Rosa Parks, considered the mother of the Civil Rights Movement, refused to give up her seat to a white man, and the Civil Rights Movement was born and dominated the political landscape in the 1950s and 1960s. In 1957, Congress passed the Voting Rights Bill, followed by the Civil Rights Act in 1964. Discussed later in this chapter, systemic racism has not abated in the post-civil rights era, nor has it abated after the election of the first black president. To sum, throughout this country's history, the government and other social institutions reinforce racism by providing blacks and whites with unequal access to opportunities and resources based on racial differences. In U.S. society, white superiority has been the norm, and race is treated as a metaphor to determine what Americanness is "in the creation of our national identity. 'American' has been defined as 'white.'"[19]

AFRICAN AMERICANS AND THE REPUBLICAN PARTY

When African Americans pledged their allegiance to the Republican Party after the Civil War, the Party welcomed them, but the Democratic Party led by southern planters rejected their participation. The Republican Party politically supported African Americans receiving their civil rights. However, the Party began rolling back the political gains and civil rights of African Americans that ended the Reconstruction era from 1865 to 1877. Had African Americans not learned the necessary strategies for economic survival, they would have perished under the weight of systemic racism.[20] The next several paragraphs offer some historical explanations and reasons why most African Americans abandoned the Republican Party after the Reconstruction era and ultimately pledged their allegiance to the Democratic Party from 1877 to the present day.

During the late nineteenth century and first half of the twentieth century, it must be noted that both the Republican and Democratic parties viewed African Americans as racially inferior to whites.[21] But the Democratic Party, the more powerful of the two parties, was the party of southern planters that opposed black participation in politics and were determined not to end slavery. On the other hand, the Republican Party welcomed African American participation and contributed to the establishment of the Freedman's Bureau. Consequently, the majority of the African American community voted for the Republican Party until the Great Depression.

In 1866, the thirty-ninth Republican Congress passed the Fourteenth Amendment, a major civil rights bill, granting former slaves U.S. citizenship. In 1867, Thaddeus Stevens, a powerful leader in the Republican Party from Pennsylvania presented the Reconstruction Act that would grant black males the right to vote. The Republican Party of that day was considered radical by the Democratic Party of southern planters because they did not want former slaves given the right to vote. Southern planters moved swiftly to prevent this voting right, but the Act was passed because these planters only believed that white men of property should govern and vote.[22] However, we could extrapolate some evidence from historical fact that southern planters were not interested in social mingling with former slaves.

Under the Reconstruction Act in 1870, African Americans were concerned about the government's land division policies and became part of the Republican Party. But their concerns went unheeded and state amendments were passed in favor of the planters. When Lincoln signed the Emancipation Proclamation on January 1, 1863, to free blacks from slavery, the government gave them land, after several southern states seceded from the union. When these states agreed to return to the union, the government returned the land to the Confederate soldiers. Herein lies part of the black economic problem. When the government denied blacks a portion of the land, this destroyed their ability to determine their economic future because land is a valuable commodity. In essence, the government is responsible for African Americans' inability to provide for themselves and future generations. With land, blacks could have amassed enough wealth to pass on to future generations but whites kept them impoverished. The taking back of the land kept the masses of blacks dependent on whites for their economic sustenance through a sharecropping system. This system kept blacks enslaved to whites, while fueling illiteracy and impoverishment among blacks in the South. This system was kept in place for several decades and is one of the reasons the masses of African Americans are trapped in poverty in urban areas, when they migrated to the North after the Reconstruction era. Overall, the Reconstruction era (1865–1877) lasted about 12 years and turned African Americans into a potent political force. During this period, African Americans enjoyed political, economic, and cultural progress, even though the black codes—whites treating free blacks as slaves—instituted by the legislature stalled the progress they made.[23]

In 1876, Republican president-elect Rutherford B. Hayes (1877–1881), who initially supported black rights, struck a deal over a disputed close election between himself and his Democratic opponent, Samuel Tilden, in support of the interests of the South that ended the Reconstruction Era.[24] With the help of a conservative U.S. Supreme Court, the political safeguards African Americans enjoyed were removed after Hayes took office. This opened the door for political and economic oppression through segregationist Jim Crow laws that lasted for almost a century. Since African Americans traditionally voted for the Republican Party from 1867 to 1932 and saw a roll back of their civil rights and no economic progress, they abandoned the Republican Party, switched their loyalty to the Democratic Party, and voted for Franklin Roosevelt. Although Roosevelt was unmoved by the plight of African Americans, he invited notable blacks to participate in his administration and challenged state-imposed limitations on their civil rights only during his third term in office.[25] The damage had been done and the losses African Americans experienced during the post-Reconstruction period still resonate today. Had powerful politicians followed in the footsteps of Thaddeus Stevens, a man of great political vision, African Americans' situation could have been different. The hostility toward African Americans, the destruction of their prosperous communities, the white society taking away their economic self-determination after Reconstruction, and forcing them to receive government assistance, while blaming blacks for not achieving economic success equal to whites has been a cruel ideology that has perpetrated and reproduced itself into the twenty-first century. In this backdrop, we can understand the reason for the vitriol and the systemic racism that Obama has endured since taking office in 2009 and the former Speaker of the House, Newt Gingrich calling the first African American president, the "Food Stamp President."

MODERN-DAY IMPLICATIONS OF SYSTEMIC RACISM

Systemic racism is a blister on the soul of America. Since the days of slavery, America has relied on this system of oppression to enrich whites and impoverish Americans of color, specifically African Americans.[26] From slavery to the pre-civil rights movement, African American males were denied the ability to determine their destiny, could not protect and defend their families, had no paternity rights, and were subject to unspeakable acts of lynching. Sociologist Anthony Lemelle argues that there is no other group of men that teaches their children to discriminate against Americans of color than white men.[27] One of the sole purposes of embedding systemic racism into the infrastructure of U.S. society was to deny African Americans their constitutional rights, to instill in them a consciousness of inferiority, a sense of helplessness to create a habit of dependence on the government, and to keep white exploitation and oppression of blacks in place.[28] With systemic racism embedded deeply within the infrastructure of U.S. society, even after the civil rights movement, blacks have been fighting to enjoy the same opportunities and privileges whites take for granted, but whites still remain 250 years ahead of African Americans in every area of life. As discussed below, this disempowerment has become a way of life for the black American masses, affecting everything from their income to their family structure to mis-treatment in the criminal justice system, and to their health, which also affects their ability to secure sufficient life insurance to protect their fami-lies upon the death of the breadwinner. By swelling the prisons with black males who commit petty crimes, it is difficult for black males to secure gainful employment unlike white males in a similar position.

Ideally, whites make convenient IQ, educational, and economic com-parisons with African Americans, making themselves feel more educated and economically well-off. I have seen blatant examples of this in my teaching experience. When I teach race, class, and gender, I have asked students the reason why whites do not compare themselves to Asians; they said that whites would not shine as bright in comparison to Asians, but African Americans make them look brighter. One of my graduate students wrote that "whites expect black America to struggle. It is the natural order of things." When I was a graduate student in the doctoral program at a predominantly white prestigious research institution, a number of white students informed me that African Americans tend to be the topic of discussion at their dinner tables. These students were taught that African Americans are the blame for the ills of society, and their families would refer to blacks as "niggers." "White-created epithets like 'nigger'" are used to deingrate African Americans to justify systemic racism.[29] Even Obama, the President of the United States, has not es-caped this epithet.

Some whites have argued (and some have taken legal action in sup-port of this argument) that Affirmative Action is unfair and disadvan-tages qualified whites in favor of minorities. Given today's economic condition of the masses of African Americans, it is too easy for white America to "blame the victim" for "not making it," completely overlook-ing the historical nature of systemic racism, how it has affected and still affects black economic and educational progress, and the social institu-tions that play a major role in sustaining and reproducing its devastating effects. "The majority of whites are willfully ignorant or very misin-formed when it comes to understanding the difficult life conditions that African Americans and other Americans of color face today,"[30] argues social theorist Joe Feagin.

Is the rage and discontentment of the white working class the result of misdirected hostility for their failure to make it in an individualist society that embraces the elusive American dream? Or is this hostility directed at a black president who, like the African American community, has been held responsible for their loss of jobs? But a more potent question we should ask is "when will America take full responsibility for the racism that has poisoned the American way of life"? White Americans have been blinded by systemic racism, Americans of color are visibly affected by it, and the first African American president is held in contempt by it. Before moving on to the impact racism has on the Obama presidency, the next several paragraphs discuss the impact of racism and colorism on black America and Obama.

IDEOLOGY AND THE LEGITMATION OF RACIST MEANING STRUCTURES

Both African American men and women have been marginalized by black and white paternalism and welfare reform by white decision makers. African American women have been ideologically stereotyped as welfare queens, breeders, and immoral, and the buttress of racialized gender politics and gendered racism.[31] Ronald Reagan constructed the "welfare queen" stereotype directed at African American women, when he told the story of the Chicago welfare queen who had several names, addresses, Social Security cards, and collected benefits from four deceased husbands, milking the government of thousands of dollars. The real welfare recipient to whom Reagan referred was actually convicted of using two different aliases for collecting more than $5,000 in welfare benefits. After the press informed Reagan about misrepresenting the case, he continued to use his version of the story, ignoring the facts.[32] When well-respected political leaders use the politics of misinformation to mislead their audiences, they not only benefit politically from these inaccuracies, but also they strengthen individuals' beliefs about certain racial groups "as incompetent and lazy rather than victims of an [exploitative] economic system they cannot change."[33] After all, Reagan was the great orator who has been raised to sainthood. Why should anyone reject the validity of his racialized rhetoric, meant for reinforcing white prejudice? Reagan constructed this "welfare queen" metaphor to support the white racial frame that only African American women are welfare recipients. Given Reagan's racialized rhetoric, African American women are viewed as breeding children outside the sanctity of marriage, having a deficient value system, engaging in other pathological behavioral practices, and abusing the welfare system.[34] Republican presidential candidate Rick Santorum relied on racist politics to pander to his white audience when he said he did not want to improve the lives of African Americans by giving them other people's money, specifically white people's money. What Reagan, Santorum, and most whites perhaps refuse to face is that "more whites are on welfare, use more food stamps, and public health services" than African Americans and other Americans of color.[35] Reagan and Santorum had actually racially framed African Americans as abusers of government aid or the welfare system. Since Santorum was running for president for 2012, he was actually charging Obama with giving "black" or "blah" people other people's money by contaminating the perceptions of his base against Obama as well as African Americans. Politically speaking, whites would vote against their own economic interests to avoid voting for Obama. Can we blame this on systemic racism, an opaque white racial frame, or misinformation about Obama?

Reagan's fictitious welfare queen was a representation of everything that was wrong with the welfare system.[36] Today, "the words welfare mothers evoke one of the most powerful racialized cultural icons in contemporary U.S. society."[37] Newt Gingrich has called Obama the "Food Stamp President." He supports deep cuts and would harm vulnerable whites who receive federal and state-government support. Even though white women have relied on state supported programs to feed, clothe, and house their children, some may vote for a Republican who is against a welfare state, which makes no logical sense.[38] However, it does make sense if we factor in systemic racism to destroy Obama's legacy. Reagan's racialized rhetoric also created black welfare recipients as lazy immorals that fit the "social stereotype of blacks" and "eliminating welfare is giving those unworthy blacks what they deserve—nothing."[39] As a result, African American women are one of the most marginalized groups in American society. We now look at the uneducated and unemployed men in the lives of African American women, men who see themselves without power and authority in U.S. society that treats them like criminals and they in turn treat black women with the same disdain and abuse with which society treats them.

THE BLACK MALE'S WOES: DESIGNED FOR FAILURE

Most black males saw their fathers, grandfathers, and great-grandfathers, as well as President Obama, treated with overt disrespect by a white paternalistic racist system and never saw them assume any real leadership roles in a repressive employment system that continued to exploit and cheat them out of their hard-earned wages. Their role models were broken fathers who knew their "place" in a racialized society. During slavery, black fathers had no paternal rights. During the Jim Crow era to the pre-civil rights movement, black fathers were forced to leave their families in search of work and their authority in the family was transferred to the black mother. Even during the post-civil rights movement, black fathers could not attain the kind of employment critical for supporting their growing families. As a result, many young black males turned to crime "to obtain the material needs of life,"[40] but "much of the crime committed by poor black men can be seen as an individualized revolt against unemployment, substandard housing, and the other by-products of economic discrimination. Whites, especially those in the upper economic classes, helped create the high cost of such crime by perpetuating the wasteful system of racial exploitation."[41] Here, we see the impact of racial exploitation on the subproletarians, the working class, and the lumpen proletariat that do not fit into mainstream society because the system created them.[42]

While systemic racism is the root of black males' long history of economic oppression, their refusal to work can also be seen as a revolt against discriminatory employment practices where equal pay for equal work, compared to white males of comparable skills, is nonexistent. Evidence has shown a wage gap between black men with a four-year college degree and white men with a high school diploma.[43] Black men with felony convictions are discriminated against for the rest of their lives and denied employment, housing, and public benefits. For this reason, they are not able to take their legitimate place in the home and rule as loving patriarchs over their children. Systemic racism has denied black men the dignity of providing for their families. They continue to rebel against a racist economic system and refuse to be exploited by it, which has hurt the economic survival of many black families.

BLACKS AND THE CRIMINAL JUSTICE SYSTEM

From slavery to Jim Crow to pre-civil rights, black males suffered the most from racial discrimination, and were hired to do the most demeaning jobs that paid low wages, thus hindering their ability for career advancement. Slavery undermined the black male's role as an economic provider, forcing black women to re-prioritize their roles and work outside the home.[44] The only job black women were qualified to do was that of a charwoman, which paid even lower wages than what black men received. Since both mother and father had to work, the home began to deteriorate over a period of time, and the harshness of economic life forced many black fathers to abandon the home. Consequently, lawlessness among black males began to abound. Black males received lengthy sentences for crimes that otherwise carried shorter sentence terms. These long racially motivated sentences affected and currently affect the black household. Thus, black men have never achieved the ability to self-determine their destiny and the black community has suffered harsh economic woes.

African American men have not had a positive experience with the U.S. legal system since they were emancipated from slavery. Studies have shown that when African Americans and other Americans of color victimize whites, they are seen as a social threat, warranting longer prison sentences. But when whites victimize African Americans and other Americans of color, they are usually exonerated of the crime or receive shorter prison sentences,[45] a process that supports the self-imposed destruction of a race. The race of a defendant makes a difference in legal situations. Sheri Johnson, a law professor, argues that

> Nine very recent experiments [found] that the race of the defendant significantly and directly affects the determination of guilt. White subjects in all these studies were more likely to find a minority-race defendant guilty than they were to find an identically situated white defendant guilty. Four studies find a significant interaction between the race of the defendant [and] guilt attribution.[46]

Johnson illustrates how a verdict is affected by the balance of the jury. The only jury unable to reach a verdict is a racially balanced one (50 percent black and 50 percent white). The social construction of race plays a major role in criminal sentencing, where unconscious racism "through the design and promulgation of statutes that, while facially neutral, will inevitably result in the discrimination against non-Whites."[47]

The white construction of the African American male criminal has created a polarizing effect on society, and the large-scale imprisonment of African American males has gone unnoticed by middle-class whites.[48] White America has removed itself from the plight of poor blacks and view black incarceration only in the "role of distant, approving spectators, cheering on legislators, prosecutors and judges to incarcerate an ever higher proportion" of black male criminals who violate laws against white society.[49]

Michelle Alexander points out that

> the future of the black community may depend on those who care about racial justice and are willing to re-examine their basic assumptions about the role of the criminal justice system in our society. The fact that more than half of the young black men living in urban America are currently under the control of the criminal justice system or saddled with criminal records is not just a symptom of poverty or poor choices, but rather evidence of a new racial caste system at work.[50]

Nationally, forty-nine percent of the prison population comprises black males, and they comprise thirteen percent of the overall black U.S. population.[51] The plight of the black male and his problems with the criminal justice system has its beginnings in the nation's history.[52] This is another form of slavery in which the new Jim Crow laws rely on the prison system to re-enslave black men. Bill O'Reilly, a political commentator for Fox News, spoke before an audience at the National Action Network on April 14, 2010, about race-related issues and believes race issues are gone. He was correct about one thing: he does not know black people's struggles any more than black people know his struggles as a white man. When he told his audience, we have dropped this "race stuff" after 9/11, because we are all Americans, the audience disagreed. O'Reilly was suggesting that only "real" Americans do not experience racism. What O'Reilly failed to understand was that African Americans, Native Americans, and other Americans of color have not been treated as "real"

Americans. Contemporary research shows that "white" is synonymous with "America."[53]

With many black males burdened with felony convictions, it was and is still impossible for them to secure substantial employment to help their mothers provide for the home and family. Naturally, black women turned to the welfare system for help, putting themselves at the mercy of a racist paternalist welfare system that stereotypes and persecutes them. Consequently, African American women have faced difficulty raising a normal family and "living in accordance with the norms of a family ethic constructed around male dominance."[54] Black women and children also have been the constant victims of physical and sexual assault by the men in their lives.[55] When black men cannot financially contribute to the household economy, they perceive themselves as victims of a racist society and misdirect their anger toward black women and children, which is not a justification for solving their problems.

In addition, systemic racism has played a major role in the intergenerational transmission of psychological and physical health problems of African Americans, such as psychosis, high blood pressure, diabetes, and hypertension, among other debilitating ailments that prevent African Americans from securing decent health and life insurance. Systemic racism has crushed the life out of African Americans, and they are held responsible for the health problems caused by it through the denial of life insurance. In addition to these ailments, African Americans have suffered "physical and psychological violence at the hand of white oppressors" oppressors who are still legally protected by the power elite.[56] Given this analysis on the criminal woes of African American males, Obama has been treated like a criminal. Oversight Committee Chairman Darrell Issa (R-CA) threatened Obama with legal action over the Troubled Asset Relief Program (TARP) and stimulus funds and called his government the most corrupt in history.[57] Ben Quayle (R-AZ), son of former vice president Dan Quayle has echoed a similar statement in a video. U.S. presidential history is replete with corruption such as Watergate, Iran-Contra, and Teapot Dome scandals, but some have gone unnoticed. A number of these scandals have resulted in criminal convictions, "but no such allegations have been made against the Obama administration."[58]

BLACK MALE PATRIARCHY IN RACIALIZED AMERICA

From slavery to these contemporary times, black females have faced triple oppression due to the race, class, and gender divide. The evolution of patriarchal institutions within black society has contributed to this problem, where the black church is still dominated by men who serve as pastors and deacons.[59] Under these circumstances, black pastors and deacons have found power and authority in the only social institution they control—the black church. They have consciously and/or unconsciously adopted the ideology of white patriarchy they currently practice in the institutions in black society. Black men did not and still do not to a certain extent consider the black female their equal and the black church supports this attitude. Consequently, the black church used and still uses biblical scripture to teach black male patriarchy and the marginalization of black females, which have gone unchallenged by black women. Black women accepted their station in the black community, based on the authority of the scripture. From slavery to the civil rights era, black women seldom demanded social equality between themselves and their men.

Since many black females today are unmarried, and many black males cannot find gainful employment to make them marriageable, a number of black females are conceiving children outside the sanctity of marriage and a large number of them and their children live in persistent poverty. Many have limited education by present day standards. With a limited educational background, they cannot compete in today's technological age, a reason Obama has increased funding for student loans and encourages mothers of disadvantaged backgrounds to seek an education. African Americans cannot make substantial progress and affirm their humanity unless black poverty is eliminated.[60] Although systemic racism will not disappear, African Americans can make some progress with an education. Given Obama's election to the presidency, a few race scholars argue that we live in a post-racial society and that Obama's election meant America became colorblind. But this is an overstatement, now that Obama has served a full term and his first-term presidency was battered with racialized rhetoric and at times overt racism. The post-racial society ideology does not challenge what legal scholar Ian Haney Lopez calls "colorblind white dominance."[61]

DIFFICULTY CREATING BLACK FAMILY NORMS IN RACIALIZED AMERICA

From slavery to the civil rights movement, black households typically had a mother and father, but two-parent unions began to erode between the post-civil rights era and the election of Barack Obama. The African American community has one of the highest numbers of children born out of wedlock compared to whites and other women of color. A large number of black households are headed by females and many black males live with their single mothers or girlfriends and have little to no control over their behavioral practices. Roy L. Brooks, Warren Distinguished Professor of Law at the University of San Diego, provides us with "diagnostic and prescriptive external and internal inquiries" for addressing the post-civil rights problems of African Americans.[62]

Brooks suggests that, during the age of Obama, the traditionalist viewpoint does not see the problems facing African Americans and this view may not be motivated by racism alone. Brooks suggests that internal and external factors equally contribute to the problems of the black community. Brooks does not dismiss systemic racism and oppression but gives equal weight to racism and oppression as an external factor. Brooks goes on to inform us that African Americans' behavioral practices are influenced by a "dysfunctional cultural orientation," as an internal factor contributing to their lack of achievements. Black intellectuals who embrace the traditionalist frame, such Shelby Steele and Thomas Sowell, argue for racial neutrality and dismiss racism as an external factor that contributes to African Americans' inability to secure opportunities in this society. When the government creates race-based policies, history has shown that whites become angry and these policies may do more harm to African Americans than good.[63] But Steele's and Sowell's analyses of the black problem do no justice to blacks who seek racial parity with whites because they dismiss the effects of discrimination and believe it cannot be measured in this post-civil rights era because of wealth and income disparities.[64] Brooks also suggests that other conservatives, like Sowell and Steele, see racial preferences as divisive tools that stir white hostility.[65]

As for internal factors, traditionalists claim that "destructive behaviors, the breeding of babies out of wedlock, broken families, drugs, and black-on-black crime" are the real culprits that prevent the masses of poor African Americans from securing opportunities.[66] Perhaps the internal factors, as a starting point, slow the process for African Americans to advance in the educational realm to securing substantial economic opportunity. Yet we cannot dismiss the fact that African Americans were emancipated from physical slavery and forced into another form of slavery, a Jim Crow economic system that exploited African Americans' labor through the share-cropping and cotton system and low-wage jobs up to the 1960s. To add to this, African Americans were turned out of slavery into a hostile racist society where minimal to no material assistance was given to them to help them build their lives. Brooks offers the most plausible answer to African Americans' inability to achieve racial equality in U.S. society since slavery. This allegory helps clarify the problem more clearly:

> Two persons—one white, the other black—are playing a game of poker. The game has been in progress for almost four hundred years. One player—the white one—has been cheating during much of this time, but now announces: "From this day forward, there will be a new game with new players and no more cheating." Hopeful but somewhat suspicious, the black player responds, "That's great. I've been waiting to hear you say that for some four hundred years. Let me ask you, what are you going to do with all those poker chips that you have stacked up on your side of the table all these years?" "Well," says the white player,

somewhat bewildered by the question, "I'm going to keep them for the next generation of white players, of course."[67]

This allegory suggests that if the power elite wanted to create a just society where racial equality and racial justice could exist, they would have shared a portion of the wealth with newly freed slaves, giving them the necessary resources to provide for themselves, their families, and their posterity. By doing so, government sponsored programs on which many African Americans have relied to sustain themselves and their families would not have been an issue and stirred the hatred of whites who lack any real knowledge of black history or American history in general. The "welfare" meaning structure that demeans African American women's "sexual immorality and so-called preference for welfare over work" would not be a legitimate debate.[68] Instead, from slavery and post-civil rights, whites continued to exploit the labor of blacks through the economic system, enriching themselves and their children, passing on their wealth to them as well as non-financial assets such as cultural and social capital that promote social mobility and social networking. Their children, who are several generations removed from slavery, are enjoying the stolen wealth as a result of black exploited labor, and white children have been socialized to chant the same mantra to their posterity that African Americans are lazy and prefer government handouts rather than a job. They have been socialized to dismiss the damaging effects of systematic racism on African Americans' psyche and only view the plight of African Americans through a white racial frame to justify their conscious and/or unconscious racist practices. Successive generations of whites have acquired wealth, the top white-collar jobs, and claim they had nothing to do with slavery or African Americans' current economic condition. But new generations of whites have practiced racism to protect their interests and passed this practice on for posterity.

A modern-day example of how African American families continue to be viewed through the lens of systemic racism is the recent statement former presidential candidate Michele Bachmann (R-MN) made as part of a Christian pledge. She believes that black children are more likely to be raised by a mother and a father in slavery than after the election of Obama. Coming from a white racial frame and believing the founding fathers "worked tirelessly" to end slavery, Bachmann does not understand that black families were broken up and sold like chattel on the auction block during slavery. Her constant gaffes throughout the 2012 presidential primaries suggest that this congresswoman has little to no working knowledge of American slavery or American history and has less understanding about what blacks suffered during and after slavery. During slavery, marriages between black men and black women were not legal, but took place with the blessings of the slave master. "But the wedding vows they recited promised not 'until death do us part,' but 'until distance' or, as one black minister bluntly put it, 'until the white man' – 'do us part.'"[69] Children were separated from their mothers and wives from their husbands at the slave owners will. Since Bachmann compares the moral standards of black families in slavery to that of blacks today, during Obama's first term in office, she has overlooked the moral behavior of slave masters, such as Thomas Jefferson, a founding father, who sired many children by Sally Hemings, an enslaved woman.

Why does the happy-go-lucky-wanting-to-be-owned black myth continue to surface? We can best answer this question by pointing to deliberate historical amnesia and blatant historical ignorance of dominant society and the denial of racial oppression by black conservatives who do not want to be exposed to the ugly truth about the role their ancestors played in slavery by producing, reproducing, and sustaining the system of racial oppression. "Refusing to be honest about how racial inequality has burdened our shared history and continues to shape our society will not get us to that post-racial vision,"[70] writes Tera Hunter.

Diverting attention from the real causes of social inequality, the beneficiaries of this stolen wealth have adopted what Dennis Mumby, a critical theorist, calls "cultural deformation."[71] Cultural deformation is a phenomenon when symbolic practices are systematically deformed so that relations of domination and dependency between African Americans and whites are rationalized, justified, and uncritically accepted.[72] But there were times in U.S. history when the power elite shared some of this wealth with a few black advocates who lessened white guilt and blamed blacks as the culprits of their own condition to make it difficult for well-intentioned social theorists to have honest debates that society is partly responsible for the conditions in which African Americans find themselves. The problems facing African Americans in this mythical post-racial era of Obama are still racial inequality and racial injustice. White America refuses to acknowledge that the unearned wealth and privileges whites enjoy are the results of an age-old problem, racism, that concentrates wealth in the hands of the whites.

America is a society where segregation and separation between whites and Americans of color in some parts of this country still prevail, where social class and color distinction divide them. In the next several paragraphs, we expand on color distinction, or "colorism," because the color of one's skin still determines who gets access to what resources and how much of these resources they can acquire.

THE ROOTS OF COLORISM

Colorism originates from slavery. It is the rejection of dark-complexioned blacks by light complexioned blacks. Colorism is a stain on African Americans' self-concept, self-esteem, self-image, and self-identity, an issue relating to race and beauty and black self-hatred. Historically, colorism has played a major role in the social, political, economic, and legal institutions of U.S. society and determined which African Americans have received the greatest access to resources as long as access to these resources does not exceed the resources that whites enjoy. African American access to certain resources and jobs still poses a problem today. The legal "dismantling of a racial state does not dismantle the racial hierarchies that perpetuate inequality" in African American communities and U.S. society.[73] Colorism "sometimes operates to confound and re-structure racial hierarchies."[74] That is, American society remains deeply afflicted by racism. Long before slavery became the mainstay of the plantation society of the antebellum South, white attitudes of racial superiority left their stamp on the developing culture of Colonial America. Today, "over a century [and a half] after the abolition of slavery, [minority] citizens suffer from discriminatory attitudes and practices, infecting our economic system, our cultural and political institutions, and the daily interactions of individuals. The idea that color is a badge of inferiority and a justification for the denial of opportunity and equal treatment is deeply ingrained."[75] In short, the ideology of colorism has become "re-ified," a term that means to give material existence to an abstraction. For colorism, the practice of discrimination is the material existence. It is the practice that gives us the ability to see what a just or unjust practice is.

Obama has defied the reified system of colorism. Although Obama has chosen to identify himself as an African American, he is not defined by it. Since Obama is of biracial pedigree, many African Americans at first thought he was not "black enough," but this attitude soon changed. African Americans supported his initial candidacy in droves and over-whelmingly rallied around his bid for re-election, which defied the political talking points that Obama disappointed them in his first term. During the 2008 presidential campaign, Obama faced challenging questions about race and addressed this issue in a speech he gave in Philadelphia. His speech received unparalleled praise from major cable networks and newspapers such as CNN, MSNBC, *The New York Times*, and the *Philadelphia Inquirer*, but colorism within the black community and our dominant society remains a problem. Colorism is a subject worthy of discussion and how Obama fits into this colorism scheme. Given the political back-lash against Obama, racism emerged in full force from underground, and African Americans understood the ravaging effects of this social and po-litical disease against the first black president and were determined to support him.

Colorism affects African Americans, other Americans of color, and white Americans in the social realm.[76] Contemporary research indicates that the color complex operates in the African American community and that lighter skinned African Americans have a clear advantage over dark-er skinned African Americans in the social, economic, political, and educational sectors.[77] Within the black community, colorism operates similar to white racism with darker-complexioned blacks being rejected by light-complexioned blacks. This phenomenon includes attitudes and beliefs that African Americans are more attractive and more intelligent when they have straight hair and narrow facial features that resemble that of whites, where whiteness is the standard-bearer of beauty.[78] Lillian Fears describes Afrotypic appearance as one that is characterized by dark skin, a broad nose, thick lips, and wooly hair. Speaking to the issues of beauty and the black woman, colorism establishes the impression that straight hair is more attractive than thick, wooly hair, and that black men are drawn to light-complexioned women with straight hair and white women. In bell hooks' "Straightening Our Hair," she writes that, "White women's . . . straight hair set a beauty standard black women were struggling to live out," since the days of slavery.[79] Female slaves did not have access to hair care salons or make-up. They would wrap their hair with head rags because they did not have the proper hair products to maintain it. Even after slavery, African American women did not have access to hair care salons until Madam C. J. Walker (1867–1919), the first black female entrepreneur and hair care business woman, invented black hair care products during the turn of the twentieth century for black women. From 1910 to the present, black women have taken great pride in caring for their hair. Or they would sport the short Afro that speaks to the ability to determine their own identity. More recently, in October 2012, Rhonda Lee, a black female weather reporter in Shreveport, Louisiana, was criticized by a viewer through Facebook because she sported a very short Afro, and was eventually fired under some unknown pretext that she brought this white wrath down on herself for not embracing the white notion of beauty, considering she was operating in a "white" public space. The viewer said, "The black lady that does the news is a very nice lady. The only thing is she needs to wear a wig or grow some more hair. I'm not sure if she is a cancer patient, but still it's not something myself that I think looks good on TV." [80] The article suggests that the viewer would have preferred that Lee wore her hair in a style that met the white racial frame standards of beauty. The article goes on to suggest that this issue was racialized and that white women receive more protection in the workplace than women of color, even if white anchor women are overweight.

For African American women, skin tone has been a determining factor for their self-concept, self-esteem, and self-identity. Historically, dark-skinned African American women have been positioned at the base of the social pyramid and were considered unattractive and unmarriageable.[81] As a result, they attempted to lighten their skin with Black and White ointment, straighten their hair with chemicals, and Anglicize their physiognomy to live up to the white notion of beauty.[82] Some have begun dyeing their hair from light auburn to a pale yellowish brown.

From a psychological fixation about colorism, some lighter skinned African Americans during the post-civil rights era separated themselves from darker skinned African Americans in the social, intellectual, and educational realms. This behavioral practice supports Frantz Fanon's *Black Skin White Masks*'s notion that some blacks wish they were white to avoid further damage to their already fragile self-esteem. Fanon believed that black men who desire to turn the black race to a white one are as miserable as blacks who preach race hatred.[83]

Grounded in historical research, light-skinned blacks were given power and privilege over dark-skinned blacks. Light-skinned blacks, or mulattoes, were the children of slave owners or what some historians call "children of the plantation." Lighter-skinned blacks were given jobs in the "big house," while darker-skinned blacks worked the fields. To this end, lighter-skinned blacks perceived they had an advantage over darker-skinned blacks because the plantation system encouraged them to believe that light skin, like white skin, gave them more privileges. Since our forty-fourth president of the United States is of biracial pedigree, a discussion on genetic makeup and the "one-drop rule" is of significant importance here. As mentioned in an earlier paragraph, the one-drop rule posits that anyone born with one drop of black blood is considered black.

HISTORICAL NOTE ON GENETIC MAKEUP

In further examination of colorism and the resurgence of racialized rhetoric leveled at Barack Obama, it is important to note that blacks and whites cannot be certain about their genetic makeup, given the act of miscegenation during and after slavery. During slavery, white males owned black women's bodies and used them for their pleasure. Children were born of these forced unions, enslaved by their own white fathers, and treated like any other slave, or, in some cases, treated well and set free. Some children of these unions looked white and were able to pass into white society undetected. For example, there is no historical account that Thomas Jefferson was the father of Hemings' children. Jefferson "freed all of Sally Hemings' children."[84] Two daughters were freed in 1822 and two sons freed upon Jefferson's death in 1826. Contemporary research indicates that some of Hemings' children resembled Jefferson and DNA evidence suggests that Jefferson was the father of Hemings' children.[85] It was a common practice for white male planters to rape the bodies of black female slaves. What white planters and their sons would not do to white women's bodies, they instead did to black women's bodies, as if they were beasts, calling it "sowing their oats." Under the slave system as well as the years following the so-called emancipation of African Americans, black women were not in control of their bodies. Under the slave and Jim Crow systems, black women were treated like sexual beasts to justify

white men's bestial desires for black women's bodies. I liken black wom-
en's situation to any oppressed group of women. For example, under
Nazi tyranny, Jewish women were raped on the streets, sexually ravaged
in concentration camps, and ultimately blamed for unconsciously appealing to the base nature of their Nazi rapists. Since extermination camps
such as Auschwitz, Majdanek, and Treblinka were states within a state
with no rules to govern the moral behavior of the perpetrators towards
their victims, Nazi murderers and rapists held institutionalized sexual
power over Jewish women and women of other nationalities.

White men could at any time rape a black woman. Blacks were not
protected under the law. If a white man desired to have a black man's
wife, he could tell the black man to leave his home and engage in conju-
gal relations with his wife. Southern racialized sexual politics prevented
black men from protecting black women from the bestial behavior practices of white men. Systemic sexism and white men's institutionalized
sexual power over black women's bodies were the norm from slavery to
the civil rights era. White women were well aware of the forced sexual
dynamics between white men and black women. White women remained
silent and accepted this nineteenth-century normalized behavior in white
men because they were bound by institutional sexism. Consequently,
white mistresses took out their frustrations and envy on the helpless
black female victim. Ida B. Wells-Barnett described the "rape of black
women as of a piece with the lynching of black men," and together they
"formed a web of racist sexual politics designed to subjugate all African
Americans."[86]

MISCEGENATION

In his three-volume treastise, J. A. Rogers' extensive research on race and
sex provides an unparalleled account of race-mixing between those of
black African and European ancestries where many Europeans were sent
to America during the colonial period. Both American and European
white historians have not accurately reported the historical events and
achievements of people of black African ancestry.[87] These historians have
supported the dominant value system and report information that produces, reproduces, and sustains white cultural and historical hegemony.
Many European monarchs have black African ancestry in their bloodline.
Queen Elizabeth II's great-great-great grandmother, Charlotte of Mecklenburg-Strelitz, queen consort to George III of England, was of black
African ancestry. She was called the "black queen of England." In America, we hardly hear about Queen Charlotte, although Charlottesville, Virginia; Charlotte, North Carolina; and a number of other important North
Carolina judicial and social institutions and historical sites are named in
her honor. Rogers claims that the present royal family of Sweden is de-

scended from Jean Baptiste Bernadotte who was of Moorish ancestry with swarthy skin and wooly hair.

Joel Augustus Rogers (1883–1966), a Jamaican-American author, historian, and journalist, has written extensively on the history of Africa, the African Diaspora, and African Americans in the United States. He challenges prevailing "ideas about race, demonstrates the connections between civilizations, and traces African achievements."[88] Rogers illustrates that race-mixing, between blacks and other racial groups, has existed since the beginning of time. He provides an exhaustive discussion on race-mixing between blacks and whites in the ancient East, the Middle East, Asia, and Europe. He also writes that even Hitler and Mussolini claimed that race is a fraud but is useful when they want to politically unite ill-informed followers to adopt their race-based policies for discrimination purposes, specifically against Jews. Rogers further points to the hypocrisy of America and Great Britain that condemned the racist doctrines of Nazism and Fascism, but pride themselves on the doctrine of equal justice for all while using race as a fetish to keep Americans of color from achieving fair treatment and justice and keeping a social division between people of color and whites. Rogers' work suggests that whites were set against blacks by the bogey of miscegenation for centuries.[89] Since the fifteenth century, Europeans have projected their ignorance and fears onto the blackness of Africans, creating in whites a distorted image of themselves.[90]

Rogers emphasizes that the power of race in U.S. society plays a major role in reifying social relations between blacks and whites in particular. The whole "phenomenon of race prejudice arises more from the questions of social expediency [rather] than from mere personal taboos."[91] Rogers, like critical race scholar Ian Haney Lopez, suggests that race must be seen as a social construction based on human interaction rather than natural differentiation. People rather than abstract social forces produce races. At any given time in history, it can determine the outcome of interpersonal and sexual relations between racial groups and invoke the notion of colorism when it is convenient to divide groups within themselves, for example, African Americans versus the light and black phenomenon.

COLORISM AND BLACK STEREOTYPING

From the beginning of U.S. slavery to the late 1960s, African American stereotypes were rampant. Contemporary research shows that stereotypic images still cast African Americans as apes and monkeys with thick white lips. Contemporary research also "documents the reality of centuries-old racist stereotypes and [apelike] images of African Americans still remain commonplace."[92] Many whites and other Americans of color have accepted these stereotypic realities about African Americans, believing that African Americans, specifically black males are violent oversexed criminals.[93] And much earlier research supports the notion that African Americans have been socially identified as being, to name a few, mentally inferior, morally primitive, emotionally unstable, overly assertive, boisterous, religious fanatics, superstitious, dirty, depreciators of property, lazy slackers at work, low class, ignorant, happy-go-lucky, troublesome, musical, and given to crimes of violence with razors and knives. Furthermore, African Americans are stereotyped as having a high fertility rate and low standards compared to other racial groups.[94] Of interest here is how language politically and ideologically situates stereotypes of African Americans in relation to whites in particular, but Asians are seen as the model minority.[95]

Countless representations of African Americans with ink-black skin, large thick white ashen lips, and bulging eyeballs have appeared almost everywhere in the public arena. For example, in vintage advertisements, white graphic artists and illustrators prospered by drawing blacks as monkeys to sell products and to illustrate show bills and magazines.[96] In such ads, black dialect was the typical speech pattern of these characters, and African Americans were uniformly depicted as happy-go-lucky fools with big white lips in servile roles.[97] These apelike images had reappeared during Obama's first term indicating Obama shared a mental and physical association with apes. After Obama's first debate with his opponent Mitt Romney, Fox News contributor Ann Coulter made reference to Obama's ears, calling them big and poking out.[98] Goff and his colleagues argue that historical representations of African Americans that once depicted them like apes remains embedded in the minds of dominant society.[99] This attitude reveals that some whites still associate blacks with apes.[100] Negative images of African Americans still prevail and reinforce white stereotypes. Some products now sold on white supremacist websites debase Obama, his wife, African Americans, and other Americans of color. In fact, Obama was garbed in witch doctor attire with a bone in his nose, while his wife's physiognomy was shaped like an ape. While many activists have championed the cause of civil rights, some black entertainers (i.e., the late Richard Pryor) have capitalized on black stereotypes and have made lucrative careers for reinforcing these stereotypes on public television, making great use of the *n*-word.[101] Because of these negative historical representations depicting blacks as unattractive, oversexed, musical, and court jesting idiots, many African Americans have bought into the colorism ideology, where dark skin is ugly, and light skin is beautiful. These past overt stereotypes of blacks "highlight common forms of discrimination that previously have gone unrecognized" and are hidden in the everyday activity of white society, where covert racism still prevails.[102] Since Obama has become president, the racism that was covert for many years has now become overt.

AFRICAN AMERICANS STILL VICTIMS OF COLORISM

Colorism is prevalent and insidiously ingrained in U.S. society, manifesting itself externally in the society and internally within the psyche of African Americans, even among the most prosperous African Americans who struggle with the black identity. In the next several sections, I explore the lives of a few notable African American icons whose lives illustrate the effects of colorism on their psyche: O. J. Simpson, Michael Jackson, Tiger Woods, and Clarence Thomas. Said in the fashion of Frantz Fanon, these men have black skin, but wear white masks, masks that help them to culturally denude themselves of their heritage. First, let me clarify that I do not oppose interracial unions, but I believe that many interracial marriages between blacks and whites are the result of colorism. When African Americans cross racial lines to deracinate themselves from the African American culture, it is a natural for those of black African ancestry to express concern. Historically, black men were legally forbidden to associate with white women. White women were the forbidden fruit and accepted this social construction regardless of their feelings for men of color. Given the historical realities of race, more African American men date and marry outside the African American community because they perceive that interracial dating and marriage could elevate their social, economic, and political status. Although there are some exceptions, relationships between African American men and white women are hypergamous. That is to say, African American men tend to have a higher economic status than the white women they marry.

BLACK MEN OF SUBSTANCE AND COLORISM

O. J. Simpson, a retired American NFL player and currently incarcerated, was charged with the murder of his wife, Nicole Brown-Simpson, and her friend Ronald Goldman. He was acquitted of these murders after a lengthy, highly publicized criminal trial in 1995. His first wife, whom he divorced, was African American; his second wife, Brown-Simpson, was white. That Simpson associated himself mainly with whites, played the white man's sport (golf), and permed his hair to make it straight, suggest that he embraced colorism.

Although African Americans emotionally supported Simpson during his trial of the century, some questions remain unanswered. Did Simpson believe his wealth could secure him a permanent place in white society and shield him from his blackness and ignore the centuries-old system of racism? Is he a victim of colorism? After Simpson was acquitted of the murders, he experienced a backlash of white hostility. Simpson's acquittal angered white America. What caused this blacklash of white anger against Simpson's acquittal was simply white racism and white retribution. Simpson thought his economic position could gain his acceptance in a white society that merely tolerates well-off African Americans. Contemporary legal research reveals that the legal system is designed for notable white acquittal, but not notable black acquittal. When I was in graduate school during Simpson's trial, professors ended classes early to hear the verdict. When they heard "not guilty," the whole university stood silent. When students of color stepped into an elevator of white professors discussing the verdict, they went silent. Whether we were Simpson fans or not, the white racial frame linked us to Simpson. Whites did not appear to care about any exculpatory evidence that set Simpson free. White racism had already condemned him. Whites were outraged over the Simpson acquittal because the white dominant racist legal system failed to secure the conviction of a well-known, wealthy black man. Much like the famous *Roots* scene that will be discussed later, Simpson had become another "nigger" and should have been convicted, regardless of his guilt or innocence. "The white tendency to view people of African descent as deviant and threatening is centuries old." [103]

The late Michael Jackson, the King of Pop, was married to two white women, Lisa Presley and Deborah Jeanne Rowe, but both marriages ended in divorce. Looking at photos of Jackson from the 1960s, Jackson sported an Afrocentric hairstyle and his facial features were Afrotypic: wide nose, brown skin, and wooly hair. In later years, he began transforming himself into the image of "whiteness." He underwent cosmetic constructive surgery to Anglicize his physiognomy and to whiten his skin. As he traveled throughout Europe, he learned that he could alter his appearance, using various procedures. According to Frantz Fanon, "For several years certain [European] laboratories have been trying to produce a serum for 'denegrification'. With all the earnestness in the world, laboratories have sterilized their test tubes, checked their scales, and embarked on research that might make it possible for the miserable Negro to whiten himself and to throw off the burden of that corporeal malediction." [104] Did the King of Pop find the magical serum that would "denegrify" his genetic appearance? Was Jackson a victim of colorism?

The third example is U.S. Supreme Court Justice Clarence Thomas, who has distanced himself from all Afrocentric activities and adopted the dominant value system. Alvin Wyman Walker, a clinical psychologist and psychotherapist, notes that Thomas himself was a beneficiary of affirmative action but now believes that affirmative action implies black inferiority and that African Americans and other Americans of color should educationally lift themselves without relying on government programs. Based on Walker's assessment, Thomas reacts to colorism in both his personal and professional life and has worked against any programs (i.e., affirmative action) that could help African Americans and other Americans of color. Thomas has said he does not fit in with whites and does not fit in with blacks. He claims he has gone "through a self-hate stage where you hate yourself for being part of a group that's gotten the hell kicked out of it. . . ."[105] Thomas suffers from what Dubois calls the "double consciousness of twoness." The notion of "twoness" is a divided awareness of one's racial identity that African Americans are trapped between two worlds, a black world and a white world—an American, a black; two souls, and two thoughts in an ebony body, a color that denies him true liberty and the pursuit of happiness.[106] Contemporary research reveals that African Americans will always see their existence through the eyes of others, especially through the eyes of the white racial frame.

The last example, Tiger Woods, has, like Simpson, the late Jackson, and Thomas, culturally denuded himself from the Afrocentric culture. Woods, an American professional golfer whose achievements rank him among the most successful golfers of all time, claims he is "Cablinasian" because of his mixed ancestry: Caucasian, black, Native American, and Asian. By claiming this packaged heritage, Woods appear to be a victim of colorism. Does the white dominant culture view him as an African American only or Native or Asian?

Woods's racial identity recently was the subject of racialized rhetoric. When Fuzzy Zoeller, the 1979 Masters champion, spoke to reporters at a tournament, he referred to Tiger Woods as "that little boy" and urged him not to order fried chicken or collard greens for the 2010 Champions Dinner. A CNN camera crew recorded the comments, which aired on CNN's "Pro Golf Weekly." There is a connection between the vintage racist rhetoric of the 1960s and Zoeller's depictions of Woods. First, Zoeller referred to Woods as a "little boy," which suggests that it is acceptable to call black men's manhood into question to deny them the right to be treated as autonomous, self-determining adults. Second, Zoeller's offensive remarks bring the days of slavery and the Jim Crow era to the forefront, re-creating the master-slave relationship. Third, Zoeller's racialized rhetoric denies Woods, black men in general, and Obama the recognition to be treated with respect. Denying black men and the president this recognition is to disrespect their manhood, a rage black men usually feel when they are treated like "boys." Most black men have been raised by female matriarchs without the benefit of a strong black male presence. Zoeller may not be aware that he has brought back the bad memories of slavery when black men were treated and disrespected like boys in front of their own sons. Zoeller's racialized comments may suggest that Woods is a successful golf pro, but he and other men of color will never be treated with the same degree of respect accorded to white men. Finally, Zoeller's racialized remarks suggest that black men should remain located in the "little boy" space because they have no power or authority in U.S. society and that social relations between black men and white men are only reified and no white man has to respect a black man. Given Zoeller's attitude toward Tiger Woods, we can understand the reason many black males are racially profiled and treated like violent criminals.

When racialized rhetoric stirs the historical pot, it conjures up the typical debasement to which Clarence Thomas refers.

Further evidence indicates that dominant society views Woods as a person of African ancestry. Kevin Blackistone asserts that *Vanity Fair*, a predominant white magazine industry, refused to validate Woods's desire to identify himself as Cablinasian.[107] Blackistone goes on to inform us that the magazine would not legitimize Woods's suburban upbringing, mastering golf, and marrying a Swedish blue-eyed blond. Instead, *Vanity Fair* identified Woods with his late father's black African ancestry, which supports the one-drop rule argument.[108]

Overall, these examples suggest that the one-drop rule is a powerful signifier of racial identity, racial purity, racial acceptance, as well as racial distinction for the sake of social significance. The power elite define what "blackness" is, making it easy for the purveyors of racism to deny African Americans and other Americans of color the same privileges that whites enjoy on an unmatched scale. Simpson, Thomas, and Woods may need to re-acquaint themselves with the one-drop rule. No matter how much they deny their black ancestry or try to augment it with the dominant value system in order to enjoy the material trappings it offers, U.S. society will always view black African ancestry through a white racial frame. Since we live in "a society pervaded by racism, then racism prescribes our experience," as Lisa Ikemoto notes. Racism is such as significant part of the African American experience that they cannot always recognize those moments when they participate in it.[109] Said differently, a racist culture infects the oppressed as well as the oppressor, where the oppressor mystifies "race" designed to engender collective false consciousness among dominant group members.[110]

THE ROOTS EXAMPLE

In describing oppression, storytelling has particular value. Racism operates in, part, through the narratives about race, and the politics that construct our reality.[111] Even if the narratives are based on facts, they can be typical or descriptively accurate, emphasizing the emotional dimensions of the narratives.[112] In Episode 5, Scene 13 of Alex Haley's miniseries *Roots: The First Generation*, there is a communication exchange between a slave named Chicken George, Alex Haley's great-great grandfather, played by Ben Vereen and his poor white ruthless drunken slave owner, Tom Moore, played by Chuck Connors. Whether this particular segment in the miniseries is fiction or nonfiction, it reveals the relationship dynamics between whites and blacks and whites' brazen attitudes toward blacks, regardless of their status—slave or manumitted.

The story presents Chicken George as a renowned cockfight trainer for his alcoholic slave owner, Tom Moore. Cockfighting was a form of gambling. Cockfighting involved two roosters trained to aggressively fight to death, while cockfighting owners placed bets on the fight. When Chicken George and his slave master's rooster lost the cockfight against the rooster of an English aristocrat, the only way Moore could settle his huge debt was to grant Chicken George permission to return to England with the Englishman to train his roosters. Moore agreed to these financial terms and assured Chicken George that he would set him free, showing him the manumission papers, upon his return to the plantation. Moore also gave his word that he would keep Chicken George's family together: his wife, two sons, and mother, Izzy, whose body was sexually ravaged by Tom Moore on a regular basis when Izzy was sold to him at the age of 14 and Chicken George was conceived as a result of Moore sexually ravaging Izzy's body. After Chicken George left for Europe, Moore went deeper into debt because of his heavy drinking. Moore's wife asked what he was planning to do to save them from further economic depression. Moore told her that he would sell off the slaves, and his wife warned him of the promise he made to Chicken George and what he was going to tell Chicken George, when Moore had promised his "son of the plantation" he would keep the family together. Moore proclaimed, "[Chicken George] will not come back white, my dear. He'll still come back a nigger. Really, what's a nigger to do?"

This exchange between Moore and his wife suggests that in American society, as subtle as it may be in modern times, regardless of African Americans' social status or educational attainment, white society does not always keep its word to blacks. We have seen this attitude played out through slavery, after slavery, during Reconstruction to the Civil Rights movement, and now in contemporary society. America may think it has improved in race relations or may believe we live in a post-racial society with the election and re-election of Barack Obama, but racism cuts across the lines of dishonesty, integrity, and the power elites' lack of commitment to honor their word to African Americans and other Americans of color. This is the reason a Native American proverb states that "white man speak with a forked tongue," meaning to say one thing but mean something different, especially in race-related social situations.[113] Having explored the historic roots of systemic racism, we now turn to modern-day racial implications for Barack Hussein Obama.

BARACK HUSSEIN OBAMA

Who is this first black president that has heaped much white racism, radicalism, and white retribution upon himself? Obama was born on August 4, 1961, to Stanley Ann Dunham and Barack Hussein Obama, Sr., in Honolulu, Hawaii. Obama's mother was a white professional from the state of Kansas and his father was an African from Nyang'oma Kogelo,

Kenya. He is a graduate of Columbia University and Harvard Law School and the first African American president of the *Harvard Law Review*, one of the most cited and well-respected law reviews among the greatest legal minds in the United States. Before he received his law degree, Obama as a community organizer and as a civil rights attorney. After he received his law degree from Harvard, he taught constitutional law at the University of Chicago Law School from 1992-2004. He served three terms in the Illinois Senate from 1997-2004. In July 2004, he gave the keynote address at the Democratic National Convention and won the U.S. Senate seat for Illinois and served in the Illinois legislature from June 2005 until November 2008, which he resigned when he was elected president of the United States. In February 2007, he sought the presidency and clinched the Democratic nomination after several close races against Hillary Rodham Clinton. In the 2008 general election, Obama defeated Republican candidate John McCain and was inaugurated as the 44th president of the United States on January 20, 2009. He served a full term and went on to win re-election on November 6, 2012.

Obama, a charismatic pragmatist, represents a new idea of race with political and social awareness, challenging people's notions of what it means to be African American in a postmodern world.[114] An enlightened intellectual, Obama possesses a sense of self-determination and self-dependence that has eluded the majority of those living in the larger African American community. This notion gives him an advantage to change a sociopolitical base and to build a racial and ethnic coalition that could foster change in the social and political realms.[115] Obama's pragmatic approach to politics has become a pragmatic practice. Even though Obama says "Yes, we can," his conservative critics say "No, we can't," and use the adverb "no" to thwart his progress, the major reason he "faced intractable political and economic problems as president"[116] in his first term. In his writings, Obama reveals his

> debts to earlier American traditions that demonstrate he has a deeper interest in, and a firmer grip on America's past than has any president of the United States since Theodore Roosevelt and Woodrow Wilson. The strands, on which Obama has drawn, however, differ from those that have appealed to many Democrats in recent decades. In part for that reason, and even more significantly because his sensibility reflects the profound changes in American intellectual life since the 1960s, Obama's ideas and his approach to American politics have thrown political observers off balance. His books, his speeches, and his political record make clear that he represents a hybrid of old and new, which explains why he puzzles so many contemporaries—supporters and critics alike—who see him through conventional and thus distorting lenses. Placing him in American intellectual history illuminates both the genuinely novel dimensions of his worldview, which have gone largely unnoticed, and the older traditions he seeks to resurrect. [117]

Obama's writings further reveal that he embodies liberation, the liberation of the rich and poor, the elite and non-elite, the educated and non-educated, blacks and whites, Americans and legal immigrants, and the political and non-political. He has been recognized as a political black presence among Americans as well as among the international community whose message of "hope" in his first term and "forward" in his second term encourages the underclass to interrogate their own interests and to exercise their voting rights. Obama's critical presence has opened up a "theoretical terrain where difference and other can be considered legitimate issues in the academy," as well as legitimate issues for political debate.[118] A Pew Center Poll conducted in March 2008 indicated that majority of the people they polled found Obama to be honest, patriotic, and down-to-earth, and a majority of them felt hope and pride about themselves.[119] A *CNN* poll conducted in August 2012 reveals that more than half of Americans believe Obama cares about their economic well-being.[120]

Obama has restored in the oppressed the faith in American democracy for all Americans for which he shows considerable concern. His ascent to the presidency helps the marginalized and the oppressed to see it is possible to rise from economic obscurity to a relative position of affluence. Shelby Steele claims that Obama used the race card to bargain and compromise with other politicians to get his way.[121] But the 112th Congress, Congressional Republicans, has refused to compromise with Obama. Compromise is "difficult, but governing a democracy without compromise is impossible."[122] Congressional Republicans would not compromise on taxes because they wanted to protect the top one percent that would fill their coffers with campaign funds. Like the 38th Congress, specifically Congressional Democrats, comprising southern planters, they, too, rejected any form of compromise with Lincoln to end slavery because they benefited from slavery and wanted to protect their interests. But history reveals that bargain and compromise are necessary to protect the entire electorate's interests and not just the wealthiest citizens who sometimes use the corrupting influence of money to get legislation passed in their favor. Lincoln compromised with the 38th Congress to get the Thirteenth Amendment passed to outlaw slavery.[123] LBJ compromised with the 88th and 89th Congresses to get the Civil Rights Act of 1964 and the Voting Rights Act of 1965 passed. Although Obama was elected with more than 50 percent of the popular vote for both presidential terms, he has politically reached out to all Americans, regardless of race, class, gender, and sexual orientation. Obama has not found it necessary to use the race card or his "blackness" to achieve his goals. Instead, he relies on pragmatic ideas and stresses the importance of U.S. democratic ideals. In one of his 2009 inaugural excerpts, he said:

In reaffirming the greatness of our nation, we understand that great-ness is never a given. It must be earned. Our journey has never been one of short-cuts or settling for less. It has not been the path for the faint-hearted for those who prefer leisure over work, or seek only the pleasures of riches and fame. Rather, it has been the risk-takers, the doers, the makers of things, some celebrated but more often men and women obscure in their labor that carried us up the long rugged path towards prosperity and freedom. For us, they packed up their few worldly possessions and traveled across oceans in search of a new life. For us, they toiled in sweatshops and settled in the West; endured the lash of the whip and plowed the hard earth.

If we link Obama's writings to the intellect and traditions from which he has drawn, in *Dreams from My Father* and *The Audacity of Hope*, Obama can be located in the context of American political and social thought and not in the context of his blackness, as his critics would want us to be-lieve.[124]

Alain Locke and Martin Luther King, Jr., had once put forth the notion for social change, hope, and the possibility for the day the United States would elect its first African American president. Locke and King explain that it would take someone who is endowed with certain inalienable abilities, a politician with a new sense of dignity and destiny, a person with self-respect, who is diplomatic and polite, willing to stand up coura-geously for what he believes is just, based on the laws of the land, and a person with a growing honesty. [125] King goes on to say that such a politi-cal figure would need to be cognizant of the American traditions of liber-ty and justice and know how to stand up for himself and the American people and demand to be treated as a full citizen of U.S. society with access to the same rights and privileges that the power elite take for granted. [126] Obama is the representation of a "new" kind of politician, the "new African American," as Locke and King have described, capable of making history. Indeed, Obama was the first black president and the first U.S. president to be awarded the Nobel Peace Prize during his first year in office, which angered elite white journalists and politicians who tried to discourage him from accepting the prize. The five-member Norwegian Nobel Committee—four of whom spoke to *The Associated Press*—said that by "awarding Obama the peace prize could be seen as an early vote of confidence intended to build global support for the policies of his young administration. They lauded the change in the global mood wrought by Obama's calls for peace and cooperation." [127] Obama's continued fight for democratic principles of fairness has upset the power elite because they want to keep in place a system from which only they benefit, a major reason Obama has met with unrelenting obstruction from the conserva-tive right in his first term that has been carried into his second term. For example, after the 2012 election, Obama and Congress agreed to focus their attention on the fiscal cliff, but the U.S. House of Representatives

Speaker John Boehner abandoned this responsibility, when his Plan B did not receive sufficient support from Congressional Republicans. Having lost political control over his caucus that is controlled by the extreme elements of the Party, this author believes Boehner was influenced by casino mogul Sheldon Adelson, who met with him and other Republican leaders a month after the election, perhaps under the pretext of changing the Foreign Corrupt Practices Act, the anti-bribery law under which Adelson's Las Vegas Sands is being investigated, to resist any negotiations with the White House that would inflict tax pains on the top one percent because of the Bush-Era Tax Cuts.[128] There does not seem to be any logical reason for the Speaker to abruptly end all negotiations with the White House and require the Senate to "Act First."[129] After all, Adelson contributed millions of dollars to Super Pacs to help presidential contender Mitt Romney defeat Barack Obama and to help other Republicans who ran for re-election, including House Speaker John Boehner and House Majority Leader Eric Cantor.

Even with his goodwill, Obama faced an insurmountable task to lay claim to the American traditions of liberty and justice for all. Obama's intellectual prowess, diplomacy, politeness, and awareness of the American traditions of liberty and justice for all transcend his blackness. In the next few paragraphs, I discuss the racism Obama experienced in his first term as president. Only time will tell if these attacks will tone down, since the first attacks did not prevent him from winning re-election.

ATTACKS ON OBAMA: RACISM, RADICALISM, OR RETRIBUTION

U.S. society cannot redeem itself from its racist past and go on to call itself a post-racial society with the election of the first African American president. "The substantial white consensus on the decline of racism is not based on empirical evidence. On the contrary, research shows that black men and women [including President Obama] still face extensive racial discrimination in all arenas of daily life."[130] Freedom, justice, and equality cannot happen until America cleanses itself of white supremacy, white privilege, and white racism and practices the tenets of the Declaration of Independence that all men and women are created equal. America's institutions are stained with a racist ideology that only whites should enjoy freedom, justice, and have full access to resources in America's coffers. Since taking office, Obama has been the subject of multiple racist attacks, portrayed as subhuman in graphics, and emails and posters used to undermine his leadership, to attack his manhood, credibility as a leader, and to turn the American people against him. In his first term, he experienced daily, a rogue's gallery of pundits who doubled down on their racialized rhetoric. From the very beginning, these attacks on the president have been personal and venomous and mostly came from the extreme conservative right, the Tea Party adamantine, to disgrace his presidency.

When Obama gave a speech that pre-empted "A Charlie Brown Christmas," the mayor of Arlington, Tennessee, called Obama a Muslim president.[131] Many denigrating cartoons of the president and the First Lady were portrayed in various media. A Florida neurosurgeon who opposed The Affordable Care Act portrayed Obama as an African witch doctor and his wife a gorilla.[132] While politicians have often been the targets of cartoon caricatures, such images of Obama still reveal racism in the American way of thinking. Journalists revealed President Clinton telling the late Senator Ted Kennedy that a few years earlier, Obama would have been serving them coffee let alone running for the presidency.[133] With disheartening regularity, the issues of race continue to surface in the Obama presidency, and white retribution is its driving force.[134]

While other presidents have been turned into caricatures, the caricatures used to criticize Obama have strong racial overtones—some are overt and some are disrespectful and outside the bounds of civil discourse. His critics repeatedly charge that he is ill-suited for the presidency, inexperienced in the extreme, lacks leadership capacity, and is an ineffective leader.[135] Obama has also been referred to as a "tar baby" by top conservative right leaders. The term "tar baby" refers to "19th-century Uncle Remus stories about Br'er Rabbit but has taken on a negative connotation towards African-Americans."[136] Pat Buchanan referred to the president as "your boy," when Al Sharpton asked him to comment on the debt ceiling debate.[137] Congressman Joe Wilson (R-SC) screamed "you lie" during Obama's first state of the union speech, when he discussed the Affordable Care Act.[138] It is worth noting that former President Jimmy Carter has taken the position that an overwhelming number of those who oppose Obama's policies and actions have engaged in racist behavior. Clearly, systemic racism has emerged full speed from underground to remind the first African American president that the "economic power is still in the hands of whites," that white men still shape the political, social, and cultural consciousness of U.S. society, and that the Republican Party will continue to constrain his legislative efforts.[139]

Questions regarding Obama's citizenship, the true location of his birth, his relationship with his controversial former pastor, Reverend Jeremiah Wright, and other issues have their roots in racism.[140] Cartoons portraying President Obama as a monkey appeared in a New York tabloid during his first two months in office. A California mayor was forced to resign after distributing a picture of watermelons on the White House lawn, and an email was widely distributed referring to the president as the "magic mulatto" with exaggerated ears and nose.[141] Former Speaker of the House Newt Gingrich called Obama the "food stamp president." A conservative Florida neurosurgeon activist forwarded a racist photo portraying Obama as a witch doctor with "Obama care: Coming soon to a clinic near you" inscribed beneath it. Delegates to the American Medical Association condemned the racist behavior of this neurosurgeon.[142] Obama has been portrayed with the same exaggerated smile and black rimmed eyes as Heath Ledger's joker character from the movie *The Dark Knight*. This poster is a distorted replication of the president's "hope" poster that is clearly designed to make the president look sinister.[143] Some critics of the poster argue that it is offensive because Obama is in white face and the image is a reverse of a black and white minstrel. Finally, a southern California Tea Party activist and member of the central committee of the Orange County Republican Party sent an email portraying Obama with chimpanzee parents and the caption titled "Now you know why—no birth certificate."[144] These caricatures of the first African American president strongly suggest that Obama is battling America's racist history.

SIDE NOTE ON THE BIRTHER MOVEMENT

Many Americans continue to believe Obama is a Muslim who was born in Kenya rather than the United States. Others use the Internet to assert that Obama is ineligible to be president because they believe his Hawaiian birth certificate is not authentic. A federal judge dismissed a lawsuit that questioned Obama's citizenship and said that the case was a waste of the court's time, but many individuals including Senator Richard Shelby (R-AL) and Representative Bill Posey (R-FL) seem to be convinced that there is room for debate on this issue. Donald Trump, a business magnate and television personality, pandered to a subset of Americans who needed to believe that Obama is not a U.S. citizen. These "birthers" cannot "reconcile the legitimacy of an African American being president with their own self-image. In order to understand the birther movement," it would help to read *The Prostrate State: South Carolina Under Negro Government* by James Shepard Pike, a book published in the nineteenth century.[145]

The rise of the "The Birthers Movement" should cause concerns for African Americans and other Americans of color. White retribution is still part of U.S. cultural production and reflects the country's early history of discrimination. Under *jus soli*, also known as birthright citizenship, for the first one-hundred years of American history, Americans of color were not considered citizens.[146] The import of the Birthers Movement emerge out of another century, particular that of *Dred Scott*. Scott was an enslaved man and went before the federal courts to argue for his citizenship rights to secure his freedom.[147] Access to the courts was predicated on citizenship.[148] Dismissing his claim, U.S. Supreme Court Chief Justice Roger Taney declared in 1857 that Scott and all blacks, regardless of their status, were of an inferior class and could never become full U.S. citizens.[149] In 1868, the Fourteenth Amendment was adopted, overruling the *Dred Scott* decision, making African Americans full citizens. In 1896, however, African Americans were legally forced into racial segregation under the notorious doctrine of "separate, but equal," making them second class citizens until the Warren Court in 1954 struck down the separate but equal doctrine.

In light of the Birthers Movement, the Arizona House passed House Bill 2177 that would require presidential candidates to show their birth certificates if they wanted their names placed on the state's ballot, but Governor Jan Brewer vetoed the birther bill, calling it "a bridge too far." This action by the majority white legislators in the Arizona state house and other state houses is a form of white radicalism. Had Obama been a white male, we are certain Arizona would have given scant attention to this issue.

Obama's experience with white racism on the political macro level should also inform African Americans and other Americans of color that racism is deeply rooted in the American culture and that the most powerful office of the land cannot even shield Obama from its grip.

OBAMA AND COLORISM

Obama, unlike Simpson, the late King of Pop, Thomas, and Woods, has rejected the reified system of race and group social relationships. Although he knows this country suffers from systemic racism, Obama is aware that dominant society views him as a person of African descent because the one-drop rule prevails in the minds of older whites. As he describes in his own writings, Obama has not given in to the illusion that an Ivy League education, a white mother, and a white middle class upbringing could wipe away his "blackness" and brought into the fold of the power elite. Obama has learned how to slip back and forth between his bi-racial world to accommodate the situation.[150] In a sense, he embraces an assimilationist, nationalist, and humanist ideology. As an assimilationist, he understands the commonalities between Americans of color and the rest of American society. As a nationalist, he understands the uniqueness of being of African ancestry. As a humanist, he understands the common features of all racial groups of U.S. society that make up its national character. However, Obama is living in a world where "white supremacy still pervades [U.S.] culture" and the reified system of social relations between blacks, whites, and other Americans of color is governed by the politics of race and white dominance. We can see the reified social relations between himself and prominent Republicans and the racist reactions to his election and re-election to the presidency, as will be discussed in chapter 2.

During the 2008 presidential campaign, Obama and his wife were depicted as terrorists in a cartoon published by *The New Yorker*. In this cartoon, Obama was garbed in a Muslim robe, sported a turban, and was likened to Osama Bin Laden, while Michelle Obama was dressed in fatigues with a gun hoisted over her shoulder and portrayed as an angry, hostile black woman supposedly having issues with white society. The artist positioned both Obama and his wife in the Oval Office bumping fists, a posture that evoked fear in white society that white-hating black terrorists would control the White House and destroy all that whites hold dear. Conservative cable news networks described this fist bump as a "terrorist fist jab," while the burning of the American flag in the background represented the desecration of America and for what it stands, suggesting that Obama was anti-American and his wife, un-American. After Obama's first-term election, a former Los Alamitos, California, mayor sent a mass email with an attachment, illustrating watermelons strewn on the lawn of the White House. This racist image was a way to dehumanize Obama and African Americans and suggested that watermelon is a negative produce only associated with black people. To this day, a number of elderly African Americans will not eat watermelon because of its negative connotations, based on their experiences during the Jim Crow era.[151]

After he was elected president in 2008, even the Tea Party adamantine nihilists reverted to creating racist advertising about Obama. Maureen Dodd notes that these nihilists believe Obama "looks down on them and sneers at their value system."[152] The Tea Party adamantine has also displayed Obama with a bone through his nose and watermelons strewn over the lawn of the White House at many of their rally parties.[153] Mark Williams, a conservative activist and now defunct leader of the Tea Party Express, likens Obama to an Indonesian Muslim turned welfare criminal who wants to destroy the country.[154] Williams writes a fictitious letter to Abraham Lincoln satirizing African Americans that demean the humanity of both Obama and the African American community. He wrote in the voice of slaves, Dear Mr. Lincoln:

> You were the greatest racist ever. We had a great gig. Three squares, room and board, all our decisions made by the massa in the house. We Coloreds have taken a vote and decided that we don't cotton to that whole emancipation thing. Freedom means having to work for real, think for ourselves, and take consequences along with the rewards. That is just far too much to ask of us Colored People and we demand that it stop!

He went on to say blacks don't want taxes cut because "how will we Colored People ever get a wide screen TV in every room if non-coloreds get to keep what they earn?"[155]

Williams's satirizing of African Americans suggests his racialized rhetoric accuses African Americans, or trifling "coloreds," of not wanting to work, and of "striving for welfare." Walt Minnick of Idaho, the only Democrat whom the Tea Party Express endorsed, publicly rejected the Party's endorsement and expressed his concerns over Williams's satirizing African Americans as lazy, which reinforces white thinking about African Americans as welfare cheats.[156]

In *Game Change*, journalists Mark Halperin and John Heilemann reported Senate Majority Leader Harry Reid as saying in private that Obama "could become the country's first black president because he was light-skinned and had no Negro dialect, unless he wanted to have one."[157] Even though Reid apologized for his insensitive remarks, there is genuine concern about the use of racialized language in both private and public spaces about white feelings and views toward African Americans and other Americans of color in general. Richard Delgado, a legal and critical race scholar, observes that the use of racialized language and stigmatization is one of the leading causes of human misery.[158]

THE REAL CULPRITS BEHIND SYSTEMIC RACISM: THE POWER ELITE AND THE INVISIBLE WHITE HOOD

As during the Jim Crow era, the power elite are the real culprits behind systemic racism. They approved the activities of the Klan through coded racist language. They did not want to be perceived as the real culprits behind the violence of the Klan, as many of them were Klansmen, were officers of the law, and held judgeships. But African Americans knew too well that the power elite upheld Klan activity. Since the power elite politically support and encourage systemic racism, this explains the slow progress this country has made in fruitful interracial relations. As during the Jim Crow era, the power elite today sends subtle messages to average white Americans with anti-racial sentiments that discrimination and oppression of African Americans and other Americans of color are age-old practices and will be politicized to an extent to lessen its effects. That is to say, they send messages that are politically expedient for white survival to oppress Americans of color in social institutions and in the workplace. Political pundits and cable network commentators have reported that the color of this society is slowly changing due to the changing demographics. This support and encouragement also explains the reason that the justice system is skewed negatively against African Americans and other Americans of color because it is incapable of rendering fair and just verdicts in criminal cases motivated by race. U.S. District Judge Richard Cebull of Montana forwarded a racist Obama email to six of his colleagues comparing African Americans to dogs and implying that Obama's mother had engaged in unwholesome bestial sex. He justified sending the email not as a racist but "anti-Obama." As a result, he has agreed to step down in March 2013, so Obama can replace him. When the power elite use racialized rhetoric and send anti-Obama messages that reach the public, they support centuries-old behavioral practices in which some white Americans with pro-racial tendencies probably would not engage if these behavioral practices were not encouraged in action by the power elite. This also explains the heightened disrespect for Obama and for his presidency. Alex Haley's *Roots* miniseries illustrated this fact that poor white males would only terrorize African Americans and other Americans of color with the blessings and approval of the power elite who in turn would shield them from prosecution by covering up the crime, similar to what history records in the killings of black male teenagers such as Emmett Louis Till in 1955 and Trayvon Martin in 2012.

CONCLUSION

It is difficult at best to ignore the power of race, class, and gender, as an important issue in the United States. It is highly likely that many of Obama's critics who challenge his policies and leadership are motivated in part by racial antagonisms, tensions, radicalism, and retribution. Cable news commentators and part of the electorate believe these racist attacks on Obama have been dampening the spirit of the country and creating political divisions among the American citizens who perhaps are already sensitive to issues regarding race.[159] As David Sessions notes, it is quite clear that there is a "very angry, small group of folks that just didn't like the fact that Barack Obama won the presidency."[160] The hegemonic influence of the white racial frame has created and continues to create a racial order based on dominance and privilege vis-á-vis Americans of color, working class white Americans, women, and immigrants. In response to the systemic racism engendered through this dominant worldview, Obama has learned to rely on psychological counter-frames aimed at resisting this dominance.

Overt and subtle racist attacks on Obama's race, religion, and patriotism are certain to occur, but Obama's predecessors have not been subjected to such attacks based on race. George W. Bush was called a "privileged white boy" by many on the political left, but they did not disrespect him.[161] They worked and cooperated with him. Bush was also likened to Adolf Hitler, and Bill Clinton dealt with anti-government sentiments. Yet the impact of these anti-sentiments was not as severe as what Obama has experienced in his first term. Research reveals that these anti-sentiments are race-based. What makes the attacks on Obama more difficult and disconcerting is that Obama is the first African American elected to the presidency and the days of race baiting and pandering to a select group of people are far too recent to take any potential racial criticism at face value. There is something unsettling about these *ad hominem* attacks on the first African American president. Of course, some of these attacks are motivated by a dislike of the president's policies and politics that embrace fairness and justice, and others are likely informed by racism, radicalism, and retribution, and the fact that an African American is the head of state and >head of government of the United States. While Obama is withstanding these challenges with dignity on the national stage, these *ad hominem* attacks stifle progress, distract attention from important issues, and ultimately hurt the American people, as we will explore in the next chapter.

Overt and subtle racist attacks on Obama's race, religion, and patriotism are certain to occur, but Obama's predecessors have not been subjected to such attacks based on race. George W. Bush was called a "privileged white boy" by many on the political left, but they did not disrespect him.[162] They worked and cooperated with him. Bush was also likened to Adolf Hitler, and Bill Clinton dealt with anti-government sentiments. Yet the impact of these anti-sentiments was not as severe as what Obama has experienced in his first term. Research reveals that these anti-sentiments are race-based. What makes the attacks on Obama more difficult and disconcerting is that Obama is the first African American elected to the presidency and the days of race baiting and pandering to a select group of people are far too recent to take any potential racial criticism at face value. There is something unsettling about these *ad hominem* attacks on the first African American president. Of course, some of these attacks are motivated by a dislike of the president's policies and politics that embrace fairness and justice, and others are likely informed by racism, radicalism, and retribution, and the fact that an African American is the head of state and head of government of the United States. While Obama is withstanding these challenges with dignity on the national stage, these *ad hominem* attacks stifle progress, distract attention from important issues, and ultimately hurt the American people, as we will explore in the next chapter.

NOTES

1. James T. Kloppenberg, *Reading Obama: Dreams, Hope and the American Political Tradition* (Princeton, NJ: Princeton University Press, 2010), 4.

2. D.T. Pollard, *Obama Guilty of Being President While Black* (Kindle Electronic Edition, Location 13–15, Grand Prairie, TX, Book Express, 2009),

3. Robert E. Denton, Jr., "Identity Politics in the 2008 Presidential Campaign: An Overview," in Robert E. Denton, Jr. ed., *Studies of Identity in the 2008 Presidential Campaign* (Lanham, MD: Lexington Books, 2010), 7. (As citing Shelby Steele, a black republican).

4. Robert Draper, *Do Not Ask What Good We Do: Inside the House of Representatives* (New York: Free Press, 2012), xix.

5. Ishmael Reed, *Barack Obama and the Jim Crow Media: The Return of the Nigger Breakers* (Canada: Baraka Books, 2010).

6. Erica Brown, "Congress Honors Slaves Who Built United States Capitol," http://www.thecincinnatiherald.com/news/2011-02-12/News/Congress_honors_slaves_who_built_United_States_Cap.html. Erica Brown is an NNPA Special Correspondent in Washington, DC. See also 111th Congress 1st Session, S. CON. RES. 24. http://www.gpo.gov/ fdsys/pkg/BILLS-111sconres24is/pdf/BILLS-111sconres24is.pdf (accessed April 11, 2012).

7. Irving M. Zeitlin, *Ideology and the Development of Sociological Theory, 6th Edition* (Upper Saddle River, NJ: Prentice Hall, 1997), 93.

8. Frederick K.C. Price, *Race, Religion & Racism*, Volume 1 (Los Angeles: Faith One Publishing, 1999), 109.

9. Paul Griffin, *Seeds of Racism in the Soul of America* (Naperville, IL: Sourcebooks, Inc., 2001), x.

10. Ibid., 39.

11. Frederick K.C. Price, *op. cit.* (see reference 8), 109.

12. "First Confiscation Act of 1861," June 24, 2011, http://teachingamericanhistory.org/library/index.asp?document=557 (accessed February 4, 2012).

13. Joe R. Feagin, *Systemic Racism: A Theory of Oppre*ssion (New York: Routledge, Taylor & Francis Group, 2006), 7.

14. Ronald Takaki, *Iron Cages: Race and Culture in 19th Century America* (New York: Oxford University Press, 1990), 12.

15. Jud Sage, "The Mississippi Black Code," http://chnm.gmu.edu/courses/122/recon/code.html (accessed June 21, 2012).

16. Ibid.

17. David Neiwert, *The Eliminationists: How Hate Talk Radicalized the American Right* (Sausilito, CA: PoliPointPress, 2009), 175.

18. Ibid.

19. Ronald Takaki, "A Different Mirror: A History of Multicultural America," in *Revisiting America: Readings in Race, Culture, and Conflict*, edited by Susan Wyle (Upper Saddle River, NJ: Pearson/Prentice Hall, 2004), 771.

20. Manning Marable, *How Capitalism Underdeveloped Black America* (Boston, MA: South End Press, 1983), 62.

21. James D. Bilotta, *Race and the Rise of the Republican Party, 1848–1865* (Philadelphia, PA: Xlibris, 2002).

22. Meltzer Milton, *Thaddeus Stevens and the Fight for Negro Rights* (New York: T.Y. Crowell Co, 1967).

23. Eric Foner, *Reconstruction: America's Unfinished Revolution, 1863-1877*, New American Nation Series (New York: HarperCollins, 1988).

24. Morris Roy, Jr., *Fraud of the Century: Rutherford B. Hayes, Samuel Tilden, and the Stolen Election of 1876* (New York: Simon & Schuster, 2004).

25. Kevin J. McMahon, *Reconsidering Roosevelt on Race: How the Presidency Paved the Road to Brown* (Chicago: University of Chicago Press, 2003).

26. Joe R. Feagin, *op. cit.* (see reference 13), 4.

27. Anthony J. Lemelle, Jr., "Racial and Cultural Minorities," Graduate course taken with Professor Lemelle at Purdue University in Fall, 1998.

28. Velma Maia Thomas, *Lest We Forget: The Passage from Africa to Slavery and Emancipation* (New York: Crown Publishing Group, 1997), 16.

29. Joe R. Feagin, *The White Racial Frame: Centuries of Racial Framing and Counter-Framing* (New York: Routledge, 2010), Kindle Electronic Edition, Paragraph 1, Location 410 of 7147.

30. Ibid., Paragraph 1, Location 187 of 7147.

31. Kenneth Neubeck and Joel A. Cazenave, *Welfare Racism: Playing the Race Card Against America's Poor* (New York: Routledge, 2001), Electronic Kindle Edition, Paragraph 1, Location 180 of 9458.

32. The Mendacity Index, "Cadillac Queens," http://www.washingtonmonthly.com/features/2003/0309.mendacity-index.html (assessed on January 4, 2012). See *New York Times*, 1976-02-15, p. 51. See also George Lakoff's *The Political Mind: Why You*

Can't Understand 21st-Century American Politics with an 18th-Century Brain. "Confronting Stereotypes: Sons of the Welfare Queen" (New York: Viking, 2008).

33. Murray Edelman. *The Politics of Misinformation* (Cambridge: Cambridge University Press, 2001), 2.

34. Ibid., 159.

35. Earl Ofari Hutchinson, "Why So Many Whites Vote Against Themselves," http://www.huffingtonpost.com/earl-ofari-hutchinson/why-so-many-whites-vote-a_b_1342425.html (accessed May 25, 2012).

36. Ibid.

37. Kenneth J. Neubeck and Noel A. Cazenave, *op. cit.* (see reference 31), 14.

38. George Lakoff, *The Political Mind: Why You can't Understand 21st-Century American Politics with an 18th-Century Brain* (New York: Viking, 2008), 161.

39. Ibid.

40. Joe R. Feagin, Hernan Vera, and Pinar Batur, *White Racism: The Basics*, 2nd ed. (New York: Routledge, 2001), 17.

41. Ibid.

42. Manning Marable, *op. cit.* (see reference 20), 63.

43. Shimon Shkury, "Wage Differences between White Men and Black Men in the United States of America" (master's thesis, University of Pennsylvania, 2001), 22–23. http://lauder.wharton.upenn.edu/pages/pdf/ SimonShkury_Thesis.pdf (accessed February 2, 2011).

44. Shirley A. Hill, *Black Intimacies: A Gender Perspective on Families and Relationships* (Lanham, MD: AltaMira Press [The Gender Lens Series], 2005), 8.

45. Ian Haney Lopez, *White By Law: The Legal Construction of Race*, 10th Anniversary Ed. (New York: New York University Press, 2006), 98.

46. Sheri Lynn Johnson, "Black Innocence and the White Jury," in Richard Delgado, ed., *Critical Race Theory: The Cutting Edge* (Philadelphia, PA: Temple University Press, 1995), 183.

47. Ian Haney Lopez, *op. cit.* (see reference 45), 98.

48. Murray Edelman, *Constructing the Political Spectacle* (Chicago, IL: University of Chicago, 1995), 38.

49. Ibid.

50. Michelle Alexander, *The New Jim Crow: Mass Incarceration in the Age of Colorblindness* (New York: The New Press, 2010), Kindle Electronic Edition, Paragraph 2, Location 115, 2847.

51. Marc Mauer, "The Crisis of the Young African American Male and the Criminal Justice System," prepared for the U.S. Commission on Civil Rights, April 15–16, 1999. http://www.sentencingproject.org/doc/publications/rd_crisisoftheyoung.pdf (accessed March 25, 2012).

52. Ibid.

53. Thierry Devos and Mahzarin R. Banaji, "American = White," *Journal of Personality and Social Psychology* 88, no. 3 (March 2005): 447–66.

54. Kenneth J. Neubeck and Noel A. Cazenave, *op. cit.* (see reference 31), 19.

55. Manning Marable, *op. cit.* (see reference 20), 72.

56. Ibid., 8.

57. Michael McAuliff, "Darrell Issa: Obama's Government Most Corrupt in in history," http://www.huffingtonpost.com/2012/04/24/darrell-issa-obama-corrupt-government_n_%201449521.html (accessed May 12, 2012).

58. Ibid.

59. Ibid., 76.

60. Cornel West, *Race Matters* (New York: Vintage Books, a Division of Random House, Inc., 1994), 97.

61. Ian Lopez, *op. cit.* (see reference 45).

62. Roy L. Brooks, *Racial Justice in the Age of Obama* (Princeton, NJ: Princeton University Press, 2009), xvi.

63. Ibid., 17.

64. Ibid., 16.

65. Ibid., 17.

66. Ibid.

67. Ibid., 10.

68. Kenneth J. Neubeck and Noel A. Cazenave, *op. cit.* (see reference 31), 4.

69. Tera W. Hunter, "Putting an Antebellum Myth to Rest," http://www.nytimes.com /2011/08/02/opinion/putting-an-antebellum-myth-about-slave-families-to-rest.html (accessed August 2, 2011). Hunter is a professor of history and African American Studies at Princeton University.

70. Ibid.

71. Dennis K. Mumby, *Narrative and Social Control: Critical Perspectives* (Newbury Park, CA: Sage, 1993), 145. Cited by Melissa Steyn (see reference 2), 21.

72. Ibid., *op. cit.* (see reference 1), 21.

73. Angela P. Harris, "Introduction: Economies of Color," in Evelyn N. Glenn ed., *Shades of Difference: Why Skin Color Matters* (Stanford, CA: Stanford University Press, 2009), 4.

74. Ibid., 2.

75. Richard Delgado, "Words That Wound: A Tort Action for Racial Insults, Epithets, and Name-Calling," *Critical Race Theory: The Cutting Edge* (Philadelphia, PA: Temple University Press, 1995), 159.

76. Margaret L. Hunter, *Race, Gender, and the Politics of Skin Tone* (New York: Routledge, 2005).

77. Margaret L. Hunter, "The Persistent Problem of Colorism: Skin Tone, Status and Inequality," http://muse.jhu.edu.www.mills.edu/academics/faculty/soc/mhunterThePersistentProblemofColorism.pdf (accessed May 4, 2012).

78. Lillie M. Fears, "Colorism of Black Women in News Editorial Photos," *The Western Journal of Black Studies* 22, no. 1 (1998), 30–36.

79. bell hooks, "Straightening Our Hair," In Lester Faigley and Jack Selzer, eds., *Good Reasons with Contemporary Arguments* (Needham Heights, MA: Allyn & Bacon, 2001), 446–52.

80. Jason Johnson, "Was News Anchor Rhonda Lee Fired Over Her Short Natural Hair? Not Likely," http://politic365.com/2012/12/12/was-news-anchor-rhonda-lee-fired-over-her-short-natural-hair-not-likely/ (accessed December 13, 2012).

81. Verna M. Keith, "A Colorstruck World," in Evelyn N. Glenn ed., *Shades of Difference: Why Skin Color Matters* (Stanford, CA: Stanford University Press, 2009), 32.

82. Ibid.

83. Frantz Fanon, *Black Skin, White Masks* (New York: Grove Press, 1967), 8–9.

84. The Jefferson Monticello, "Thomas Jefferson and Sally Hemings: A Brief Account," http://www.monticello.org/site/plantation-and-slavery/thomas-jefferson-and-sally-hemings-brief-account (accessed November 16, 2012).

85. Ibid.

86. Patricia A. Schechter, "The Anti-Lynching Pamphlets of Ida B. Wells, 1892–1920," dig.lib. niu.edu/gildedage/idabwells/pamphlets.html (accessed March 18, 2013).

87. Joel A. Rogers, *Race and Sex* (St. Petersburg, FL, Helga Rogers, 1968).

88. "Critical Assessments of Joel Augustus Rogers," http://www.africawithin.com/bios/joel_rogers.htm (accessed July 12, 2011)

89. Joel A. Rogers, *op. cit.* (see reference 87).

90. Joe R. Feagin et al., *op. cit.* (see reference 40), 97.

91. Ibid, as cited by Rogers in Volume II, 175.

92. Joe Feagin, *The White Racial Frame: Centuries of Racial Framing and Counter-Framing* (New York: Routledge, 2009), 104.

93. Ibid.

94. Gordon W. Allport, *The Nature of Prejudice* (Reading, MA: Addison-Wesley Publishing Company, 1979), 196–99.

95. Stephen Nathan Haymes, *Race, Culture, and the City: A Pedagogy for Black Urban Struggle* (Albany, NY: State University of New York Press, 1995), 44.

96. Jeff Mays, "How Racist Are You?" http://www.bvblackspin.com/2009/10/28/racist-test (accessed June 5, 2012).

97. Ibid.

98. Alex Alvarez, "Ann Coulter On Debate: Obama Looked Depressed, Could See 'Michelle Wanted To Go Home With Mitt'" http://www.mediaite.com/tv/ann-coulter-on-debate-obama-looked-depressed-could-see-michelle-wanted-to-go-home-with-mitt/ (accessed January 23, 2013).

99. Phillip A. Goff, Jennifer L. Eberhardt, Melissa J. Williams, and Matthew Christian Jackson, "Not Yet Human: Implicit Knowledge, Historical Dehumanization, and Contemporary Consequences," *Journal of Personality and Social Psychology* 94 (2008): 292–306.

100. Ibid, 292.

101. Ibid.

102. Phillip A. Goff *et al.*, (see reference 96), 1.

103. Joe R. Feagin *et al.*, *op cit.* (see reference 40), 97.

104. Frantz Fanon, "The Fact of Blackness," in David Theo Goldberg ed., *Anatomy of Racism.* (Minneapolis: University of Minnesota Press, 1990), 109.

105. Alvin Wyman Walker. "The Conundrum of Clarence Thomas: An Attempt at a Psychodynamic Understanding." http://www.raceandhistory.com/historicalviews/clarencethomas.htm. Retrieved May 13, 2011.

106. W.E.B. Dubois, *The Souls of Black Folk* (College Station, PA: The Pennsylvania State University Press, 2006), 9.

107. Kevin Blackistone. "As Vanity Fair Cashes In, Tiger's Image Gets Tossed Into the Gutter," http://www.aolnews.com/2010/01/06/as-vanity-fair-cashes-into-tigers-image-crawls-into-the-gutter/ (accessed January 12, 2012).

108. Ibid.

109. Lisa C. Ikemoto, "Story of African/Korean American Conflict," in Richard Delgado, ed., *Critical Race Theory: The Cutting Edge* (Philadelphia, PA: Temple University Press, 1994), 307.

110. David Theo Goldberg, *Racist Culture: Philosophy and the Politics of Meaning* (Oxford: Blackwell, 1993), 69.

111. Ibid.

112. Daniel A. Farber and Suzanna Sherry, "Telling Stories Out of School: An Essay on Legal Narratives," in Richard Delgado, ed., *Critical Race Theory: The Cutting Edge* (Philadelphia, PA: Temple University, 1995), 283.

113. Donald E. Worcester, *Forked Tongues and Broken Treaties* (New York: Caxton Printers, 1975).

114. Personal conversations with Dr. Dominique M. Gendrin, Professor and Bell-South Endowed Professor, Department of Communications, Xavier University of Louisiana, 1 Drexel Drive, New Orleans, LA 70125-1098.

115. Alain Locke, *The New Negro: An Interpretation* (New York: Arno Press, 1968).

116. James T. Kloppenberg, *op. cit.* (see reference 1), xi.

117. Ibid., 2–3.

118. bell hooks, *Postmodern Blackness* (New York: Columbia University Press, 1994), 422.

119. John R. Talbott. *Obamanomics: How Bottom-Up Economic Prosperity Will Replace Trickle-Down Economics* (New York, NY: Seven Stories Press, 2008), 17.

120. Paul Steinhauser, "CNN Poll: Which candidate cares more about you?" http://politicalticker.blogs.cnn.com/2012/08/26/cnn-poll-which-candidate-cares-more-about-you/ (accessed October 23, 2012).

121. Robert E. Denton, Jr. *op. cit.* (see reference 3), 7.

122. Amy Gutmann and Dennis Thompson, *The Spirit of Compromise: Why Governing Demands It and Campaigning Undermines It* (Princeton, NJ: Princeton University Press, 2012), 1.

123. Doris Kearns Goodwin, *Team of Rivals: The Political Genius of Abraham Lincoln* (New York: Simon & Schuster, 2005).

124. James T. Kloppenberg, *op. cit.* (see reference 1), xvi.

125. Open Mind with Dr. Martin Luther King, Jr., who shares his insights on The New Negro during a televised panel discussion. Black History, Volume 3, Disk 3. Black History, Civil Rights Movement: From Civil War Through Today.

126. Ibid.

127. Karl Ritter and Matt Moore, "Obama Wins Nobel Peace Prize," http://wwwhuffingtonpost.com/2009/10/09/obama-wins-nobel-peace-pr_n_314907.html#. (accessed January 12, 2010).

128. Jake Sherman, John Bresnahan, and Kenneth Vogel, "Sheldon Adelson Met with John Boehner, Eric Cantor," http://www.politico.com/story/2012/12/sheldon-adelson-met-with-john-boehner-eric-cantor-84692.html (accessed December 27, 2012).

129. "US House Speaker Boehner Urges Senate to Act on 'Fiscal Cliff,'" http://www.reuters.com/article/2012/12/26/usa-fiscal-boehner-idUSL1E8NQ7TJ20121226 (accessed December 27, 2012).

130. Joe R. Feagan, *et al., op. cit.* (see reference 41), 13.

131. Sarah Netter, "Racism in Obama's America One Year Later," http://abcnews.go.com/WN/Obama/racism-obamas-america-year/story?id=9638178 (accessed January 3, 2013).

132. Ibid.

133. Mark Halperin and John Heilemann, *Game Change: Obama and the Clintons, McCain and Palin, and the Race of a Lifetime* (New York: HarperPerennial, 2010), 218.

134. Ibid.

135. David Sessions, "Democrats Sense Racism Is Driving Obama Critics," http://www. politicsdaily.com/2009/09/14/democrats (accessed September 16, 2011).

136. Becky Brittain, "Congressman Calls Obama a 'Tar Baby,'" available at http://whitehouse. blogs.cnn.com/2011/08/01/congressman-calls-obama-a-tar-baby/.

137. Natasha Lennard, "The Real Problem With Buchanan Calling Obama 'Boy,'" http://www.salon.com/news/politics/war_room/2011/08/03/pat_buchanan_boy_comment (accessed March 30, 2012).

138. "Rep. Joe Wilson Yells Out 'You Lie!' During Obama Health Care Speech" (video) (accessed September 16, 2011).

139. Ismael Reed, *Barack Obama and the Jim Crow Media: The Return of the Nigger Breakers* (Montreal: Baraka Books, 2010), 9.

140. Ibid., 1–2.

141. Anonymous, "Racial Slurs Continue against Obama Despite Historic Achievement," March 30, 2009: 1. www.foxnews.com/politics/2009/03/30/racial/.

142. Roth Zachary, "Conservative Activist Forwards Racist Pic Showing Obama As Witch Doctor." http://tpmmuckraker.talkingpointsmemo.com/2009/07/conservative_activist_forwards_racist_pic_showing.php (accessed October 2, 2011).

143. Lola Adesioye, "Why So Serious about Obama as Joker?" August 5, 2009, p. 1. Available at www.guardian.co.uk/comments free/cifamerica/2009 .

144. Lena Sullivan, "'Now You Know Why There's No Birth Certificate' Jokes Tea Party Member in Racist Email Showing Obama and Parents as Chimps," http://www.allmetronews.com/politics/65356-now-you-know-why-there-s-no-birth-certificate-jokes-tea-party-member-in-racist-email-showing-obama-and-parents-as-chimps.html#ixzz1MlR4Nl8w (accessed October 3, 2011).

145. Kris Broughton, "President Obama Chumps Donald Trump and the Birthers," http://bigthink.com/ideas/38111 (accessed September 11, 2011).

146. Ian Haney Lopez, *op. cit.* (see reference 45).

147. Ibid.

148. Ibid.

149. Ibid.

150. Barack Obama, *Dreams from My Father: A Story of Race and Inheritance* (New York: Crown Publishers, 1995, 2004), 82.

151. "Stereotypes of African Americans: Essays and Images," http://www. authentichistorycom/diversity/african/chickenwatermelon/index.html. (accessed February 8, 2012).

152. Maureen Dowd, "Tempest in a Tea Party," http://www.nytimes.com/2011/07/31/opinion/sunday/dowd-tempest-in-a-tea-party.html?_r=1&emc=eta1 (accessed January 5, 2012).

153. Patricia Zengerle, "Analysis: Race Issues Beset Obama's 'Post-racial' Presidency," http://www.reuters.com/article/idUSTRE66K6JN20100721 (accessed July 5, 2011).

154. Helen Kennedy, "Tea Party Express Leader Mark Williams Kicked Out Over 'Colored People' Letter," http://www.nydailynews.com/news/politics/2010/07/18/2010-07-18_tea_party_express_leader_mark_williams_expelled_over_colored_people_letter.html (accessed July 5, 2011).

155. Ibid.

156. Ibid.

157. Jeff Zeleny, "Reid Apologizes for Remarks on Obama's Color and 'Dialect,'" http://www.nytimes.com/2010/01/10/us/politics/10reidweb.html (accessed January 15, 2012).

158. Richard Delgado, "Words That Wound: A Tort Action for Racial Insults, Epithets, and Name-Calling," *Critical Race Theory: The Cutting Edge* (Philadelphia, PA: Temple University Press, 1995), 159.

159. David Sessions, *op. cit.*, (see reference 129).

160. Ibid., 2.

161. Warner Todd Huston, "AP Confuses Criticism of Obama with 'Racial Slurs,'" http://www.redstate.com/warner_todd_huston/2009/04/01/ap-confuses-criticism-of-obama-with-racial-slurs/ (accessed March 30, 2012).

162. Warner Todd Huston, "AP Confuses Criticism of Obama with 'Racial Slurs,'" http://www.redstate.com/warner_todd_huston/2009/04/01/ap-confuses-criticism-of-obama-with-racial-slurs/ (accessed March 30, 2012).

TWO

The Obama Presidency

A Backlash of Racism and Conservative Radicalism

"Our nation's greatest strength is the enduring power of our ideals."
— President Barack Obama

America has become a nation of different worldviews, polarizing ideologies, and conflated philosophical disagreements. Some conservative right-wing Americans are looking for reasons to validate their anti-government rage and frustrations, and much of the American populace has found itself overcome with a struggling hopelessness, a hopelessness rooted in a failing economy that Obama is trying to fix. Obama, the pragmatist, understands the source of the American people's struggle and the reasons behind them.[1] The election of Barack Obama brings with it reasoned deliberation and a pragmatic philosophy that some Americans cannot seem to accept. Obama's ability to inspire and persuade the American electorate and Congress at a time when extreme white racism, radicalism, and unyielding partisanship have displaced reasoned deliberation and a commitment to solving the economic problem, has only enraged the conservative right and frightened his own party.[2] As I discussed in chapter 1, white racism is the driving force behind many anti-Obama narratives, and Obama has been faced with insurmountable ideological warfare and Republican obstructionism.

The power elite's ability to create a just and fair economic and political system has been replaced with partisan politics of race, class, and gender discrimination. The system of inequality and injustice designed for Americans of color and maintained and perpetuated through social forces is now experienced by ordinary white American citizens. As will be explored later in this chapter, corporations are participating in the global economy and outsourcing factory jobs abroad. The power elite,

47

with the help of Congressional Republicans, is creating a culture of reductionism that is hurting the American economy. In this chapter, I present a systemic racism perspective on the structural forces that have affected Obama's presidency and his political agenda.

THE MAKING OF A PRESIDENT: SOCIAL CHANGE OR SOCIAL CONSTRAINT

Obama inherited a myriad of problems from the prior administration, and the GOP has yet to accept blame for the problems, but instead has stymied Obama's effort to solve the nation's problems from special interest, reified politics, and ideological hegemony. Obama, a product of philosophical pragmatism, reflects the power of America's enduring ideals. His inaugural address illustrated that he understood the plight of the American people and the ocean of difficulties that lie ahead. Obama has the ability to capture America's past and understands its current political narrative based on that past. Reading Obama's *Audacity of Hope* and *Dreams of My Father*, one senses a renaissance man of post-modernity, a man who understands not only America's history and the Constitution, but also its democracy and founding principles.

Despite his readiness to tackle America's challenges, Obama may not have been prepared for the merciless constraints and resistance his administration would endure from the conservative right. About six months into his presidency, we witnessed an onslaught of Tea Party adamantine carrying signs and bearing arms depicting him as Hitler and a despot. In the 2010 midterm election, white America and conservative blacks turned on Obama, while the Republicans refused to acknowledge the problems their party created during the preceding eight years when they controlled the White House, the Senate, and the Congress. They passed legislation that protected the rich and power elite and got America involved in two wars that contributed to America's current economic condition. From the start, the Republicans began using negative hyperbolic rhetoric against Obama, making it seem that his policies to solve these problems were a failure:

> It is no small irony that those who are complaining the loudest about the length of time it takes to see the results of economic stimulus were standing shoulder to shoulder with President George W. Bush in rejecting a much-needed boost for the economy. . . . Having helped to push the economy over the cliff, they are now complaining about the mess that was made in the valley below.[3]

History records a similar problem left by a Republican administration when Franklin Delano Roosevelt (FDR) assumed office, after the stock market crashed in October 1929 (see chapter 4). It is worth noting, however, that Bush could not have created these problems if his own party had not supported his political agenda and the agenda of the wealthiest citizens who filled their coffers on an unprecedented scale for placing federal policy and decision making at their service.[4] Bush called them the haves and the have-mores, his elite base. What is happening in the American economy began more than three decades ago, but these problems intensified under the Bush administration and now hover over the Obama administration like a dark looming cloud.[5] In sum, Obama inherited two wars, an economic recession, a progressive base with a litany of unrealistic demands, and a hostile Republican Party.[6] Adding to this list, he inherited a corrupt banking system, a weak dollar and high foreign debt, a high demand for public services, a widening gap in income levels, a major collapse in the housing industry, an energy crisis, a dire economic condition of average American citizens, and a job market that was taken abroad.[7] Since gaining control of the U.S. House of Representatives, the Republicans have focused on policies that destroy job creation, such as proposing deep spending cuts, obstructing Obama's agenda, culture wars, and defunding programs that benefit women and racial minorities. Republicans have been extremely uncivil, contentious, confrontational, and aggressive in nearly every area of politics and governing, since Obama became the first African American president. In addition, many ordinary Americans have embraced the conservative right viewpoint that Obama's approach to resolving the economic problem and extending healthcare to 30 million uninsured Americans may be "ill-suited to our own cultural moment."[8] Many ordinary Americans are also convinced that Obama is "a Manchurian president born in Kenya and trained in the Muslim madrassas of Indonesia to destroy America from within."[9]

As the first African American president, Obama is not immune to the age old problem of white racism. His rapid rise to the presidency is owed to the struggles and achievements of those who went before him in that the

> achievements of the civil rights and feminist movements that produced the institutions and the cultural characteristics that made possible [his] rise . . . are those same democratic institutions, and the unfinished cultural project that we call American democracy, now constrain him as president. The immediate circumstances that led to his election—public dissatisfaction with the greatest economic collapse in the United States since the Great Depression of the 1930s—have now become the single greatest obstacle impeding the realization of his most ambitious plans. The economic crisis resulted directly from policies of deregulation put in place during the preceding two decades by his predecessors Bill Clinton and George W. Bush. Yet many . . . Americans who now hold Obama himself responsible for failing to restore prosperity also criticized the steps he took, the stimulus package and bank bailout, which most observers agree helped prevent an even deeper crisis.[10]

Given this analysis, we must ask how much of this public dissatisfaction with Obama is

> rooted in old-fashioned racism as the first black president; how much of it is new-fashioned and genuine—yet arguably misdirected—rage over an economy that increasingly has nothing to offer its working class, and how much of it is the result of a political system that caters solely to the affluent or to the elite classes? And how come nobody was watching the vultures circling overhead—the media superstars whose ratings grew in proportion to their ability to scare regular Americans, the other hucksters making a quick buck on that fear, and the political opportunists quick to embrace radical and often bogus ideas to keep their elected positions? [11]

Viewing Obama through a systemic racial lens, what can we know about a pragmatic man who is relatively new on the stage of national and international politics; a man racially demonized for his domestic, international, and war policies; a man who was willing to risk the wrath of his own party and base to compromise with the conservative right during his first term? Since these questions are worth addressing, I now turn to an analysis concerning the political consequences Obama is still experiencing in his second term as president and how the established Republicans and radical Tea Party adamantine obscured his record with ideological hyperbole by putting a spin on his talking points. We start with a look at the Bush-era policies on low corporate taxes and job outsourcing, the major culprits of the current economic crisis that Obama has been saddled with, as well as a prime example of corruption and the constraint caused by special interests.

THE BUSH-ERA POLITICS

Foreign outsourcing is no new phenomenon in America, and increased globalization has opened up markets for goods, services, and labor around the world, which has had devastating effects on all Americans, including Americans of color. Outsourcing provides an avenue for businesses to reduce labor costs, the most significant costs that businesses face. Outsourcing "ultimately places American workers in effective competition with the vast pool of lower-wage foreign labor, and exerts downward pressure on worker wages. This competition will result in the so-called 'race to the bottom' between domestic and foreign workers." [12] To make matters worse, dramatic technological changes revolutionized the workplace—changes that eliminated many of the jobs that less skilled workers once relied upon for their survival. The loss of manufacturing jobs not only hurt white America, but also helped to push the unemployment rate of African Americans over 15 percent, which exceeded the national average of 7.9 percent, a week before Obama was re-elected.

Foreign outsourcing increased under the George W. Bush administration, resulting in businesses having ten years of insurmountable tax breaks. Since foreign outsourcing is important to big businesses, Congress kept the tax rate low for big businesses, resulting in these businesses sending jobs overseas.[13] During Bush's presidency, several corporations repatriated billions of dollars to the United States in 2003, but cut thousands of jobs between 2005 and 2006 (see table 2.1). These corporations could afford to repatriate billions of dollars because they prospered from foreign cheap labor and little to no environmental regulations.

In addition, table 2.2 illustrates that top U.S. companies paid tax rates much lower than the required 35 percent for the purpose of creating jobs. Instead of creating jobs, these corporations reduced their labor force and contributed millions of dollars to Republican candidates to secure a smaller tax rate, according to MSNBC.

The Bush era tax regulations favored big business to the detriment of American workers. In addition to this, the trade policy served to encourage outsourcing. In 2002, the United States ran a merchandise trade deficit of $484 billion, which hit $550 billion in 2003. In the first 38 months of Bush's presidency, 2.6 million manufacturing jobs disappeared.[14] A study by Forrester Resources found that 3.3 million U.S. sector jobs, jobs that fall into the at-risk category, will be outsourced to foreign countries by the year 2015. On top of that, tax breaks for middle and lower income Americans were cut. The Bush administration wiped out the $236 billion surplus left by the Clinton administration and turned it into a $1.2 trillion deficit, which devastated the economy and contributed to a massive job losses. According to conservative commentator Pat Buchanan, the globalists and corporatists, together with the GOP, plotted the evisceration of American manufacturing with the collusion of free-trade fundamentalists.[15] American jobs are being eliminated rather than created, and the Obama administration has inherited this economic downturn.

Table 2.1.   Repatriation in 2004.

Corporation	Amount Repatriated	Layoffs in 2005-2006
Pfizer	$37 billion	10,000
Merck	$15.9 billion	7,000
Hewlett-Packard	$14.5 billion	14,500
Honeywell	$2.7 billion	2,000
Ford	$900 million	30,000
Colgate-Palmolive	$800 million	4,000

Source: thinkprogres.org.

Table 2.2.   What Some Top U.S. Companies Pay in Taxes.

Corporation	Tax Rate Paid	Employee Job Loss
Citigroup	16.9%	525,300 (2009–2010)
Johnson & Johnson	21.3%	589,500 (2006–2010)
General Electric	7.4%	591,000 (2009–2010)
Hewlett-Packard	20.2%	Sent jobs overseas

Source: *The Rachel Maddow Show* (July 6, 2011).

POLITICAL IMPLICATIONS FOR THE OBAMA ADMINISTRATION

In his State of the Union address on January 25, 2011, Obama informed the American people that technological innovation is the future and America is in danger of lagging behind countries such as China and Japan that are already embracing technological innovation and are far superior in science, technology, education, and mathematics. Even though Obama has put forth legislation that could help Americans prepare themselves to compete in a global economy, GOP obstructionism continues to thwart his efforts to move the country in this direction, under the guise that too much spending occurs under a liberal government. The working class in America has become a "loathsome form of humanity" in the eyes of conservatives.[16] The GOP has not created any jobs legislation but had weakened the Obama stimulus package. The Obama administration made concessions to the conservative right to demonstrate a willingness to work in a bipartisan manner and extended olive branches to reach across the aisle in his first term, but none of the Congressional Republicans voted for the package and attacked it as a socialist one.

The congressional conservatives went on record hoping that Obama's initiatives would fail, so they could foist their political agenda on the American people.[17] John Boehner, Speaker of the House, said that "President Obama has created over 200,000 federal jobs since he's been president, but if some of these jobs get lost in the budget cuts, 'so let it be.'" What Boehner's eliminationist rhetoric suggested was that the Republican Party was not interested in job creation, even though Republicans campaigned on this issue during the 2010 midterm elections. Recent polls consistently showed that Americans blamed the Bush administration policies for the downturn of the economy, and *The New York Times*/CBS News poll indicated that Congress had an 82 percent disapproval rating on the way they did their job. Had Bush used the surplus inherited from the Clinton administration for economic development, the American economy would have been much stronger when Obama took office in 2009. Consequently, the Republicans, in collusion with big corporations, used a depressed economy that occurred under their watch as a political weapon against Obama, claiming his economic policies failed. In other words, in a Clintonian fashion, during the Democratic National Convention, Obama had not cleaned up their mess fast enough, so their plan was to defeat Obama and deny him a second term. If the Obama administration had done as well as the Republicans in getting its message to the Americans, the 2010 election probably would have turned in the Democratic favor. Instead, Republicans were "swept into power on a Tea Party tide of discontent."[18] And now the Tea Party is hijacking established Republicans, the Obama presidency, and America in general, preventing any real debate over important issues or getting anything done. For the Republicans, scapegoating Obama "lays the groundwork for purging an enemy and has become the impetus used to defeat and to eliminate the opposition" by any means necessary.[19] Republicans have successfully repackaged their talking points for general consumption by stripping out any overt reference to racism and xenophobic hatred of the "other."[20] It is no secret that many Republicans share Minority Leader Senator Mitch McConnell's (R-KY) feelings to make Obama a one-term president, using a failed economy they caused to achieve this goal. As mentioned earlier, the Republicans ran on job creation. But when their white electorate base, 78 percent, gave them control of the U.S. House of Representatives and 26 state houses, the GOP focused its energies on gutting the financial reform law, repealing the Affordable Care Act, defunding Planned Parenthood, and tried repeatedly to gut Medicare, Medicaid, and Social Security. By focusing on these goals, the GOP slowed down the economy, sabotaging an already fragile economy, but it appears to be on slow recovery. Republicans changed their job creation campaign script to one that laid the responsibility of job creation at the feet of businesses and not the government, yet many large businesses and corporations are sitting on large sums of cash and not hiring people or spending on new investments that could result in job creation. Large corporations are using this cash to acquire or merge with other companies, which rarely results in job creation. Still other corporations are using their excess cash to invest in facilities overseas, and exporting jobs to China and India. Overall, policies pursued by the Republicans, particularly after the 2010 elections, are intended to stall the economic initiatives by the Obama administration to prevent a double-dip recession. Such a recession, or continued slow economic growth, could have enhanced the Republicans' prospects of winning back the White House in the 2012 general presidential election, but the American people took note of the GOP's obstructionist behavior and gave Obama a second chance.[21]

Outsourcing alone cannot be blamed for the current economic condition, as the racist and classist partisan politics of the conservative right and extremist Tea Party is keeping the economy from making any substantial recovery, abrogating their campaign promise to create jobs and benefitting special interests at the expense of the rest of the country. As jobs are relocated overseas, it becomes more difficult for retrenched American workers to find work at the previous income level. This, in turn, affects their participation in the local economy. Therefore, Obama is faced with the grueling task of reversing a three-decade old problem that slowly devolved upon the American people but was exacerbated under Congressional Republican control. Moreover, the Republican's "blame Obama" ideology and Democratic complicity with the Republicans gave them a free hand to pass legislation that benefited the wealthiest citizens and corporate America before Obama took office.[22] Meanwhile, the Republican racist reprobation of Obama remains unabated, civil dialogue nonexistent, and the "normative rules of give and take and fair play" abated.[23]

OBAMA'S VISION FOR INSOURCING

When Obama made a trip to Wisconsin, the birthplace of unions, he laid out his vision before Wisconsinites on how he would bring jobs back to American soil by rewarding those companies that choose to bring jobs back to America and hire Americans. By doing so, according to MSNBC, Obama would double the tax deduction for companies making products in the United States, sell those products to Americans, help finance new plants and equipment, and invest in community college training programs and trade enforcement unit.

OBAMA'S PRAGMATISM

In his inaugural address, Obama speaks about unifying the national audience by reconstituting the concept of "American Community," one of his primary concerns. He employed regenerative rhetoric to reinterpret the core values of America.[24] This regenerative rhetoric launched his administration in an attempt to reaffirm the American people's allegiance to renewed political values based upon the nation's welfare. To restore new political values, it requires social change in the current infrastructure, a change that will favor all American citizens and not just the power elite. The Bush administration lavished tax cuts on corporate America and pushed through unfair tax legislation for the wealthiest individuals over the middle-class. Most important, the Bush administration had "operated under a cloak of secrecy, which is deeply antithetical to the principles of our nation."[25] But the conservative right currently shows no intentions of investigating these secrecies, and has sounded off on Obama, claiming his administration is the most "corrupt" in history and should be investigated for financial irresponsibility. However, this lashing out against Obama is just another way to distract him from carrying out his duties as president. Unlike his predecessors, Obama informed the Muslim world that

> We seek a new way forward, based on mutual interest and mutual respect. To those leaders around the globe who seek to sow conflict, or blame their society's ills on the West—know that your people will judge you on what you can build, not what you destroy. To those who cling to power through corruption and deceit and the silencing of dissent, know that you are on the wrong side of history; but that we will extend a hand if you are willing to unclench your fist.[26]

Obama makes it clear that he seeks peace in place of conflict and mutual interest and respect in the place of dissidence and strife, cooperation rather than discord, and nation-state sovereignty in the place of nation-state hegemony. But a few 2012 conservative presidential candidates create dissidence and strife through their divisive and hyperbolic rhetoric to divide the American people. But what they really did was put forth a violent radical message that points fingers at Obama because many Americans believe he is a Muslim and not a Christian. But Obama's call for social change and the rise of conservative radicalism and retribution have been difficult for him. In his first two years in office, he was not able to carry out his agenda of hope, optimism, and bi-partisan politics. Instead, his progressive agenda was met with "unparalleled anger on the far right that eventually twisted important national discussions and pushed ideas from the conservative fringe into the mainstream media, playing on the apocalyptic fears of the American people."[27] Given the above excerpt from Obama's inaugural speech, Osama Bin Laden, the greatest threat to America's national security, was finally killed by order of Obama. Obama made good on his regenerative rhetoric from the campaign trail that the hunt for bin Laden was one of his top priorities.

Obama's politics appear to be an enigma and a contradiction compared to traditional politicians. His pragmatic politics contradict the traditional ways individuals have practiced politics, his ideology is somewhat different, and he is an idealist. Up to the midterm elections, Obama may have lost sight of his promise to the American people to solve the economic crisis, and his use of apologia for his Party's losing the House during the midterm elections and gridlock with the conservative right did not restore total confidence in the American people. Since we live in a mass society with so-called formal freedoms and crippling economic pressures, social change is needed if the American people want to see true prosperity restored to this nation.[28]

Obama appears to be his own person with his own ideas, and will act on behalf of the American people if this means to compromise or what Shelby Steele calls to "bargain" with the devil to seek "common ground." This does not mean he has turned his back on the American people and their interests, but his philosophical pragmatism reveals why he sees

American politics as he does and responds accordingly. Leaders win acclaim and their followers win reassurance and hope from courses of action that reaffirm accepted ideologies while displaying boldness, intelligence, change, and paternal protection.[29] But the deprivations and powerlessness that characterize the lives of working class whites and most Americans of color "furnish the incentive to believe in leaders who give them hope, inspiration, and a talent for coping with complex forces, where mass education and mass communication become potent."[30]

OBAMA'S PROLETARIAT

Obama represents the interests of ordinary working Americans. This class represents at least ninety-nine percent of the American population while the conservative right represents the wealthiest one percent. Obama's representation of the poor, politically oppressed, the voiceless, the inarticulate, the decentered, the alienated, and the marginalized are Americans that are treated as mere passive objects rather than active subjects in a democratic society. Generally speaking, conservatives are hostile to a welfare state and acknowledge their disdain for the have-nots.[31] Clearly, if they can successfully repeal the Affordable Care Act, they would further acknowledge their disdain for the well-being of working Americans who cannot afford the high cost of health insurance.

The deep cuts Congressional Republicans proposed in 2011 will hurt the poor and the middle class. Prominent members of the clergy have come together to protest the budget cut. Some clergy were arrested for protesting on Capitol Hill. They believe that the deep spending cuts by Congress would hurt the poor. These men and women of the cloth, including Jim Winkler, General Secretary of the United Methodist Church's General Board of Church and Society; Rabbi Arthur Waskow of the Shalom Center in Philadelphia; and the Rev. Jennifer Butler, head of Faith in Public Life, came together in prayer. Rev. Michael Livingston, a past president of the National Council of the Churches of Christ (USA) lamented that

> Our elected officials are protecting corporations and wealthy individuals while shredding the safety net for millions of the most vulnerable people in our nation and abroad. Our faith won't allow us to passively watch this travesty unfold. . . . Today, we offer our bodies as a living sacrifice.[32]

Since Obama's position has been to represent racial, class, and gender equality for all Americans, he has enforced laws to prevent discrimination.

OBAMA, THE COMPROMISER?

To understand Obama's challenge, we must understand his "conception of democracy as deliberation."[33] Most Americans, Democrats, Republicans, and Independents believe Obama compromised too much with the Republicans in his first term because he tended to give in to their hostage-taking behavior practices. But, at the same time, Americans believe the GOP should compromise and work with the president. Perhaps, there is a point when a president should not compromise. For most Americans, Obama, under no circumstances, should compromise the big three (social security, Medicare, and Medicaid). A large percentage of Americans receiving these benefits are considered economically vulnerable, and Obama and the Democratic Party should protect their interests the way the Republicans protect the interests of the richest Americans. But if compromising on unemployment benefits meant releasing Americans as hostages from the callous grip of Congressional Republicans, so the jobless could receive their unemployment benefits, then a short-term compromise may be in order. Systemic racism has hindered Obama's progress. Many media commentators, comedians, and talk show hosts believe racism is behind the vitriol rhetoric Obama experienced in his first term. The Republicans have consistently distracted Obama's attention from the area of job creation and forced his hand to deal with a looming deficit, under the pretense that America's coffers are already depleted because of overspending. In fact, it was Republican policies before Obama became president that caused the country's massive deficit. However, Obama has demonstrated the psychological strength to deal with the political ill-treatment and racism he endured in his first term.

It is worth noting that MSNBC aired a poll that indicated fifty-six percent of Americans approved the way Obama handled the "lame duck session," while forty-one percent disapproved. In that same poll, when Americans were asked if Obama was doing enough to cooperate with the Republicans, fifty-nine percent said he was doing enough, while thirty-seven percent said "no." On the other hand, the Republicans received a twenty-eight percent approval rating for their cooperation with Obama, while sixty-eight percent of the Americans did not believe they were doing enough to cooperate with the president. Given these statistics, many of Obama's legislation bills were passed during the "lame duck session," and an annual Gallup Poll ranked him as the most admired man in America, suggesting that the demonizers' political discourse was losing its potency.[34]

Obama has used political savvy to contend with the philosophical-ideological forces that would locate him in a position of a failing president. For this reason, Obama needs to pick arguments to make a case that economic growth and fairness go together. He may need to talk more about innovation, investment, and education and make a case to the

American people that there is a place for the public sector to make the economy grow, although he touched on many of these issues in his State of the Union address in January 2011. By doing so, he has the power to appeal to the middle of the road individuals and to his own base. By the end of 2011, Obama was no longer seen as the "compromiser." He refused to compromise with the Republicans on the payroll tax holiday for the middle class. He took certain action without the help of Congressional Republicans who controlled the House. Congressional Republicans made no attempt to confirm any of Obama's appointments and have continued to obstruct his agenda, which has forced him to exercise the power bestowed upon him by the office of the presidency. Therefore, Obama has shown leadership by exercising the authority of the presidency to make recess appointments, and Congressional Republicans are calling his appointments unconstitutional. Comparing Obama's recess appointment record to that of former presidents, Reagan averaged 30 appointments per year; George H. W. Bush, 19; Bill Clinton, 18; George W. Bush, 21; and President Obama, 9, according to MSNBC. Even though Obama is a pragmatist, it may not be enough to bring about economic growth and serious fiscal responsibility for change in the social, economic, and political infrastructure, given the obstructionist behavior of the conservative right to block Obama's success.

THE DEBT-CEILING DEBACLE

After the 2010 midterm elections, the Obama administration began to signify responsiveness to the economic discontentment of Americans. With an 8.3 percent unemployment rate, which is lower than it was a few years ago and could be lower now, Obama's ability to effect economic policy has been consistently sabotaged by the Republican-controlled Congress. Is there a relationship between the federal budget and the debt ceiling? There is no relationship between the two, but the Republicans "have linked the two together, and used a routine, legally technical vote to raise the debt limit as a means of holding the nation hostage to their own political goal of shrinking the size of the federal government."[35] Since 1962, the U.S. House of Representatives has raised the debt ceiling 74 times, and it was raised 19 times during the Bush administration. The debt limit provides the U.S. House of Representatives with the strings to control the federal purse, allowing Congress to assert its constitutional prerogatives to control spending.[36] The debt limit also imposes a form of fiscal accountability, which compels Congress and the President to take visible action to allow further federal borrowing when the federal government spends more than it collects in revenues.[37] When the debt limit had to be raised under Obama, Congressional Republicans and the

Tea Party adamantine changed the rules of the game and began using hyperbolic rhetoric to justify their actions.

Our power elite "resist change that would reduce their power, status, and financial resources and the strategies they use to maintain the cooperation of the mass of the population," furthering their own interests.[38] Change means altering statutes, administrative regulations, rules, and laws that will not be enforced politically if these changes go against the interest and practices of the power elite.[39] In fact, changes to old practices that "maintain established inequalities" between the working class, the middle class, and the power elite will be resisted at all cost, a reason the conservative right is adamant about using eliminationist racist rhetoric against Obama.[40] Obama cannot make a change to the infrastructure without the full cooperation and agreement of Congress. The U.S. Constitution requires both the President and Congress to work together. With respect to the Constitution, it is based on intellectual tools and ideas from the eighteenth century Enlightenment thinkers. Given today's politics, these tools and ideas have proven inadequate because politicians and Constitutional scholars interpret it differently. For example, when President Obama and the Congressional Republicans were in gridlock over raising the debt ceiling, many high ranking officials, even former President Clinton, suggested President Obama invoke the Fourteenth Amendment. But the President did not believe this amendment provided him with the necessary effective tools to exercise his executive authority independent of an intransigent Congress to raise the debt ceiling. In fact, President Obama was perhaps wise enough to reject using the Fourteenth Amendment because the many voices encouraging him to do so were subtle enemies in his own camp. We can infer from the Constitution that the democracy the framers "designed leaves open the possibility of revolutionary change."[41] Had Obama invoked the Fourteenth Amendment, would the Tea Party adamantine encouraged or even forced a revolution and then blame the President for "calling their bluff"?

Did President Obama get rolled on in the debt debate, as suggested by staunch progressives or did House Speaker Boehner get pushed into a corner by the extreme right in his own conference? If we look at what both the Democrats and the Republicans gained from the outcome of this manufactured crisis, many commentators and political analysts believe the Republicans drove and won the debate. Granted, there are deficit cuts. A close examination of this debt-solving plan revealed that when the Bush tax cuts expired at the end of December 2012, the deficit cuts would take effect in January 2013. The revenues from the expired Bush taxes would be restored to the treasury to help America pay its bills and stimulate the economy. In the meantime, the debt deal spending cuts would cost the economy close to 2 million jobs.[42]

During the debt-ceiling debate, Boehner, representative of the 8th district in Ohio, introduced a house plan that would hurt many Americans,

particularly African Americans, Americans of color, the indigent, the elderly, and students. Boehner's bill would have hurt hundreds of thousands of his most vulnerable constituents. For example, all budget legis-
lations for the past quarter of a century have exempted low-income
Americans in reductions from programs such as Medicaid and food
stamps, but Boehner's plan does not exempt them. In Boehner's own
district, according to MSNBC, about 90,000 of his constituents or 14 percent live below the poverty line. His budget plan had deep cuts to Medicare and Medicaid that would affect 180,000 of his constituents. There
would have been deep cuts to approximately 70,000 households that receive social security benefits. Over 30,000 low-income people would have
difficulty securing food stamps; 20,000 low-income children would be
affected by cuts in food and nutrition services. It would cut 4,000 people
who rely on public housing assistance.[43] When the Boehner Debt Plan
was voted down in the Senate, Minority Leader Senator Mitch McConnell
(R-KY) refused to negotiate with Majority Leader Harry Reid (D-NV), but
wanted to negotiate with President Obama, an unprecedented practice.
McConnell's political posturing to filibuster the Reid Bill would not only
hurt the American people but also would imperil America's credit rating.
McConnell threatened a filibuster because his real purpose was to keep
the debt ceiling from being extended beyond the 2012 elections. He
wanted this ruckus to turn voters against Obama. McConnell, a staunch
Obama nemesis, believed if he negotiated with the president, Obama
would cave and give into his political antics but Reid would not cave.
"Whatever the criticisms of Obama, it is Republicans who are overtly
playing politics. Even though Obama compromises . . . easily, the Republicans are showing no willingness to compromise at all."[44] The CNN/
ORC Poll also indicates that 51 percent of those surveyed would blame
the Republicans if the debt ceiling is not raised as opposed to 30 percent
blaming President Obama.[45] This same poll indicates that 63 percent of
those surveyed believed the Republicans acted irresponsibly during the
debt ceiling debate, while 33 percent believed the president acted irresponsibly, a three percent increase for the GOP and a one percent increase for the president over a three-month period.[46]

It is worth noting that Americans want cuts to government spending,
but they do not want Congress to cut programs that affect them. The
American people contributed to this deficit-reducing debacle because the
Tea Party Caucus claims the American people sent them to Washington
to cut spending. However, the American people were unaware how
deeply these cuts would harm their programs and how far the Tea Party
adamantine would push the economy and America's credit rating over
the cliff.[47] Table 2.3 illustrates the programs Americans support and the
cuts they oppose, which contradicts both their position and the Tea Party's position.

In a number of polls, a large percentage of conservative voters supported the ideology of the Tea Party during the midterm elections because they wanted a change to the status quo, but not "because they considered reducing the federal debt the nation's biggest concern."[48] Polls indicated that 66 percent of the Tea Party supporters thought the GOP should compromise with the Democrats to raise the debt limit.[49] Some Tea Party supporters wanted this debacle over and did not want to see an already-fragile economy go into default.[50] Did Tea Party Republicans misunderstand their assignment to change the status quo? In short, "their intransigent demands for deep spending cuts, coupled with their almost gleeful willingness to destroy one of America's most invaluable assets, its full faith and credit, were incredibly irresponsible."[51] Overall, the Republicans appear to have successfully distracted Obama's attention from the most important issues, an anemic recovery, staggering high unemployment rates, declining home prices, and falling wages, by dragging him into a politically manufactured budget crisis, created by the Republicans to exact fear on the American people and make Obama appear a failed leader.

Table 2.3. Where Americans Favor and Oppose Cuts.

Program	Favor	Oppose	No opinion
Cutting federal subsidies to farmers	31%	66%	2%
Cutting pensions and benefits for retired government workers	30%	68%	2%
Cutting defense spending	47%	52%	1%
Cutting the amount the government spends on Medicaid, the federal health program for the poor	22%	77%	*
Cutting the amount the government spends on Medicare, the federal health program for the elderly	12%	87%	1%
Cutting the amount the government spends on Social Security	16%	84%	1%
Increasing the taxes paid by oil and gas companies by ending federal subsidies for those businesses	73%	26%	1%
Increasing the taxes paid by businesses that own private jets	76%	23%	*
Increasing the taxes paid by people who make more than $250,000	73%	26%	*

Source: CNN/ORC Poll (July 18–20, 2011).

LABELING OBAMA A "SOCIALIST"

During 2011, the middle-class was under attack by the newly elected GOP governors. Upon taking office, some of these governors in collusion with each other began passing draconian legislation that would strip collective bargaining rights of K–12 teachers, university professors, firefighters, police officers, and other public employees. They also targeted Planned Parenthood to defund it under the pretext that they existed only to provide abortion services. Republicans at both the state and national levels were oblivious to the devastating effects of their shenanigans on the poor, elderly, and middle-class, but they underestimated these citizens. The sole purpose of destroying the democratic base was to gut social spending, to abort a fragile economic recovery, and to humble the president by undercutting his re-election chances, thus turning the country into a one-party country. Consequently, conservatives have socially constructed Obama as a socialist president, and former House Speaker Newt Gingrich has called Obama a "Food Stamp President" to demonize him and de-legitimate his economic initiatives. But Gingrich knew his statement would appeal to those whites who detested American becoming a welfare state. When politicians want to "exploit white racist animus for political gain, they need not say the words Niggers or Nigras, as did white southern segregationists. They now need only mention the word welfare."[52] Given this statement, is Obama a socialist and what is socialism?

Unlike capitalism, socialism puts the means of production and material resources in the hands of the working class. Critics of capitalism argue that capitalism concentrates power and wealth into the hands of a small percentage of individuals in society. With the capital concentrated in the hands of a few, the labor of the working class is exploited and equal opportunity becomes an illusion. To be a black socialist in America means one would be seen as a nonconformist.[53] But Obama is not a nonconformist in the sense of the word. His platform to rally around the cause of the working and middle classes may make him seem a nonconformist compared to his predecessors. Billy Wharton, a *Washington Post* contributor, says Obama is no socialist.

> Socialists know that Barack Obama is not one of us. Not only is he not a socialist, he may in fact not even be a liberal. Socialists understand him more as a hedge-fund Democrat—one of a generation of neoliberal politicians firmly committed to free-market policies. The first clear indication that Obama is not, in fact, a socialist, is the way his administration is avoiding structural changes to the financial system.[54]

Staunch Republican and Fox News political commentator Bill O'Reilly, an Obama critic, believes ill-informed Americans, who do not understand the difference between types of governments, give Obama too much credit for being a socialist. There's a major difference between Obama and a true socialist like Karl Marx. Until Barack Obama "begins to insinuate himself into the livelihoods of American workers, he cannot accurately be described as a socialist."[55] Perhaps Congressional Republicans filibuster a majority of Obama's bills, even those that could help the economy, because they want to give the illusion that he is a socialist. Until the Republicans got the Bush tax cuts extended, they filibustered the different parts of the healthcare bill, the stimulus package, Wall Street Reform bill, FDA Food Safety Modernization Act, bills they agreed with, and bills they did not agree with, and all the regular business of the Senate. Many bi-partisan politicians, Americans, and news contributors and commentators noted that these filibusters represent a strategy of the GOP to deny the Obama administration any degree of success and make his policies and his ability to lead this country a failure.

Consequently, the vitriol has accelerated and in town hall meetings across the country, Obama has been likened to Adolf Hitler and alternatively called a socialist or an outright communist.[56] One poster has been circulated in emails in which Obama is compared to the Nazis and the word "socialism" appears under each of the four images of the president on this poster.[57] More recently, we received on our faculty listserv a poster from a hostile Republican colleague who claims a friend sent him a photo of Obama standing in the forefront of a city in ruins with smoke bellowing so thick that it hid the sun, giving an impression on the impact of Obama policies on the country. The caption read, "My work here is done." This photo suggests that Obama rose to power for the sole purpose to destroy America through socialism. Exploring this type of ideological warfare, the next several paragraphs analyze how ideology functions under the cloak of systemic racism to hinder the Obama administration's efforts to regenerate the nation.

SYSTEMIC RACISM AND OBAMA'S CONSTRAINTS

Why would any politician, progressive or conservative, constrain the efforts of a new president as soon as he is sworn into office? Was there something cynical afoot to sabotage Obama or is this centuries-old racist system not willing to give a black man a chance to serve his country in the same capacity as white men? Obama may have executive power, but how much of it can he exercise, when a Republican-controlled House with a radical right wing Tea Party attached to it, refuses to cooperate, even with established conservatives. Keeping black men in their "place" and affecting their ability to lead goes back to slavery and the Jim Crow era where overt racism was a normal practice. Some scholars argue that "Republicans believed Obama was [not ready] to lead, presumptuous, and a profligate liberal. Into this set of indictments, they then insinuated the suspicion that his temperate demeanor masked an unpatriotic radical who disdained basic American values" a justification to undermine his credibility, which would clear the way for radical conservatives and hucksters to pen white racially framed anti-racist Obama narratives to play on the apocalyptic fears of the American people.[58] Some liberal commentators have become frustrated with Obama and believe he should be more aggressive with the Republicans by using the bully pulpit. They overlook the fact that the more Obama becomes aggressive with the GOP, the worse the GOP will get. We have learned from history that systemic racism is so deeply embedded in U.S. culture that if African Americans and other Americans of color demonstrate aggressive behavior towards white racists, they would become more aggressive in their hostile behavior.

Martin Luther King, Jr., was well aware of this fact and therefore fought for the civil rights of African Americans and other disenfranchised groups on a nonviolent platform. King knew the movement could not fight hatred with hatred, stirring white hostility, giving white racists the justification to spew out their venom on the black bodies of those they were socialized to detest. King knew if movement members had not turned the other cheek, the movement would not have achieved its goal. The racist establishment was already angry with King and his followers for boldly thinking about equal justice and economic empowerment of African Americans and other Americans of color. Therefore, King rightly tried to achieve this goal through peaceful resolutions to off-set white racism, hostility, and retribution against members of the movement.

For Obama, it does not matter what he does or does not do. His enemies will always take the counter position. Bill Maher argues that racism undoubtedly exists in America and that Obama should get tough with the GOP. If Obama got tough with the GOP, would they heighten their malevolent behavior against him? Maher goes on to say that if Obama saved forty percent of the white Americans who hated him from drowning, they would still unleash their racist hostility on him. Maher's assertion supports how deep systemic racism runs in the American culture which is clear to the international community. The deep racial animus that has inspired white supremacy is alive and thriving in politics, and Obama has become the scapegoat for the discontentment of white racists.

Some political commentators argue that racism and hatred guide the behavior of radical Republicans against Obama, working class Americans, and immigrants. They are anti-tax, anti-union, anti-welfare, and will decry any program they classify as "giveaway programs" that help the low-income whites and Americans of color. For example, majority of the Republicans in both the House and Senate signed Grover Norquist's tax pledge. This pledge means they will stop at nothing to prevent tax increases on the wealthiest citizens. Although this pledge does not physically destroy the working class, it destroys them economically and would contribute to the downfall of the economy because revenues from taxes help to stimulate the economy.

The Republicans initially railroaded Obama into supporting their economic policies that almost destroyed the economy because they took advantage of Obama's bi-partisan compromising nature. When the Republicans insisted on extending the Bush tax cuts for the wealthiest top two percent to strengthen their political power base, Obama engaged his pragmatic philosophy to release the unemployment benefits from the hostage grip of the Congressional Republicans who showed no mercy for the downtrodden. Obama "understands that democracy requires deliberation, an ethic of reciprocity and a culture committed to the peaceful resolution of conflicts. He also knew he would have to impose his veto powers with the barrel of a gun."[59] So the forces against Obama after the 2010 midterm elections were so powerful that he found himself in compromise with an unrelenting, Republican-controlled house.

IDEOLOGY AND REIFIED POLITICS

On the national stage of politics, Obama has transformed the reified dominant social and political systems into a reality for Americans of color. The ideology of reification means to give material existence to the abstract. Reification treats abstractions as if they are concrete or corporeal entities that are perceptible to the senses. The U.S. dominant political system is a reified system of abstract entities that exclude rather than include the real participation of the American people. Americans have been convinced to some degree that they have real political power. But what they may not understand is that political parties control what candidate will run or not run for the presidency, with the wealthiest individuals throwing their full financial support behind the candidate of their choice, a candidate, if elected, who will support the ruling elite. Sarah Palin and Michele Bachmann have been pushed to the political front to distract the American people's attention away from the real issues of job creation with their anti-intellectual rhetoric. Palin and Bachmann have learned to mask the GOP's real agenda to cut, cap, and balance the budget that would destroy jobs and gut the big three: social security, Medicare, and Medicaid. Instead of focusing on job creation policies, the GOP has been focusing on deficit reduction, obsessing over repealing the Affordable Care Act, and making Obama a one-term president. It is worth noting that it was the Republicans who initially put healthcare on the table, but later withdrew from it because Obama favored it. The GOP has convinced the American people that they hear their concerns, but these are only talking points, and many average Americans have bought into this ideological rhetoric because it is racially framed against Barack Obama. The political system is a reified system and the electoral voting process appears to be illusory, making the American people believe they have a real voice in a racist, sexist, and classist society. However, Americans have been given a voice and ideological power by the U.S. Constitution, but many of them are unaware of this fact. Many can hardly tell you what is in the Constitution besides citing the First Amendment.

Americans operate under the illusion that our political system treats them as active political participants. They have been socialized to accept the authority of public officials and the power elite and have learned not to challenge their misguided political rhetoric. As mentioned earlier, many anti-narratives have been written to vilify and demonize the president and raise calumny upon him and liken his rise to the presidency to that of Hilter's rise to power. Vilification and demonization are two potent weapons that stir the fears of individuals, when their fears are based on the unknown and they have limited access to power. What is most conspicuous is that ordinary Americans do not see the relationship between the economic structure and the legal and political institutions that can impede economic improvement through procedural trickery as we have seen during the manufactured debt ceiling crisis. Rather than acquiring important sources of information about the way the economy works, Americans are influenced by a radical ideology that directs their attention to Barack Obama as the real source of our economic crisis.

Our power elite, the most educated among us, exploits the intelligence of the American people. For example, during a political debate on our faculty listserv, one of my colleagues said:

> Political parties have placed the game of politics ahead of the function of government. Each party uses the tools of media and money to win rather than to govern. As a result, the people who govern us spend more time trying to misinform us, shape what we know, or hide what they do rather than actually govern in our general best interests. Corporate media is complicit in this deceit and has abdicated its role—at least in a functioning democracy—to tell truth about the powerful. There is a shell game being played that is designed to keep us all focused on petty differences and to believe that we are enemies of one another. This is done lest we discover that our "representatives" no longer represent the majority, but only the privileged few. Human corruption is at the heart of our problems. It infects Republicans and Democrats alike, rich and poor, socialist, democrat, communist, and capitalist.[60]

When some conservative right politicians, especially Tea Party members, are interviewed by major cable networks and are asked what their plans are for creating jobs, since they emphasized this point before and after the 2010 midterm elections, they claim the American people put them back in power to shrink the debt and the government. The established Republicans are held hostage by the Tea Party purists, an extreme isolationist wing of the Party, which further helps them contradict their campaign promises for job creation and point the finger at Obama. Annihilation of Obama was their real platform when the American people voted them into office: not job creation. In the meantime, the GOP is supporting and passing legislation that makes the rich richer and the poor poorer. Americans cannot see through this maze of ideological rhetoric. Many of them are ill-informed about the way the economy and the government work. There is a "closing of the mind" when it comes to political knowledge among the American electorate, a major reason they vote against their own self-interests. Murray Edelman asserts that

> Contradiction and murkiness about the role of powerful people are instruments of political influence because they make it easy to generate reasons to accept authority. Aspirants must create an impression that they deserve to be followed, and common mystifications help them do so. Regimes, educational institutions, and everyday rhetoric disseminate a familiar set of beliefs that serve their purpose [to snare the ill-informed].[61]

More so than the Democrats, the Republicans continually use the media to create the illusion that the nation's interests are best served by the GOP. Prior acts that "rationalized and perpetuated incumbent leadership were for the most part those that could readily be dramatized, consisting largely of defeats of foreign and domestic enemies and threats such as what was carried out during the Bush administration."[62] Thus, the Republicans have ultimately contrived many humbugs to foist on a gullible public to turn it against the Obama presidency.

Under these circumstances, Obama has demonstrated restraint, civility, stability, and practicality, draining the toxicity out of the political discourse, when news commentators and political analysts want him to respond emotionally to those who revile him. Since Obama does not respond emotionally but rather rationally to his critics, he has defied the stereotypical behavior and the white racial frame that views African Americans as emotional radicals. Obama stands for reaching across party lines, racial lines, class lines, and gender lines with rational discourse, and has not let "hatred and bigotry figure in any computation of his politics," says Howard Fineman of *The Huffington Post*, during an interview on MSNBC in 2011.

A SIDE NOTE ON OBAMA'S BLACK CRITICS

It is important to note that in the realm of reified politics, Obama faces opposition from both black and white conservatives. So what attracts African American men to the Republican Party and become obsessed with dissociating themselves from the slave plantation and welfare ideology? As discussed in chapter 1, slavery, Jim Crowism, and contemporary racism have affected the black male psyche and image. For one thing, many African American men from generation to generation have been brought up in households where the mother had to rely on state-supported programs, which has contributed to an already unhealthy self-image, with no male role models. Clarence Thomas has cited the "welfare" phenomenon as a problem when he criticized his own sister for accepting public assistance. Michael Steele, former RNC Chairman, also cited his mother rejecting public assistance because she "didn't [want the] government to feed and clothe her children."[63] We can make the assumption that these well-educated African American men embrace the Republican Party because it rejects a welfare state and "welfare" has been synonymous with black people. Obama, Thomas, and Steele have all matriculated through the most prestigious cognitive elite institutions in America. Even though Obama's mother relied on welfare to support him, he has not let it destroy his self-esteem or self-concept. Therefore, Thomas and Steele, like other well-educated black men, have become accommodationist politicians to the conservative right.

We can trace accommodationist thinking back to Booker T. Washington (1856–1915), an orator and author who received substantial financial support from the white power elite because he insisted that blacks should prepare themselves for citizenship through self-help programs and industrial education. Washington, like other black conservatives of his day and modern-day black conservatives, was an accommodationist. He believed African Americans were creating hostility among whites for demanding their rights, ignoring America's major role in subjecting blacks to slavery, and putting legal barriers in their way after emancipation to keep them in a slave-like state. Allen West (R-FL) and a Tea Party radical, has become a Republican claiming it was a one-way ticket off the twenty-first-century plantation. West's extreme behavior will not allow him to see that he has traded one plantation for a more radical one, and that the Republican Party will not embrace him for his intellectual abilities as an African American, his manhood, or leadership qualities. Herman Cain, a former 2012 presidential candidate, shares West's plantation ideology.[64] Both men believe that to be associated with the Democratic Party is tantamount to living on a plantation, where dependency undergirds the Democratic ideology. Simply put, these men have dissociated themselves from their black heritage. As Clarence Thomas puts it, individuals who come from a racial group that has had the "hell kicked out of it" by the white power structure is not seen as equal to whites unless they give up a part of themselves to become part of that white power structure, but it comes with a high price tag. These African American men have no desire to combat systemic racism or reach out to the masses of young African American males who need guidance through the maze of racism that keeps them incarcerated and jobless. Carter G. Woodson, considered the father of black history, informs us that elite African Americans who have been so long inconvenienced and denied opportunities for development are naturally afraid of devoting themselves to uplifting the black race.[65]

Herman Cain panders to white audiences and has scathingly denounced President Obama. He has shown prejudice against the religious rights of Muslims who love this country, and has demonstrated a prejudice that is felt by African Americans as a whole. Cynthia Tucker, a syndicated columnist for the *Atlanta-Journal Constitution* and Pulitzer Prize winner, writes that Cain has "enthusiastically castigated President Barack Obama, a tactic unlikely to lure many black voters who take great pride in the nation's first black president. Cain has not only cozied up to birthers, but he has also questioned Obama's manhood, telling *The New York Times* that the president isn't 'a strong black man.'"[66] Cain's statement suggests that he has bought into the age-old belief from slavery that black men could never be strong men, including himself. His statement further suggests that his economic success has given him a special place in the minds of the power elite. Cain perhaps fails to understand that strength is not a byproduct of wealth, as enormous riches can be gained through exploitation of others, but strength comes from individuals' refusal to give up their identity, beliefs, and value system. Cain's cozying up to conspiracy theorists would make them all outliers. Simply put, conspiracy theories are real problems that can threaten the security of American citizens as well as the president. Conspiracy theorists engage in deceptive communication that involves holding factual information from listeners and restricting their free choice, especially if the communication comes from political leaders we trust. In a nutshell, deceptive communication is no less propaganda than the dissemination of ideas for the purpose of inducing or intensifying a specific attitude in individuals. On the whole, the American electorate may not be aware that propaganda distorts facts, and is invariably false and misleading for the purpose of appealing to their passions and prejudices. It is the conservative right that uses conspiracy theories for political purposes and for contaminating the minds of the American electorate against the first African American president to make him appear as *"the Other"* who is dangerous, diminishing his chances for re-election. After all, it is up to the American electorate to critically analyze and objectively evaluate the merit of these messages.

Shelby Steele, another conservative black, has been affected by systemic racism. He claims that Obama's victory would wash away America's racist past, but would Obama, as president, keep America clean?[67] Steele also did not believe Obama could win the presidency. Now that Obama has been inaugurated as the forty-fourth president, Steele has changed his argument and claims Obama used his "blackness" to win the presidency. Given Steele's argument, can other notable African Americans run for the presidency and clinch the nomination by using their "blackness" to win? Carol Moseley Braun, Shirley Chisholm, Jesse Jackson, Alan Keyes, and Al Sharpton are African American and were presidential contenders, but their "blackness" did not help them clinch the nomination for the primaries, let alone the general election. To say Obama used his "blackness" is a naive statement and pushes Steele into the company of other Obama "nigger breakers" and haters.

A public intellectual, Shelby Steele, often finds himself at the center of controversy for his conservative position on programs that could help African Americans. This makes him a much in demand media pundit when the GOP needs him to weigh in on controversial issues involving African Americans that are highly offensive to whites.[68] Steele's analysis of African Americans is one that supports a racist conservative ideology, and conservative black thinkers who buy into the notion that African Americans will use the race card to get what they want are pandering to white hostility.[69]

Negative thinking has infected even those blacks who are not conservatives, including many of my black colleagues, who had doubts as to whether Obama could fulfill the duties of the presidency of the United States. They had difficulty liberating themselves from the systemic racism that has cloaked African Americans with an inferiority complex. But at the same time, many African Americans and other Americans of color are troubled by the white disrespect and dismissal of Obama. If occupying the highest office of this land cannot accord a black president the same respect given to a white president, then white racism has a stronger hold on the attitudes of whites than does the symbolic greatness of the White House.

RACISM AND IDEOLOGICAL HEGEMONY

Antonio Gramsci first coined hegemony as the ability of the power elite to maintain control of the populace through ideology. But they will use violent means if necessary through law enforcement.[70] Hegemony involves both coercion and consent. It is a "system of ideas worked out by intellectuals or institutions as a historically organic process necessary for any social formation; ideologies are embodied in the practices of individuals through their way of knowing as well as through the institutions" that supposedly serve us.[71] In the United States, control is maintained mainly through ideological hegemony and ideological rhetoric that politicians use to settle their differences with each other. This rhetoric has emerged from both political parties to demonize the other. Does the conservative right use ideological hegemony against Obama to turn his progressive policies into conservative ones? We can argue that ideological hegemony dominates our social, political, and economic life, but it also dominates us intellectually.

It was ideological hegemony that forced Obama to distance himself from his former pastor Reverend Jeremiah Wright of Trinity United

Church of Christ, for his inflammatory rhetoric against America's race-based hegemonic practices. Instead, the scholars who questioned Obama's relationship with his former pastor, labeling him un-American, believed that Obama's use of apologia in his 2008 Philadelphia speech on race was a failure and that he relied on identity politics to explain his membership with Trinity.[72] Consequently, many white Americans denounced Wright for his inflamed words against America and likened him to Malcolm X, viewing him as a radical time-bomb. Many media networks and communication academics did not present Wright's complete sermon, but teased out and reported the part they knew would offend white America,[73] but Wingfield and Feagin place Wright's

> prophet-like statements . . . in their larger context, which is near the end of a long sermon on societal injustice. One sees clearly that he is arguing that, in contrast to the power of God, even powerful governments such as that of the U.S. are fallible and transitory and in his views this is especially true of those that fail to treat all citizens equally.[74]

In this excerpt, Wright says,

> The government gives them the drugs, builds bigger prisons, passes a three-strike law and then wants us to sing "God Bless America." No, no, no, God damn America, that's in the Bible for killing innocent people. God damn America for treating our citizens as less than human. God damn America for as long as she acts like she is God and she is supreme.[75]

This appealed to the racist attitudes of those who did not want Obama elected as president. Every politician jumped on the bandwagon to condemn Wright. Hillary Clinton weighed in on this spectacle claiming that one does not choose his or her family, but they can choose their church, suggesting that then presidential candidate Obama should have shielded his ears from Wright's black liberation messages. Clinton cashed in on the Wright controversy and used it to her advantage by presenting Obama as un-American for his association with Wright for over twenty years. If the cable networks had presented Wright's sermon in full context, they and white America would have understood that his sermons "drew from the tradition of black liberation theology, a current of religious expression that combined black power's emphasis on racial pride, the civil rights movement's critique of discrimination, inequality, and militarism visible in the sermons of Martin Luther King, Jr."[76]

Meanwhile, Clinton and many conservative pundits have not spoken a word against declared racist politicians such as the late Senator James O. Eastland of Mississippi, Senator Strom Thurmond of South Carolina, Senator Robert Byrd of West Virginia, former Senator Trent Lott, and many others. These men not only embraced racist ideologies and southern racialized sexual politics, but also campaigned on platforms of racism, gave political speeches that denounced the NAACP and African Americans, were part of the Ku Klux Klan or supported the organization or tried to block civil rights legislation. In 1955, at an all-white convention for southern racists, the late James O. Eastland went as far as to approve the murder of Emmett Louis Till, the fourteen-year-old black boy who was beaten to a pulp by two white brothers who were not accepted as part of the southern elite class. Nonetheless, these senators were elected term after term, and were not called to the national stage to apologize for their racist behavior or why they associated with Klansmen during their tenure as congressional senators and representatives. No doubt, systemic racism creates a double standard for both blacks and whites, and whites do not have to justify or explain their past racist behavior, as Obama was forced to explain his position on race. Consequently, presidential candidate Obama was prompted to discuss his relationship with Wright and made "his most detailed statements about racism and racial inequality in the United States."[77] The most important issue confronting us now is whose framing takes precedence and is given more weight in public spaces.[78] For now, whites are doing the framing and are not required to rationalize it.

Obama has marked his fourth year in office and struggles daily to defy the status quo that is produced, reproduced, and maintained by elite white male politicians and the power elite they serve who do not want to see change. "A major reason for white male concern about change is the challenge to white men's power by those who have been oppressed. Many find it hard to accept the fact that they have been (or are) oppressors. They sense they are losing legitimacy and power, and they wish to stop this process."[79] Some politicians and media pundits have said that Obama is naïve, inexperienced, and unprepared to lead this nation. For example, Rush Limbaugh calls Obama a "little boy" with a radical agenda who holds disdain for the U.S. Constitution. Limbaugh is an ultra-conservative far-right radical and noise machine and a demagogue from the Jim Crow era. To refer to the President of the United States as a "little boy" supports the *Roots* miniseries scene discussed in chapter 1. Furthermore, as discussed earlier, Tiger Woods was referred to as a "boy." To publicly call a black man "boy" is taboo and politically incorrect. By today's ethical standards on political discourse, this epithet opens old wounds and suggests black men are still symbols of inferiority, criminality, and social deviants. Limbaugh's derogatory remark suggests that black men's perceived "boy" status prevents them from becoming "autonomous adults,"[80] having been rendered economically powerless, further suggesting their only real purpose in life is "intoxication, sex," and criminality.[81] There was no outcry from the white community to challenge Limbaugh's racist remarks, which also suggests that social relations are based on social and cultural hegemony. This hegemony is perpetuated and reinforced by the media, as will be explored in chapter 3.

Obama's critics play an important role in perpetuating ideological hegemony. A vast number of politicians and ordinary Americans know it is impossible to turn the economy around in the limited time Obama has been in office. However, the economy is slowly improving.

Is the conservative right's hegemonic political stance a reaction to Obama's rapid political rise to the presidency and the endearing attitude many Americans and the international community have about him? Even if Obama could restore America economically, the reified dominant political system will not allow for such change.[82] We have no reason to believe the 112th Congress and the Tea Party will consider the general welfare of the American people, even though they claim they speak for the American people, but have no real economic agenda to help them. Looking at the long list of problems Obama is faced with, is it realistic to believe he can restore national economic stability, political accountability, values and morality to society, personal financial security for Americans, and education reform; end race, class, and gender inequality; and narrow the gap between the haves, have-nots, and have-mores? Most importantly, can Obama restore respect for America among other nation-states in his second term in office?[83] Americans did not expect such a monumental task from any of Obama's predecessors. In fact, Ronald Reagan is forever heralded for his Reaganomics, trickle-down economics. The American people should open their minds and put away conspiratorial and paranoid politics, so they can collectively demand change in the institutions that only benefit the affluent. But they will have to demand it from both political parties and not just from the president. The U.S. Constitution is clear about how decisions should be reached about government processes, and President Obama cannot unilaterally make certain decisions without Congress. The Constitution requires a balance of power between the two. The most important issue before us is that the American electorate's voting practices during the 2010 elections inculpate them for the intransigent behavior of Congress, the division they have witnessed between the established Republicans and the Tea Party, and Congress's behavior toward the Obama administration. Our elected officials cannot assume office without the American people's vote. Clearly, we see ideological hegemony operating in the dissenting voices of the radical right. The war in Iraq, the Wall Street meltdown, the economy, and bad international relations were all signs that pointed to Republican hegemonic domination.

CONCLUSION

White racism, white radicalism, and white retribution contribute to the attacks against President Barack Obama and are the driving force behind many anti-Obama narratives that construct Obama as America's greatest enemy since fascism, Nazism, and communism. Overt representation of special interests, reified politics, and ideological hegemony from the conservative right are obstructing Obama's efforts to effect change in the infrastructure of the United States. Conservative black intellectuals like Shelby Steele, demagogues like Rush Limbaugh, and radical Tea Party activists like Sarah Palin and Michele Bachmann play on the apocalyptic fears of the American people, and they expose America's true nature of systemic racism and oppression of African Americans, other Americans of color, and immigrants. Most important, their racism, radicalism, and retribution are directed at the first African American elected to the presidency of the United States.

At the beginning of this chapter, we mentioned that we are a nation of different worldviews, polarized ideologies, and conflated philosophical disagreements. We also alluded to how the toxic political climate has divided the American people to the point where incivility influences our perceptions against Obama and our ability to engage in collective action to resolve our political differences. Following the 2011 shooting in Tucson, Obama's memorial speech at the University of Arizona "rose to the moment and transcended" the toxic rhetoric that has demonized and propagandized his presidency. Obama ran on the platform of politics of hope and the "change" platform that illustrates no distinction between race, class, gender, and religion among the American electorate. But his ability to turn the American economy around and create an environment for businesses to hire the American people may prove a mounting task due to obstructionism on the right. What should loom large in the minds of the American people is that corporations are sitting on large sums of cash and outsourcing work to foreign countries. On the macro political level are the conservative-controlled Congress, large corporations, and power elite banding together to win back the White House, the Congress, and the Senate so they can turn this country into a plutocracy.

NOTES

1. James T. Kloppenberg, *Reading Obama: Dreams, Hope and the American Political Tradition* (Princeton, NJ: Princeton University Press, 2010), xiii.

2. Ibid., 3–4.

3. Lilly Scott, http://www.americanprogress.org/issues/2009/07/whose_problem. html (accessed May 14, 2011).

4. Tom Hamburger and Peter Wallsten, *One Party Country: The Republican Plan for Dominance in the 21st Century* (Hoboken, NJ: John Wiley & Sons, 2006), 5.

5. Robert Kuttner, *Obama's Challenge: America's Economic Crisis and the Power of a Transformative Presidency* (Chelsea Green Publishing Company, 2008), Kindle Electronic Edition, Paragraph 2, Location 298 of 3263.

6. Carl M. Cannon, "The Top 15 Winners and Losers of 2009,"http://www. politicsdaily.com/ 2009/12/30/the-top-15-winners-and-losers-of-2009(accessed January 4, 2011)

7. Robert Kuttner, *op. cit.* (see reference 5), Kindle Electronic Edition, Location 313 of 3263.

8. Ibid., xii.

9. Will Bunch, *The Backlash: Right-wing Radicals, High-Def Hucksters, and Paranoid Politics in the Age of Obama*, cover flap (New York: HarperCollins, 2010), 3.

10. Ibid., x.

11. Ibid., 5.

12. Craig K. Elwell, "Foreign Outsourcing: Economic Implications and Policy Responses." Congressional Research Service, The Library of Congress, http://fpc.state.gov/ documents/ organization/50272.pdf (accessed January 23, 2012). Craig Elwell is a specialist in macroeconomics for the government and finance division.

13. Adam Hersh, Michael Ettlinger, and Kalen Pruss, "The Consequences of Conservative Economic Policies," *Center for American Progress*, http://www.americanprogress.org/issues/2010/10/conservative_economics.html (accessed June 26, 2012).

14. Patrick J. Buchanan, *Where the Right Went Wrong* (New York: Thomas Dunne Books: St. Martin's Griffin, 2005), 160.

15. Ibid.

16. David Neiwert, *The Eliminationists: How Hate Talk Radicalized the American Right* (Sausalito, CA: PoliPointPress, 2009), 29.

17. Steve Benen, "Embarrassingly Unpatriotic," *AlterNet*, February 14, 2009, http://www.alternet.org/blogs/workplace/126984/embarrassing-ly_unpatriotic:_conservatives_who_want_the_u.s._to_fail/ (accessed June 26, 2011).

18. Jay Newton-Small, "The Weak Speaker: How a Failed Debt Vote Disarmed the Nation's Top Republican," http://news.yahoo.com/weak-speaker-failed-debt-vote-disarmed-nations-top-111905041.html (accessed June 28, 2012).

19. David Neiwert, *op. cit.* (see reference 16), 39.

20. Ibid.

21. Charles Babington, "Obama Wants Big 2012 Campaign Map, GOP Wants Small," *Huffington Post*, June 20, 2011, http://www.huffingtonpost.com/2011/06/20/obama-wants-big-2012-camp_n_880205.html (accessed July 8, 2012).

22. Tom Hamburger and Peter Wallsten, *One Party Country: The Republican Plan for Dominance in the 21st Century* (Hoboken, NJ: John Wiley & Sons, 2006), 5.

23. David Neiwert, *op. cit.* (see reference 16), 41.

24. David E. Procter and Kurt Ritter, "Inaugurating the Clinton Presidency: Regenerative Rhetoric and the American Community," in Robert E. Denton, Jr., and Rachel L. Holloway (Eds.), *The Clinton Presidency: Images, Issues, and Communication Strategies* (Westport, CT: *Praeger Series in Political Communication*, 1996), 1–16.

25. Senator Robert C. Byrd, *Losing America: Confronting a Reckless and Arrogant Presidency* (New York: W. W. Norton & Company, Inc., 2004), front flap cover.

26. Barack Obama, "Text of Obama's Inauguration Speech," The Associated Press. http://www2.hickoryrecord.com/content/2009/jan/20/text-obamas-inauguration-speech/ (accessed March 19, 2012).

27. Will Bunch, *op. cit.* (see reference 9).

28. Ibid., 39.

29. Murray Edelman, *Constructing the Political Spectacle* (Chicago, IL: University of Chicago, 1995), 38.

30. Ibid.

31. Manning Marable, *How Capitalism Underdeveloped Black America* (Boston, MA: South End Press, 1983), 182.

32. United Press International, "Clergy Arrested in Capitol Budget Protest," http://readersupportednews.org/news-section2/320-80/6811-clergy-arrested-in-capitol-budget-protest.

33. James T. Kloppenberg, *op. cit.* (see reference 1), 82.

34. Will Bunch, *op. cit.* (see reference 9), 343.

35. "High Stakes Histrionics," http://seekingalpha.com/article/283896-high-stakes-histrionics (accessed August 24, 2011).

36. D. Andrew Austin, "The Debt Limit: History and Recent Increases," http://fpc. state.gov/ documents/organization/105193.pdf (accessed August 25, 2012). D. Andrew Austin is an analyst in government finance.

37. Ibid.

38. Murray Edelman, *The Politics of Misinformation* (Cambridge, UK: Cambridge University Press, 2001), 1.

39. Ibid., 19.

40. Ibid., 27.

41. Ibid., 13.

42. "Economic Policy Institute: US Debt Deal Will Cost 1.8 Million Jobs," http:// www.economywatch.com/in-the-news/economic-policy-institute-us-debt-deal-will-cost-1-8-million-jobs.03-08.html (accessed September 5, 2011).

43. Statistics presented on *The Ed Shultz Show* on Friday, July 28, 2011.

44. Maureen Dowd, "Not O.K. at the O.K. Corral," http://www.nytimes.com/2011/ 07/27/ opinion/27dowd.html?emc=eta1 (accessed July 21, 2011).

45. *Politicalticker*, http://politicalticker.blogs.cnn.com/2011/07/03/clinton-to-obama-dont-blink-on-debt-ceiling-showdown/ (accessed October 3, 2011).

46. Ibid.

47. Ibid.

48. Kate Zernike, "That Monolithic Tea Party Just Wasn't There," http://www. nytimes.com/ 2011/08/02/us/politics/02teaparty.html?_r=1&emc=eta1 (accessed September 12, 2011).

49. Ibid.

50. Ibid.

51. Joe Nocera, "Tea Party's War on America," http://www.nytimes.com/2011/08/ 02/opinion/the-tea-partys-war-on-america.html?emc=eta1 (accessed September 12, 2011).

52. Kenneth J. Neubeck and Noel A. Cazenave, *Welfare Racism: Playing the Race Card Against America's Poor* (New York: Routledge, 2007), 3.

53. Manning Marable, *op. cit.* (see reference 31).

54. Billy Wharton, "Obama's No Socialist. I Should Know," *The Washington Post*, March 15, 2009.

55. Bill O'Reilly, *Pinheads and Patriots: Where You Stand in the Age of Obama* (New York: HarperCollins, 2010), 128–29.

56. A. E. Kornblut and Krissah Thompson, "Race Issue Deflected, Now as in Campaign" September 17, 2009: 1. Available at www.washingtonpost.com/wp-dyn.

57. Ibid.

58. Kate Kenski, Bruce Hardy, and Kathleen Hall Jamieson, *The Obama Victory: How Media Money, and Message Shaped the 2008 Election* (New York: Oxford University Press, 2010), 72.

59. James T. Koppenberg, *op. cit.* (see reference 1), 237.

60. David Bringhurst, Director, University Writing Center, Wright State University, made this statement on our Faculty Listerv in response to a conversation about the allegory of *The Ant and The Grasshopper*.

61. Murray Edelman, *op. cit.* (see reference 29), 38–39.

62. Ibid., 43.

63. Jim Duffy (April 2005), "Mother Knows Best," *Johns Hopkins Magazine*, http:// www.jhu.edu/jhumag/0405web/steele.html (accessed September 29, 2011).

64. Clarence Lusane, "Why Herman Cain Will Not Become President," http://www. progressive.org/mplusane062911.html (accessed May 4, 2011).

65. Carter G. Woodson, *The Mis-Education of the Negro* (Blacksburg, VA: Wilder Publications, 2008), 39.

66. Cynthia Tucker, "Herman Cain's Bigotry," http://blogs.ajc.com/cynthia-tucker/ 2011/ 07/22/herman-cains-bigotry/?cp=6 (accessed July 24, 2011).

67. See Robert E. Denton, Jr. *op. cit.* (see reference 6), 7.

68. Shelby Steele, "Why Black Messiah Obama Won't Win," http://aalbc.com/%20reviews/%20shelby_steele.htm (accessed September 27, 2011).

69. Ibid.

70. Antonio Gramsci, *Selections from the Prison Notebooks* (New York: International Publishers, 1971).

71. Eileen T. Walsh, "Representations of Race and Gender in Mainstream Media Coverage of the 2008 Democratic Primary," *Journal of African American Studies* 13, 121–130. DOI 10.1007/s12111-008-9081-2. 2009.

72. Gwen Brown, "A More Perfect Union": Barack Obama's Failed Apologia and Successful Use of Identity Politics," in Robert E. Denton, Jr., ed., *Studies of Identity in the 2008 Presidential Campaign* (Lanham, MD: Lexington Books, 2010), 44–48.

73. Aidia Harvey Wingfield and Joe R. Feagin, *Yes We Can? White Racial Framing and the 2008 Presidential Campaign* (New York: Routledge, 2009), 129.

74. Ibid.

75. Ibid.

76. Thomas J. Sugrue, *Not Even Past: Barack Obama and the Burden of Race* (Princeton, NJ: Princeton University Press, 2009), 87.

77. Ibid., 121.

78. Joe R. Feagin, *The White Racial Frame: Centuries of Racial Framing and Counter-Framing* (New York, Routledge, 2010).

79. Joe R. Feagin, Hernan Vera, and Pinar Batur, *White Racism: The Basics*, 2nd Edition (New York, Routledge, 2001), 199–200.

80. Anthony J. Lemelle, Jr., *Black Male Deviance* (Westport, CT: Praeger Publishers, 1997), 139.

81. Ibid.

82. Murray Edelman, *op. cit.* (see reference 29).

83. Frank I. Luntz. *What Americans Really Want . . . Really: The Truth About Our Hopes, Dreams, and Fears* (New York: Hyperion Publishers, 2009).

THREE

The Media

Transmitters of Eliminationist and Racialized Rhetoric

"The American mass media have achieved what American political
might could not: World domination." —Akbar S. Ahmed

Americans are frustrated with millions of them struggling to survive in
the ruins of a once-thriving economy. Today, Americans have more access to the media to organize, protest, and challenge the status quo. From
the west coast to the east coast, Americans are railing against unemployment, income disparity, and culture wars between themselves and the
ruling elite. Occupy Wall Street and similar other movements on college
campuses throughout the country have used the media to bring attention
to social and economic inequality, corporate greed, corruption of banks,
and high unemployment rates even among the educated. Senior citizens
are filling town halls and questioning their Congressional representatives
about deficit-reduction plans that would diminish their Social Security
and Medicare.[1] Hundreds of thousands of people in Ohio and Wisconsin
have used the media to protest against the draconian legislation that
would strip them of their collective bargaining rights. Even Obama has
used the power of the media to encourage the American people to con-
verge on their Congressional representatives to raise the debt ceiling, and
work with him to create bipartisan bills to create jobs. With this said, the
media have served as a conduit for average American citizens who are
protesting the greed of the power elite that use the conservative right to
protect their interests.

The quote by Akbar S. Ahmed informs us that the media are ubiquitous and can transmit information at an exponential rate faster than the
American polity. When one surfs the Internet, reads newspapers on and
offline, uses social media, listens to political commentators or repetitive

talking points of Republican (GOP) presidential candidates on cable news blaming Obama for a depressed economy and every conceivable problem in America, one walks away with a sense of mental numbness and wonders whether politicians and political pundits are deceived by their own rhetoric. Even though the GOP uses the economy against Obama repeatedly as a talking point in the media, Republicans have yet to put forth any substantial plan for solving the U.S. economic crisis. Instead, the conservative right has incessantly used eliminationist and racist rhetoric that focuses more on blaming Obama's administration rather than working with him to find job creation solutions that could put millions of Americans back to work. This chapter focuses on media networks, and how they are used by the conservative right to transmit eliminationist and racist rhetoric, intentionally contaminating the perceptions of the American people against President Obama and constraining his ability to address the country's pressing problems. I also examine how media coverage lends itself to sectional interests, frames political discourse, and creates and perpetuates ideological hegemony that obscures and obstructs the political process.

THE MEDIA'S INFLUENCE

The media are inescapable in our lives and have a ubiquitous presence like the environment around us. They infiltrate every aspect of our lives with the same rapacity as political advertisement. The media are simply everywhere. They are, "to a large extent, the mental and cultural environment we inhabit every day, bringing us the first voices we hear in the morning, the opinions we absorb. . . . The media are the world we share."[2] They are the guardians of social and political information that shape the national debate and the national conversation. They influence our attitude and disposition towards the president and Congress, and set the tone for both progressive and conservative political discourse. The media influence public opinion and set the national political agenda. They are also considered the *Fourth Estate*. In other words, they function as the fourth branch of government because the government relies on the media to disseminate information about its functions and processes. As U.S. society grows into a mass public, political "ideas become commodities and assimilate to the economics of mass media consumption."[3] No doubt the media have pushed America onto the international stage as a global superpower, and serve as a site for international political struggle and contestation. The media are our cultural authorities and icons, and are capital-driven. They typically support the status quo and the agenda of the ruling corporate elite that owns them. However, the media play a major role in contributing to our democratic process with respect to the government. That is, the media contribute to political openness and democratic accountability, better known as transparency.[4]

Jack Balkin, a First Amendment scholar, writes that informational and political transparency of the government is important, holding government officials accountable through the legal system or by public opinion when the American people's interests are adversely affected.[5] Americans prefer transparency to secrecy, and are aware that information is often manipulated.[6] The media devote their time, energy, and resources to monitor politicians by crowding the halls of power to determine who is doing the people's work, and who is corrupting the process.[7] They should function as transmitters of objective information that people need to know. However, many of the cable networks, such as Fox News, present their own biased opinions about a given situation instead of the actual facts. Fox operates as a wing of the Republican Party and tends to politicize events, such as the Benghazi incident, and presents a partisan political agenda that goes against the standards of fair reporting and objectivity. For example, the Chrysler Super Bowl ad by Clint Eastwood was denounced by former President George W. Bush's guru Karl Rove, a Fox News contributor. Rove believed that the ad supported Obama's re-election efforts, but Eastwood said, "It was meant to be a message about job growth and the spirit of America." Millions of individuals "hang on the media's every word as Received Wisdom because every major broadcast and cable news network has presented them, and people who watch them, as serious thinkers whose words are worthy of the public's consideration."[8]

The media influence our thought process with ideological messages that often obscure reality. For example, during the past three years of Obama's presidency, the media focused too much on his critics rather than showing the American people Obama's achievements. It should be noted that an annual Gallup poll ranked Obama as the most admired man in America with Bush and Clinton following him. According to MSNBC Hardball Chris Matthews, a recent Gallup poll ranked world leaders on the job they were doing. The U.S. was ranked first in global leadership, followed by Germany, France, Japan, United Kingdom, and China. In 2008, before Obama took office, it was ranked 6th.[9] However, the media have given this poll little attention. Beyond this, the Pew Research Center reported America's positive influence and foreign countries' attitude towards America during Obama's first term (see table 3.1). BBC/GlobeScan/Pipa conducted a poll that indicated and ranked the countries' support for Obama. Many countries such as France, Australia, Kenya, and Nigeria, but not Pakistan, preferred Obama over Romney for U.S. president.

Cable networks tend to prioritize and marginalize media events in a manipulative manner. For example, Fox News, a right-wing cable network and an anti-Obama hate machine that makes up charges against the

Table 3.1.   Approval of U.S. in 16 Foreign Countries.

	2007	2012	Change
Technological Advances	69%	71%	+2%
Music/Movies/TV	60%	66%	+6%
Ideas about Democracy	35%	45%	+10%
Ways of Doing Business	32%	43%	+11%
Ideas Spreading Here	19%	27%	+8%

Pew Research Center, Date: June 12, 2012.

President,[10] hosted the 2011 Iowa Straw Poll, and prioritized this event over the Rick Perry event in South Carolina where he announced his candidacy for the presidency. Fox knew that the GOP presidential candidates in the straw poll would direct their political eliminationist discourse at Obama. Even though polls change from day to day, the media reported that Obama's performance approval ratings plunged after his bus tour in Iowa, making it seem that he had lost some of his base after he called on organized unions to make more sacrifices.

Meanwhile, the Democrats have remained silent and have not adequately defended President Obama against the onslaught of negative GOP discourse that defies facts. For example, it was stated on MSNBC during the Jobs Fair the Democrats hosted, that the party had put forth over forty economic bills but Congressional Republicans tabled the bills in order to tank the economy and blamed it on Obama's policies. Why have the Dems remained silent on this issue, allowed the GOP to overshadow their job creation effort with their vitriol, and direct eliminationist rhetoric at Obama to make him a one-term president? These were questions the American people needed to ask, and they did at the voting booths. In his second term, Obama may need to exercise whatever presidential powers to which he is entitled to counter frame the destructive rhetoric of the GOP that would destroy his chances of succeeding in his second term. However, Obama took the necessary steps to create bold jobs bills in his first term, sent them to Congress, and the American people began to see that Congressional Republicans obstructed the process and are trying to obstruct the process in Obama's second term.

RACIALIZED RHETORIC AND THE MEDIA

The media helped the American people to take the bold step of electing the first African American president. However, did the American electorate expect that a black president presiding over a racist society could change a centuries-old system that has been in the control of the whites from the very beginning where "power, privilege, and the shaping of cultural consciousness" have become a bureaucratic monolith in individuals' political thought and action?[11] This is not rational thinking, and we must reason together. President Obama has achieved a lot, for which he has received little recognition, but African Americans and other Americans of color cannot expect a black president to change racist, sexist, and classist institutions overnight or even change them at all. Nor should they believe that we live in a post-racial society because we have elected the first black president. As discussed in chapter 2, many politicians benefit from the way these institutions operate, and the GOP has consistently obstructed Obama's presidential agenda to make sure these institutions operate in favor of the power elite. Obama's critics do not want to give him the credit for being an accomplished think-tank, and are bent on attacking his agenda. When conservative right-wing commentators, such as Rush Limbaugh, present information, they purposely "make their case on the more objective grounds of factual inaccuracy or a breach of standards or ethics, precisely because, as long as there are consumers of news who share the biases of the right-wing media critics, they know that they can never be proved wrong."[12] For example, certain media outlets and politicians would make Americans believe that Obama is a Muslim; that he and his wife hate white people; that he slipped "reparations" into the stimulus package for African Americans; that his administration is the most "corrupt" one in American history; that he is a socialist and a statist; and that he is the worst president in American history.

Many Americans, including some Americans of color, have allowed racial and anti-democratic messages of conservative news media outlets blind them to accept fact-based information about Obama and themselves. Much of the information presented by the right-wing media is "marred by factual errors and by a pervasive anti-Arab" and anti-Muslim bias and tends to politicize social problems, the fiscal crisis, and worker rights.[13] When former presidential candidate Michele Bachmann touted that the "founding fathers worked tirelessly to end slavery," her statement was found to be factually and historically erroneous suggesting that she has little knowledge about American history. Fox News aired Bachmann's chaff information in such a way that the Fox audience believed her. The audience believed what Bachmann said because they did not have a full grasp of American history.

Rush Limbaugh and Fox News are examples of talk show hosts and networks that use racist language to play on the fears of dominant group members, and racially divide the American people. Fox has become the conduit for false information and extreme conservative views, and studies show that the channel actually affects the way viewers vote.[14] The network's commentators slander, misalign, attack, and humiliate anyone who opposes its conservative agenda.[15] Fox has also become a reporting machine of denouncing members of certain religious groups, especially Muslims, progressives, and racial minorities. The channel has also become a propaganda machine that uses race-baiting and portrays Obama as an unproductive president, a false ideology that supports the beliefs of its viewers. Former New Hampshire Gov. John Sununu, a Fox insider, called the President "lazy, disengaged, incompetent, and stupid,"[16] during a three-minute interview with MSNBC Andrea Mitchell of *Andrea Mitchell Reports*. Of course, Mitchell was so astonished by the former governor's unscrupulous remarks about the President that she gave him the opportunity to withdraw his statements, but he refused. Regardless of Sununu's personal feelings for the president, Mitchell did not believe the former governor should disrespect the president of the United States on national TV.[17] Moreover, Fox presents false information about politics and progressive politicians, hires contributors and pundits who are willing to validate their right-wing bias and are willing to fall in line with Fox's false coverage of the Obama administration and agenda, and downplays actual statistics. Fox portrays Obama as a president who cannot lead, but the network does not focus on the GOP's constraints on his efforts to move this country in the right direction and killing whatever little recovery the fragile economy has made. Studies show that Fox misleads the public, creating a misinformed audience.[18] With the exception of a few media watchdog groups, professional journalism reviews, and a few genuine liberal voices, most institutions and uninformed viewers accept Fox as a legitimate news organization.[19] Given conservative America's attitude on race and racism, the Republicans, with the help of Fox News, get more positive coverage than the first African American president, regardless of his many achievements.[20] Language is a very powerful conditioner in the U.S. culture. In this culture, black equates to bad and white to good.

Another example of pundits using the media to racially divide the people during the Obama presidency is from a well-known Atlanta-based conservative radio talk-show host, Neal Boortz, who called for "modern-day lynching of black male thugs." For Boortz, the subtle practice of racism against African Americans and other Americans of color is not enough. He goes on to argue that whites should take up arms to defend themselves against "urban thugs." He has extrapolated the criminal activity of a few urban black males to the entire black and Hispanic communities. Therefore, is Boortz using the phrase "urban thugs" as racist imaging of urban black men to justify some whites' attacking them? Sensible law-abiding American citizens would never approve of criminal activity by any individual, regardless of race, class, or gender. But urban black males and their families largely live in poverty because the racist and classist legal system has incarcerated more black males at a greater exponential rate than poor white males, because of the outsourcing of jobs from urban and rural communities to China, the lack of educational opportunities, and the lack of a strong male support system.

In chapter 2, we described how Rush Limbaugh referred to Obama as a "little boy" and all the racist implications behind it. While media pundits use racialized language to demean Obama and Americans of color, communication scholars are yet to question these behavioral practices in their scholarship. Instead, these gatekeepers of journals and publishing houses are as anti-Obama as the pop-culture books devoid of any real critical analysis. When Limbaugh levels criticism toward particular ideas, groups, or individuals on most of his broadcasts, his listeners tend to accept his ideological position as gospel. Constant exposure to Limbaugh's messages not only correlates with attitudes that reflect his message, but also reflects the number of ill-informed Americans who listen to his radio messages that lead to greater antipathy towards Obama and most progressives.[21] For Americans of color, especially African Americans, the process of getting around racialized discourse has provided many challenges.[22] Simply put, Limbaugh is in a game driven by the power elites' political initiatives and will use racial overtones on his program to fulfill their political goals.

Americans believe in freedom of speech, but should free speech be used to denigrate those who have an opposing ideological position by dividing the country and destroying what progress it has made toward civil rights? The opinionated information the public receives is altering their "beliefs in a systematic way that produces long-term change" in the social reality about who the political enemies are.[23] Since eliminationist discourse and violent rhetoric dominate the airwaves, we can conclude that critics like Limbaugh use the airwaves to revive Jim Crowism and feel justified to hinder Obama's presidency with the support of the power elite.

THE POWER ELITE AND SPECIAL INTERESTS

The media represent the special interests of the ruling, corporate, and political elite. "Allegations of political bias in the media are common, although there is considerable controversy concerning the nature of this bias: neither liberals nor conservatives are pleased. Conservatives allege that the media exhibit a liberal bias. On the other hand, liberals allege that the media exhibit a pro-corporate, plutocratic bias."[24] In practice, certain media outlets, such as Fox News, seem to support the conservative agenda and ideology, while others like CNN and MSNBC support the progressive agenda and ideology.

Jürgen Habermas, a German sociologist and a philosopher in the tradition of critical theory and pragmatism best known for his theory on the concepts of communicative rationality and the public sphere, argues that all knowledge reflects the interest of the ruling elite, a society's capitalist class. Consequently, it is the "role of critical social theorists to expose the interests behind knowledge and indeed the knowledge, which exists behind the interests" between the ruling elite and the proletariat, regardless of race, class, and gender.[25]

Mainstream media tend to present a "remarkably narrow, homogenous and centrist conservative view of political life that supports the status quo. This is often attributed to heavy media reliance on government officials, leaders of political groups, and large bureaucratic organizations as routine, predictable sources of information."[26] The media support and promote the dominant power structures because they are owned by the largest for-profit corporations in America, such as Time Warner Inc., Walt Disney, Viacom Inc., among others. Because the media are controlled by the corporate elite, their news reports reflect the views of the power elite these corporations serve as well as the wealthy class who control political discourse by throwing large sums of money to the politicians who support their agendas. There is no "greater power in the world today than that wielded by the manipulators of public opinion in America. No King or Pope, no conquering general or high priest has ever disposed of a power even remotely approaching that of the few dozen men who control America's mass media of news and entertainment."[27] Most often, their ideological influence goes unchallenged by the working class. This is because the working class sees it as a natural order of things and has come to accept that those with power and wealth can influence the media. Murray Edelman, a political scientist who specializes in symbolic politics, cautions us

> that public officials normally exercise little initiative and little authority; that established institutions ensure that little change will occur that such change as does take place will be superficial, making little difference in people's lives; and that confidence in constant progress and frequent innovation, in spite of the persuasive evidence to the contrary, effectively counter discontent with the conditions that persist in everyday life.[28]

Edelman's statement alludes to the fact that people are guilty of what Karl Marx calls "false consciousness," the erroneous assumption that their elected officials will serve their best interests, an idea that is not challenged in the media. Even though the media supposedly report news under the cloak of political objectivity, they (especially Fox News) slant racial, gender, and class issues. For example, looking at the flip side of racial issues, most dominant group members of society may not publicly speak ill of Americans of color for fear of being perceived as racists or bigots by the media, but what they say clandestinely is a different story. On the other hand, conservative right politicians who do not hide their hostility for the first black president have become comfortable articulating their eliminationist racist rhetoric by taking an *ad hominem* approach.

The media help politicians to socially construct images of the world for us and then tell us what to think about these images. Epistemologically, a majority of the American populace learns everything it knows from the daily newspaper, weekly news magazines, the television, and radio.[29] If we frequent certain restaurants, the owners have a television mounted on the wall, which is usually tuned in to Fox News channel. The Internet and email are adding to the list. Both the Democratic and Republican National Committees bombard us with their partisan messages, but if one analyzes the RNC messages, they spin their messages about what Obama did or should have done or liken him to the Italian Captain Francesco Schettino who not only abandoned his stricken vessel, but also the passengers. If Obama had appeared to be campaigning for re-election, which is typical of any incumbent president in the last year of his term, the RNC chair claims he is abandoning his presidential duties to the American people. This is another form of eliminationist rhetoric to put doubt in the minds of the American people, especially the conservative base. Therefore, the conservative right has formed an apparently false image of Obama for most Americans, but should Obama take on a more aggressive posture to deal politically with the conservative right?

For Obama, the media appeared to present his political discourse objectively during his first term, and it challenged him to address critical issues relating to race and gender during his 2008 campaign. MSNBC host Chris Matthews claims that Obama will be challenged and feared because he is the first African American president. Matthews goes on to say that older whites, unlike younger whites, fear African Americans.[30] Given the historical experiences of African Americans and unresolved racial issues, some dominant group members may have a paralyzed fear of what African Americans may do should they achieve the power of self-determination. More recently, the media focused "almost exclusively on Obama's critics, without holding them responsible for the uncivil, unconstructive tone of their disagreements or without holding the previous administration responsible for putting the country in a deep hole. The misinformation and [eliminationist rhetoric] that now passes for political reporting and civic debate is beyond description."[31] The following sections discuss the media's ability to construct the political spectacle to frame progressive and conservative political discourse, including eliminationist rhetoric.

USING ELIMINATIONIST RHETORIC TO CONSTRUCT A
DANGEROUS POLITICAL SPECTACLE

Eliminationist rhetoric has always been buried in the U.S. culture since John Adams and Thomas Jefferson became the first sitting U.S. presidents.[32] What do we mean by "eliminationist rhetoric"? Elimination, in a political context, refers to political discourse or rhetoric to eliminate an enemy through vitriol and hyperbolic rhetoric that spin the truth. Eliminationist rhetoric excises and exterminates, in this case, political enemies in the guise of civil means. This type of rhetoric is designed to damage a leader's reputation before an ill-informed American electorate and is based on a foundation of untruths, blatant lies, and deception. Eliminationist rhetoric is the "death of discourse itself. Instead of offering an opposing idea, it simply shuts down intellectual exchange and replaces it with the brute intention to silence and eliminate."[33]

As MSNBC's Chris Matthews notes, we have overcome slavery, the Great Depression, McCarthyism, Jim Crow, and the Civil Rights movement. And it was through our great debates that we resolved these problems. Matthews suggests that individuals who are passionate about their political views may want to replace the radical eliminationist rhetoric with meaningful debate and reasoned deliberation. Given the tragedy in Arizona in 2011, politicians and the media were called upon to tone down the eliminationist rhetoric that vilified the other side. Even though this eliminationist rhetoric is a threat to genuine intellectual debate, such as Sarah Palin's "Don't retreat, reload" metaphor, which alludes to the Second Amendment; Sharron Angles, a Tea Party favorite, invoking the Second Amendment to encourage Americans to protect themselves against a "tyrannical government"; and Michele Bachmann, a former 2012 presidential candidate and founder of the House Tea Party Caucus, touting the "armed and dangerous" slogan, this kind of rhetoric rarely contributes to the development of the great debates on which this country was founded and solved its problems, but these radicals set out to eliminate those who oppose their political ideas. Other GOP politicians are obsessed with eliminationist rhetoric directed mainly at progressives. The conservative right and Tea Party adamantine use words that imply that they will stop at nothing to get what they want, even if it means physical violence or advocating the elimination of a perceived enemy at the hands of unstable citizens who are affected by the very policies or no policies the GOP refuses to pass to help ordinary American citizens. This kind of rhetoric destroys the Republican brand and suggests the Party is anti-government, un-American, and politically hostile towards Americans of color, immigrants, and women. The GOP brand has also stifled any real intellectual debate about what true democracy is and how to move the country in a direction that embraces changing demographics.

Table 3.2 presents a short list of eliminationist rhetoric the conservative right has been using since the 2008 election of Barack Obama.

John McCain notes that "Our political discourse should be more civil than it currently is, and we all, myself included, bear some responsibility for it not being so." Ron Brownstein, contributor to the *National Journal*,

Table 3.2.   GOP Eliminationist Rhetoric.

"Don't Retreat, Instead Reload"	Vice Presidential Candidate and Former Gov. Sarah Palin
"I hope that's not where we're going, but, you know, if this Congress keeps going the way it is, people are really looking toward those Second Amendment remedies and saying my goodness what can we do to turn this country around? I'll tell you the first thing we need to do is take Harry Reid out."	Senate Candidate Sharron Angle
"We have become, or are becoming, enslaved by the government ... I dare 'em to try to come throw me in jail. I dare 'em to. [I'll] pull out my wife's shotgun and see how that little ACS twerp likes being scared at the door. They're not going on my property."	CNN Commentator Erick Erickson
"I want people in Minnesota armed and dangerous on this issue of the energy tax, because we need to fight back."	U.S. Rep. and Presidential Candidate Michele Bachmann
"Our nation was founded on violence. I don't think that we should ever remove anything from the table as it relates to our liberties and our freedoms."	Texas Candidate for U.S. Rep. Stephen Broden
"We are aware that stepping off into secession may in fact be a bloody war. We are aware. We understand that the tree of freedom is occasionally watered with the blood of tyrants and patriots."	Texas Gubernatorial Candidate Debra Medina
"Does sharia law say we can behead Dana Milbank?...I think you and I should go and beat him up."	Fox News Host Bill O'Reilly
"Put anything in my scope and I will shoot it."	U.S. Rep. Joe Barton (R-TX)
"Meet Mr. Smith and Mr. Wesson"	Conservative Radio Show Host Glenn Beck

Source: STFU with the eliminationist rhetoric.

also notes that "when political arguments are routinely framed as threats to America's fundamental character, the odds rise that the most disturbed among us will be tempted to resist the governing agenda by any means necessary."[34] Given McCain's and Brownstein's statements, the political discourse of violence is framed around the GOP's deep-seated resentment toward Obama, racist partisan rancor, unyielding conservative fanaticism and fringe political views, and a willingness by Tea Party adamantine, with the blessings of former Governor Sarah Palin, to drive the U.S. government into default to discredit the legitimacy of Obama's presidency, and ultimately blame him for the downgrade. In the end, most of the blame was shifted to Congressional Republicans for creating an unnecessary crisis, then to the Obama administration for its failure to get tough with Congress. After this fiasco, Congress's approval rating plummeted to an all-time low of 13 percent, the lowest in 40 years.[35]

FRAMING CONSERVATIVE POLITICAL DISCOURSE

Political discourse is transmitted through the media and advertising.[36] The conservative right represents the interests of large corporations and the power elite. It is a party of obedience to authority and dominance, and its political discourse is framed around robust individualism, limited government, obstructionism, and the elimination of perceived political enemies.[37] When GOP politicians repeat shared sound bites or charge the Obama administration with political corruption, they are on a quest to eliminate his chances for re-election by destroying him with violent political discourse or threatening to investigate him on abuse of stimulus money, or charging him with false civil charges to impeach him for the sole purpose of distracting him from focusing on the real issues facing this country. The GOP feeds the ill-formed average American electorate with misinformation. These repeat sound bites have become "a bedrock party principle."[38] The party elucidates a narrow worldview and a consistent rigid ideological belief system that its base must adhere to by submitting the hegemonic system that controls them. The GOP tells its base what is good for them, what is bad for them, and that they must speak those things that the party approves. Party members are very successful at articulating their talking points and hidden objectives. Their use of political discourse hides the party's true ideology to turn this society into an elite plutocracy and favor the "haves," those in power, against the "have nots," those without power and exploited by those in power. The GOP has also been successful at radicalizing the minds of black conservatives, making them believe that the party has set them free from the psychological effects of their ancestral slave status and a "welfare" mentality. The party has become an illusory haven for mentally oppressed blacks who believe the Democratic Party is a plantation party.

Black conservatives have symbolically distanced themselves from anything that resembles welfare, black existentialism, and affirmative action programs, and thus embrace the GOP. With the Tea Party enmeshed with established conservatives, the party has become radical and its political discourse has been passed off as mainstream ideas.[39] Conservatives speak in terms of right and left and the "use of the left-to-right" political continuum "serves to empower today's radical conservatives and marginalize progressives."[40]

Fox News and their conservative contributors have helped the Party's political discourse to dominate the media, and the media repeatedly use GOP-coined terminology even when it is inherently biased. We can see this in everyday conservative language and the ideas that go with it: supporting the troops, illegal immigrants, illegal consumers, squandering tax money, welfare, etc.[41] Fox and other conservative media outlets have become vehicles for their continued effort to assault the Obama administration, while experimenting with political methods for a Republican comeback in 2012. In the meantime, Fox, its commentators, and some news analysts loudly support the GOP's culture wars, and the denouncement of same-sex marriage and Planned Parenthood "as the key to conservative reformation."[42] If ill-informed Americans get to hear these media sound bites often enough, they will accept these bites as gospel.

We can see the difference between conservative and progressive media coverage in the situation that arose when former Governor of Mississippi, Haley Barbour, wanted to honor a Civil War era Confederate General, Nathan Bedford Forrest with a license plate. In 1864, the troops of Nathan Forrest slaughtered a largely black Union regiment that was trying to surrender in what became known as the Fort Pillow Massacre. After the war, Forrest became one of the founding fathers of the terrorist Ku Klux Klan, and was the group's first grand wizard. When Barbour realized he was losing his white base over this, he decided against signing into law the creation of a license plate to honor a dishonorable southern icon. Fox News gave no attention to Barbour's plan to honor a dishonorable figure in U.S. history. But MSNBC gave it coverage, allowing the Americans to see that the country has not escaped the Jim Crow era where overt racist behavior was normalized in everyday politics.

Fox News also gives negative media coverage to public employee protests against Republican governors and blames the White House and progressives for using political discourse that fuels these media events. Fox News often solicits Tea Party members to push an eliminationist ideology against public employee protesters under the pretext that Republican governors are faced with imminent liberal threats and must be protected.[43]

In the next several sections, we explain further how the political elite promote dominant power structures through ideological hegemony and reification in the media.

HEGEMONY AND RACIALIZED DISCOURSE IN THE MEDIA

In media studies, hegemony refers to the modes the media use to encourage average citizens to consent to and support the status quo and other power structures. Individuals are socialized to consent to everyday life practices that keep the power elite in power.[44] To keep systems of power in force, Americans, for example, celebrate Independence Day with parades, keep the government in power, shop at upscale and not-so upscale stores, keep corporations in power, women take care of their families and stay home as homemakers and keep patriarchy in power,[45] and cast their votes during elections and keep the political parties in power. When average citizens consent to these power structures, they help the ruling elite maintain control through ideological hegemony, using the media as the conduit to subjugate them.

Naturally, racialized societies throughout the world associate negative images to persons, groups, or things they do not understand or to those things they perceive as different.[46] In the United States, most Americans of color, especially African Americans and President Obama, have been the subject of racialized, hegemonic discourse in the media that has socially constructed African Americans as criminals and immoral human beings and Obama as an alien citizen. Such racialized discourse has its roots in slavery and is produced, reproduced, and maintained in modern U.S. society with the help of the media. When hegemonic media, for example, Fox News, use pseudo intellectuals to denounce or devalue a cultural practice or particular behavior practices of minority groups, they are, in essence, identifying these minority groups as subjects worthy of oppression, absolving a racialized, hegemonic society of all blame for the oppressive conditions it created and the reason such behavior has become normalized in the media for eliminating the marginalized in U.S. society.

Paul Griffin, a professor of religion, argues that some intellectuals are the carriers of racism and racialized discourse and their racist "comments and expressions" are rarely challenged, regardless of what platform they use to deliver their messages (i.e., church pulpits, academic lectures, the media, the Halls of Congress, corporate boardrooms, etc).[47] Griffin goes on to say that such intellectuals provide the incubative culture for race theories, and working-class whites are then provoked or impelled by these theories towards the concrete expression of what might otherwise remain irrelevant abstractions.[48] Perhaps the most blatant example of bias and hegemony is the bias practiced by Fox News.

FOX NEWS

Fox News, a conservative cable network and subsidiary of News Corporation, is self-proclaimed as "The Most Powerful Name in News." Created by Australian American media mogul Rupert Murdoch in 1996, the network dominates the family rooms of millions of viewers worldwide. A patron can walk into fast-food restaurants and notice a television on and customers tuned in to Fox News. Fox's trademark slogans say they are "Fair and Balanced" and "We Report. You Decide." Fox News claims fairness, objectivity, and impartiality, but the network practices eliminationist rhetoric to unfairly misrepresent Obama and other progressives. The network also tends to report subjective, slanted, derogatory, and biased information against Americans of color, specifically African Americans, since we have an African American President whom former Speaker of the House Newt Gingrich (1995-1999) has called a "food stamp president."

The journalistic integrity of Fox News was also questioned when the Rupert Murdoch-owned *News of the World* was shut down in London, England, a scandal in which their reporters illegally hacked individuals' cell phone messages. Former Governor Eliot Spitzer of New York says this should concern Americans:

> First, it is hard to believe that the misbehavior in Murdoch's media empire stopped at the water's edge. Given the frequency with which he shuttled his senior executives and editors across the various oceans—Pacific as well as Atlantic—it is unlikely that the shoddy ethics were limited to Great Britain. Much more importantly, the facts already pretty well established in Britain indicate violations of American law, in particular a law called the Foreign Corrupt Practices Act. . . . While one must always be cautious in seeking government investigation of the media for the obvious First Amendment concerns, this is not actually an investigation of the media, but an investigation of criminal acts undertaken by those masquerading as members of the media.[49]

Not all broadcasters agree with the way Fox reports its news. CBS producer Don Dahler quit Fox when he was asked "to play down the statistics on the progress of African Americans."[50] Another example of Fox's bias was against CNN's *Black in America* documentary that was first aired in July 2008. Fox took a subjective, ideological, and derogatory position that African Americans far exceeded the whites in the number of children they gave birth to, with a reportedly higher number of out-of-wedlock births, giving the impression that African Americans engage in irresponsible procreative activity.[51]

To support their hegemonic view, Fox courts conservative-right African Americans such as Juan Williams, Reverend Jesse Lee Peterson, Larry Elder, Angela McGlowan, and Erick Rush to expose black self-hatred, to target black women, or to call Obama a "sell-out" without offering other points of view. These racialized speakers are encouraged to make offensive and racially charged statements against other African Americans, suggesting that they are amoral people.[52] Such conservative blacks have filled their coffers by smearing black leaders and the African American culture in general. Instead of refuting Fox's or the GOP's racist behavior, they have become the mouthpiece for racist Fox. Rather than holding Fox accountable for its racist hegemonic discourse, Fox solicits, as a media strategy, some African Americans who are willing to attack an already vulnerable African American community and President Obama.[53]

Many rational-minded people view the black commentators of Fox as a hawkish and self-loathing group. But African Americans and other Americans of color who have the "intellect, poise, and emotional stability to withstand the sophistry of its anchors are verbally abused and disrespected on the air" by Fox News commentators.[54] David Brock documents that in the last several decades, the conservative right has built a powerful media machine to sell conservatism to the public, discredits its opponents, and disregards journalistic ethics and universal standards of fairness and accuracy, manufacturing "news" that is often bought and paid for by a tight network of corporate-backed foundations and old family fortunes.[55]

Fox News supports right-wing politics on most social, racial, and religious issues and misrepresents facts to the public, playing on the fragile sensibilities of their viewers. By doing so, Fox viewers typically vote against their own interests. Furthermore, Fox uses its network as a platform to instill fear and hatred in its viewers to maintain a social distance between the various racial groups in America, especially between conservative whites and the progressive "other." Fox is "bluntly critical and interpretative when it comes to covering news" on racial issues and the Obama administration, which goes against the fair and objective model of news reportage.[56] It broadcasts negative images of Obama and African Americans in general to third world nationals, elites, and white critics who passively absorb white supremacists' thinking.[57] Given Fox's position on race and race relations, we can assume that Obama's "blackness" contributes to this portrayal, but the network appears to deliberately ignore the fact that the GOP constrains his every effort. Fox also portrays black Americans as unproductive citizens who want government handouts without providing any U.S. historical information that white society has contributed to black impoverishment. In short, ideological hegemony is one way Fox News transmits its racist conservative ideology and represses competing ideologies. Most important, Fox and other conservative outlets undermine democratic media, healthy freedom of expression, and its philosophical-ideological detachment from fair and objective reporting restricts the public's ability to engage in meaningful discussions about race, class, gender, and political issues. In simple words, Fox functions as a propaganda network under the guise of freedom of expression.

A NOTE ON ADVERTISING AND REIFICATION

Reify means to give material existence to an abstraction. In critical work, the media give material existence to an abstract value system that many Americans embrace. From a Marxist perspective, reification is an impediment to critical consciousness, preventing individuals from seeing the way things actually are. Media coverage, advertising, press conferences, and sound bites have concealed individuals' social consciousness about media as a capitalist commodity, which are "crucial for the subjugation of individuals."[58] Specifically, political advertising generates illusory representations of social reality of political and economic reality.[59] Advertising "colonizes the U.S. mass media and is responsible for most of their income."[60] Due to this colonization and advertising being the main source of income for the media, advertising is full of ideology and political rhetoric and has a reifying effect on the general public's thinking processes and voting practices. For example, the GOP dragged Obama into a political war over spending cuts while simultaneously repeating the reified sound bite that they are about creating jobs. But this political war was about eliminating the president's chances for re-election. The Republicans may have campaigned on job creation, but the party began waging a war on the middle class and President Obama soon after they took control of the House. The GOP makes effective use of the media and press conferences and tries to persuade the American people that they are interested only in job creation, but the "job creation" concept has become reified in the media, in the minds of the conservative right, and has lost its economic significance for the American people. Job creation has been reified through conservative sound bites rather than given an actual material existence through the legislative process.

Advertising influences the electorate's affective, cognitive, and attitudinal behavior, specifically in the political arena. Acceptance of these fundamental categories, especially of people's thought patterns, is rooted in material existence. It follows that the working class is incapable of fully grasping the true nature of reification within relations of capitalist production.[61] Advertising wields a powerful effect on the consumer and is an influential form of social and political communication. As a commodity, it mediates social and political relations between the consumer and the product—a political activity or media event. Media advertising is "significant because, in consumer capitalism, individuals depend on it for meanings—a source of social information embedded in commodities that mediate interpersonal relations and personal identity."[62] Americans depend on media advertising to provide them meaning concerning the Obama presidency, his political relationship with Congress, and how both can create jobs. However, Americans also want to know how Obama differs from his predecessors who maintained stagnant political institutions from which the corporate and political elite benefited. But with all the wrangling between Obama and Congressional Republicans and the Tea Party as the driving force, over raising the debt ceiling and the country possibly defaulting on its financial obligations to pay America's bills, this media event dominated the financial news and frightened the American people. Consequently, Obama influenced the American people to contact their congressional representatives to encourage them to raise the debt ceiling. From the televised speeches of President Obama and the House Speaker John Boehner to the hardline tactics of the Tea Party adamantine, the rhetoric that was supposedly about deficit reduction became reified in the minds of the American people who were left wondering what this fiasco had to do with job creation and why Congressional Republicans would not work with the President.

In contrast, Obama's ad campaign during his election bid presented the flip side of the reified nature of advertising and illustrated ways he became more than just an image for American consumers, but presented him as a real person who was interested in change and not some reified deity.[63] In recent interviews comparing him to GOP presidential candidates, Obama said he wants the American people to compare him to his opponents and not to a "deity." Through ads that placed great emphasis on his language for change, we saw who he was and what he was promising. Obama's use of technology, (the Internet, email, emerging media channels, social media, mobile websites that offered news updates, and so forth) encouraged dialogue via user-generated content and electronic social interaction between him and the people, is what made his ads non-fictitious, non-illusory, and genuine to his supporters. His direct contact with the people waned after the 2008 election and has been edged out by Republican posturing to the detriment of his presidency. To sum, reification creates "modes of thought that have ideological consequences. This mistaken perception, this 'reified' or 'false' consciousness is by no means inconsequential. More than merely being a superimposed illusion, these modes of thinking serve to sustain categories of thought to which capitalism owes its very existence."[64] Having looked at conservative media and its influence on about half of the American electorate and the GOP obstruction of Obama's agenda, we now turn to progressive political discourse and the media's potential to be a catalyst for positive change.

FRAMING PROGRESSIVE POLITICAL DISCOURSE

In contrast to conservatives, progressives primarily represent the interests of the working class and the middle-class, and have a unifying moral value: empathy. Progressives frame their political discourse around "equality, justice, and freedom for all." For example, the progressives will summon the full resources of the government to provide relief for the disadvantaged, indigent, homeless, and jobless. They frame their political discourse around protecting the American people and believe it is the responsibility of the government to provide safe food through regular inspections, consumer and worker protection, disaster relief, health care for the uninsured, and environmental protection.[65] The progressive frame of thinking articulates the need to empower the people through public education, to create and maintain highways so people can go to work, to take care of business, and to travel for pleasure. The progressive frame also makes sure they hold airlines responsible for the maintenance of aircraft through government regulation, whereas the conservatives want to deregulate, putting citizens' lives at risk. The government has a moral responsibility to protect and empower the people.[66]

When the GOP took control of the U.S. House of Representatives, Obama expressed his concern that the conservative right lacks empathy for the people. This empathy deficit follows the "Golden Rule." It is a failure of politicians to care about their constituency and each other and take courageous responsibility and act powerfully for the people.[67] But some of the 2012 GOP presidential candidates claim they will make the government inconsequential in the lives of the citizens. The conservative agenda is about taking the moral responsibility away from the people. Unlike progressives, conservatives want to privatize government and call for total deregulation that led to the housing and Wall Street collapse. The problem with privatization is that "there is no moral mission involved. But when it comes to testing the safety of food or of drugs, a clear moral mission is involved: protecting the public. The danger in privatization is that the profit motive may intervene and undermine the moral mission."[68] The problem with the limited government ideology is that the average citizen will lose out, and many of these protections will be diminished if the conservative right has its way. It is up to the progressives to put forth their message of empathy and protection, and to inform the people that the conservative message of deregulation and limited government only benefits the wealthiest citizens of this country.

MEDIA AS AGENT FOR CHANGE

The media can help the electorate become active human agents in exercising their autonomy over a dysfunctional political system and economic concerns by helping them get their voices heard. Under the Bush administration, the media did not create a political scene for the working class to vent their pent up feelings and their overwhelming response that forced the media to reset their agenda to put common citizens' concerns in the forefront. Occupy Wall Street was one such example of the working class using the media to protest their concerns. "Since the mass media, especially newspapers and television, are the dominant source of political information, one of their key roles in a presidential election year may be to restore politics to a prominent position on the agendas of America's voters. This role of stimulating renewed interest in learning about politics may be the ultimate agenda-setting influence of the media."[69] The political attitude of Americans toward the 2012 presidential candidates evoked a similar response to that of the people's attitude when Herbert Hoover was blamed for the stock market crash.

The media coverage of marginalized, voiceless, and seldom humanized American citizens shows them "sick and tired" of being "sick and tired," and they simply want infrastructural changes. Americans who voted to change the political power in the Congress that gave the GOP a sweeping victory is now seen as buyers' regret. The GOP has been politicizing their talking points rather than presenting any real jobs plan bill. The major networks as well as the smaller networks focused their attention on the ability of voters to make their experiences heard and understood, on the availability of occasions for them to speak in the streets, and on the willingness of others to listen to them. Using the media, the American people are beginning to challenge some of the major priorities of the GOP that support without constraint the ruling elite. Their voices are being heard at many town hall meetings, and they have been occupying universities and major financial entities throughout the nation, for example, Wall Street. The American people want a commander-in-chief who would have their best interests at heart, a leader who would put an end to the war in Iraq, recession, layoffs, corporate greed, unemployment, and financial and housing crises. Barack Obama was the leader the American people wanted: a leader who would stand as an active agent of reform, a leader with energy and real concern for the working class, a leader whose platform of change would offer the people hope, a leader who could help America regain its former glory.

While the media, as representatives of the ruling, business, and political elite, tend to cover up the victimization of the voiceless and marginalized, when Obama arrived on the scene, the media's coverage of him clearly showed a president who wanted to represent the interests of those who had been *de*-centered from the national polity. Because of Obama's message of change, the media gave in to airing the concerns of the voiceless. Beyond this, the media reported how Obama fought for

> disability pay for veterans, worked to boost the non-proliferation of deadly weapons, and advocated the use of alternative fuels to cure our national addiction to oil. He has spoken against the vicious indifference of the Bush administration to the poor—and to political incompetence—in the aftermath of Hurricane Katrina, and rallied against genocide in Darfur. Long before it was popular, [Obama] stood against the

war in Iraq as a futile gesture of the American empire that would do little to beat back the threat of terror.[70]

Media representation of the sectional interests of the working and middle class appeared to have closed the gap in class relationships between the ruling elite and the coverage they receive. A good example is the media coverage of the political fights over union-busting legislation between the public employees and GOP governors in Wisconsin and Ohio.

UNION BUSTING PROTESTS

In 2011, Wisconsin Republican Governor Scott Walker rammed through a bill to strip public employees of their right to collectively bargain. Not willing to go down without a fight, the workers protested, the media aired every protest event, and the recall effort of GOP State legislators who voted in favor to eliminate the unions was put in place. In the end, four of the six senators retained their seats. The Democrats needed three seats to become the majority of the state house, but missed this opportunity by one recall. After successfully gaining three of the four seats, voters needed to take control of the General Assembly. Therefore, Democrats and thousands of Wisconsinites decided to recall Governor Walker. To achieve this recall, voters were required to collect over 500,000 signatures and have them verified by the State's Accountability Board. Through their efforts, voters collected over 1 million signatures.[71] Having done all they could to recall Walker, the union sector fell short of defeating Walker at the polls because those who voted in favor of Walker did not believe he should have been recalled because of ideological differences. Yet the exit polls indicated that most voters were in favor of re-electing Obama for a second term.

In Ohio, first-term Governor John Kasich, a Fox News contributor and Tea Party favorite, signed Senate Bill 5, better known as SB 5, into law in March 2011, and public-sector union workers were not given a chance to speak against this draconian piece of legislation that would strip them of their collective bargaining rights. When workers wanted their voices heard at the beginning of the process, the governor ordered the state house doors to be locked. He rebuffed union leaders and disrespected officers of the law, calling them "idiots." In protest, union workers formed a group called *We Are Ohio* and collected 1.3 million signatures of which 915,000 from all 88 counties were validated; this was four times what the organization needed by law to get a referendum on the November 2011 ballot to repeal the law. SB 5 was successfully repealed by Ohioans. It is important to note that throughout the union busting debate, Kasich and his legislators disseminated false information, offended public workers, and used eliminationist rhetoric. In August 2011, Kasich wanted to meet with union leaders, but they refused to meet with him unless he repealed SB 5. Since the governor would not repeal SB 5, union leaders refused to meet with him, and Kasich gave Ohioans the impression that union leaders' refusal to meet with him and other top legislators was reflective of their so-called non-compromising nature.[72] The repeal of Senate Bill 5 was a referendum against the governor for his overreach into unions, higher education, eliminationist rhetoric, and political actions, all of which played out as important media events for public-sector employees. The Wisconsin and Ohio protests received much media attention from MSNBC and CNN but Fox News, an ultra-conservative leaning network, hardly aired the protests because the protests were against its own conservative ideology and conservative governors.

CONCLUSION

This chapter examined ways the media frame public discourse and help to create and perpetuate ideological hegemony. Through the media, conservatives have manipulated public confidence in a democratic society and engaged in eliminationist and racist rhetoric to advance its conservative right-wing agenda, that is, to eliminate Obama from seeking a second term as president. By contaminating the perceptions of the American people, the conservative media have divided the nation, contributing to the strident and violent rhetoric that has overshadowed Obama's presidency and constrained his ability to address our nation's most pressing problem, unemployment. The GOP has reached a "booming right-wing media market . . . that is largely based on bigotry, ignorance, and emotional manipulation."[73] This kind of technological networking hinders diverse opinions, minority expression, and community solidarity.

As we can see, the media have the capacity to voice the concerns of the working class and can serve as an agent for change for average American citizens. Obama can, and has been able to use the media to communicate his vision for a better America during his State of the Union speeches. But through much of his term, the GOP has forced him into a conservative space that goes against his "change" rhetoric and those who voted for him have been left wondering whether he is a true Democrat.

As we move forward, will Americans' frustration with a depressed economy and a broken political system continue to ignite the fires of rebellion against the GOP, with Obama leading the way to reform? Or will the eliminationist and racist rhetoric continue to hinder political progress and divide the country along party lines? Eliminationist rhetoric has a long tradition in American politics with the media acting as the transmitter.

Democratic media would encourage all racial groups to understand each other, and actively participate in political life if they want to successfully bring about a change in the system.[74] Edward Herman argues that this is likely to occur where media structures are democratic as such media will be open to neighbors who want to communicate views on problems and their possible communal resolution. Moreover, here the media structures are open to individuals' perspectives on social, economic, and political problems.[75] Consequently, democratic media would allow all views to bloom regardless of their financial position and institutional power.[76]

Having observed the role that the media plays in Obama's political saga, we now turn to the next chapter for a discussion on the roots and implications of a fallacy that Obama's critics and the media have foisted onto the voting public that Obama is anti-American.

NOTES

1. Richard (RJ) Eskow, "Insanity: After the Big Crash, The GOP Wants to Deregulate . . . Again," http://ourfuture.org/blog-entry/2010083426/insanity-after-big-crash-gop-wants-to-deregulate-again (accessed October 28, 2012).

2. Robert W. McChesney and John Nichols, *Our Media Not Theirs: The Democratic Struggle Against Corporate Media* (New York: Seven Media Stories, 2002), 9.

3. Jurgen Habermas, *Stanford Encyclopedia of Philosophy* (2007), http://plato.stanford.edu/entries/habermas (accessed August 3, 2012).

4. Jack M. Balkin, *How Mass Media Simulate Political Transparency*, http://www.yale.edu/lawweb/jbalkin/articles/media01.htm (accessed July 24, 2011).

5. Ibid.

6. Ibid.

7. John Stewart, Ben Karlin, and David Javerbaum, "The Media: Democracy's Valiant Vulgarians," *America: A Citizen's Guide to Democracy Inaction* (New York: Warner Books, 2004), 133.

8. David Neiwert, *The Eliminationists: How Hate Talk Radicalized the American Right* (Sausalito, CA: PolitPoint Press, 2009), 70.

9. Jon Clifton, "Worldwide Approval of U.S. Leadership Tops Major Powers: U.S. Also Remains Top Desired Destination for Potential Migrants," http://www.gallup.com/poll/146771/Worldwide-Approval-Leadership-Tops-Major-Powers.aspx (accessed April 5, 2012).

10. Bill Press, *The Obama Hate Machine: The Lies, Distortions, and Personal Attacks on the President—and Who Is Behind Them* (New York: Thomas Dunne Books, St. Martin's Press, 2012), 244.

11. Joe Feagin and Eileen O'Brien, *White Men on Race: Power, Privilege, and the Shaping of Cultural Consciousness* (Boston, MA: Beacon Press, 2003), cover page.

12. David Brock, *The Republican Noise Machine: Right-wing Media and How It Corrupts Democracy* (New York: Crown Publishers, 2004), 62.

13. Ibid., 13.

14. Stefano DellaVigna and Ethan Kaplan, "The Fox News Effect: Media Bias and Voting," *Quarterly Journal of Economics 122* (August 2007): 1187–1234.

15. Tolu Olorunda, "FOX News Finds Another Way To Attack Black People," http://www.opednews.com/articles/FOX-News-Finds-Another-Way-by-Tolu-Olorunda-090309-876.html (accessed December 20, 2012).

16. Byron Tau, "Sununu Calls Obama Lazy, Disengaged and Incompetent," http://www.politico.com/politico%2044/2012/10/sununu-calls-obama-lazy-disengaged-and-incompetent-137529.html (accessed January 26, 2013).

17. Noah Rothman, "Andrea Mitchell Visibly Shocked After Sununu Calls Obama 'Lazy,' Asks Him If He Would Take It Back," http://www.mediaite.com/tv/andrea-

mitchell-visibly-shocked-after-sununu-calls-obama-lazy-asks-him-if-he-would-take-it-back/ (accessed January 26, 2013).

18. "Fox News Viewers Know Less Than People Who Don't Watch Any News: Study," http://www.huffingtonpost.com/2011/11/21/fox-news-viewers-less-informed-people-fairleighdickinson_n_1106305.html (accessed December 18, 2012).

19. David Brock, *The Republican Noise Machine: Right-Wing Media and How It Corrupts Democracy* (New York: Crown Publishers, 2004).

20. Devin Dwyer, "GOP Gets More Positive Press Than Obama, Pew Study Finds," http://abcnews.go.com/blogs/politics/2011/10/gop-gets-more-positive-press-than-obama-pew-study-finds/ (accessed December 18, 2012).

21. David C. Barker, *Rushed to Judgment* (New York: Columbia University Press, 2002), 24.

22. Ibid., 139.

23. Anthony DiMaggio, *When Media Goes to War: Hegemonic Discourse, Public Opinion, and the Limits of Dissent* (New York: Monthly Review Press, 2009), 211.

24. "The Mass Media & Politics: An Analysis of Influence," http://www.progressiveliving.org/mass_media_and_politics.htm (accessed January 26, 2012).

25. Caroline Ramazanoglu with Janet Holland, *Feminist Methodology: Challenges and Choices* (Thousand Oaks: Sage, 2002), 147.

26. Tawnya Adkins Covert and Philo C. Washburn, "Information Sources and the Coverage of Social Issues in Partisan Publications: A Content Analysis of 25 Years of Progressive and the National Review," *Mass Communication & Society* 10, no. 1 (2007): 67–94.

27. "Who Rules America?" Research staff of National Vanguard Books and Kevin Alfred Strom, Media Director. http://www.realnews247.com/who_rules_america_updated_2004.htm. (accessed May 12, 2012).

28. Ibid., 1.

29. Ibid.

30. "Older White People Are Bigots, Says NBC News' Matthews," http://nation.foxnews.com/chris-matthews/2011/01/17/older-white-people-are-bigots-says-nbc-news-matthews (accessed February 23, 2012).

31. Robert P. Watson, "Obama's Accomplishments to Date." Dr. Watson shared a hardcopy list with me via email in September 2011. See also http://curmilus.wordpress.com/2010/03/02/what-has-president-obama-accomplished-by-robert-p-watson-ph-d/ (accessed April 12, 2010).

32. David Neiwert, *The Eliminationists: How Hate Talk Radicalized the American Right* (Sausalito, CA: PolitiPointPress, 2009), 12.

33. Ibid., 18.

34. *National Journal*, January 15, 2011.

35. "Congress—Job Rating," http://www.pollingreport.com/CongJob.htm (accessed February 12, 2012).

36. Julia M. Bristor, Renee Gravois Lee, and Michelle R. Hunt, "Race and Ideology: African-American Images in Television Advertising," *Journal of Public Policy & Marketing* 14, no. 1 (1995): 48–59.

37. David Neiwert, *op. cit.* (see reference 32), 229.

38. Richard (RJ) Eskow, *op. cit.* (see reference 1).

39. George Lakoff, *The Political Mind: Why You Can't Understand 21st-Century American Politics with an 18th-Century Brain* (New York: Viking, 2008), 45.

40. Ibid.

41. Ibid., 46.

42. David Brock, *The Republican Noise Machine: Right-wing Media and How it Corrupts Democracy* (New York: Crown Publishers, 2004), 63.

43. Daily Mail Reporter, "Tea Party takes on pro-union protesters as 70,000 demonstrators descend on Wisconsin Capitol in biggest rally yet," http://www.dailymail.co.uk/news/article-1358675/Wisconsin-Capitol-protests-Tea-Party-

takes-70-000-pro-union-demonstators.html (accessed February 27, 2012). Read more: http://www.dailymail.co.uk/news/article-1358675/Wisconsin-Capitol-protests-Tea-Party-takes-70-000-pro-union-demonstators.html#ixzz1nc6F3VHi.

44. Naomi Rockler-Gladen, "Antonio Gramsci's Theory of the Hegemonic Media," Hegemony and Media Studies. http://medialiteracy.suite101.com/article.cfm/hegemony_and_ media_studies (accessed April 28, 2012).

45. Ibid.

46. Richard Delgado and John Stefancic, "Images of the Outsider in American Law and Culture: Can Free Expression Remedy Systemic Social Ills?" in R. Delgado (Ed.), *Critical Race Theory: The Cutting Edge* (Philadelphia: Temple University Press, 1995).

47. Paul R. Griffin. *Seeds of Racism in the Soul of America* (Naperville, IL: Sourcebooks, Inc., 2000).

48. Ibid., 7.

49. Elliot Spitzer, "Prosecute News Corps," http://www.slate.com/articles/news_and_politics/the_best_policy/2011/07/prosecute_news_corp.html. (Retrieved August 5, 2011)

50. David Brock, *The Republican Noise Machine: Right-wing Media and How it Corrupts Democracy* (New York: Crown Publishers, 2004), 319.

51. CNN's *Black in America* documentary. Aired in July 2008. See "Fox Attacks: Black America." http://www.youtube.com/watch?v=UY04gIruZ4E (accessed August 3, 2011).

52. Ibid.

53. Casey Gane-McCalla, "Top 5 Fox News Uncle Toms." Available at http://newsone.com/nation/casey-gane-mccalla/top-5-fox-news-uncle-toms/

54. Tolu Olorunda, "Fox News Is Using the Obamas to Perfect Its Racist Attacks on Black America," http://www.alternet.org/story/123574/fox_news_is_using_the_obamas_to_perfect_its_racist_attacks_on_black_America (accessed January 19, 2012).

55. David Brock, *op. cit.* (see reference 47).

56. Everette E. Dennis and Melvin L. DeFleur. *Understanding Media in the Digital Age* (New York: Allyn & Bacon, 2010), 211.

57. bell hooks, "Postmodern Blackness," in Patrick Williams and Laura Chrisman (eds.), *Colonial Discourse and Post-Colonial Theory: A Reader* (New York: Columbia University Press, printed in Great Britain, 1996), 423.

58. Georg Lukas, "History and Class Consciousness: Reification and the Consciousness of the Proletariat," available at http://www.marxists.org/archive/lukacs/works/history/hcc05.htm.

59. Val Burris, "Reification: A Marxist Perspective," *California Sociologist* 10, no. 1 (1988): 22–43. http://www.uoregon.edu/~vburris/reification.pdf (accessed November 16, 2011).

60. Robert W. McChesney interview with Edward S. Herman, "The Political Economy of the Mass Media," *Monthly Review,* January 1989, http://www.chomsky.info/onchomsky/198901--.htm (accessed May 2, 2011).

61. Tim Novak, "Mass Media and the Concept of Ideology," Media and Social New School for Social Research, http://timnovak.org/uploads/Ideology_proofed.pdf (accessed March 25, 2012).

62. John Harms and Douglas Kellner, "Toward a Critical Theory of Advertising," *Illuminations,* http://www.uta.edu/huma/illuminations/kell6.htm (accessed May 3, 2012).

63. "Claire Beale on Advertising: Obama has rewritten the advertising rules," http://www.independent.co.uk/news/mediaadvertising/claire-beale-on-obama-has-rewritten-the-advertising-rules-986254html. Retrieved 9/13/2012.

64. Tim Novak, *op. cit.* (see reference 61), 5.

65. Ibid.

66. Ibid., 48.

67. George Lakoff, *op. cit.* (see reference 40), 47.

68. Ibid., 49.

69. David H. Weaver, Doris A. Graber, Maxwell E. McCombs, and Chaim H. Eyal, *Media Agenda-Setting in a Presidential Election: Issues, Images, and Interest* (New York: Praeger, 1981).

70. Michael Eric Dyson, "Barack Obama," *Nation* 285, no. 17 (2007): 22–23.

71. Editorial, "Short Take: Wisconsin Recall Effort," *Wisconsin State Journal.* http://www.startribune.com/opinion/141237603.html (accessed March 5, 2012).

72. "What's Going on with SB 5 in Columbus?: Theatrics by Key Republicans to Stir Up Emotions and Confusion," AAUP Ohio: Ohio Conference Update. Email update received on Monday, August 22, 2011.

73. Ibid.

74. Edward S. Herman, *Triumph of the Market: Essays on Economics, Politics, and the Media* (Cambridge, MA: South End Press, 1995), 215.

75. Ibid.

76. Ibid.

FOUR

American "Exceptionalism"

Roots, Racism, and Obama

"We hold these truths to be self-evident, that all men are created equal, that they are endowed by their Creator with certain unalienable Rights, that among these are Life, Liberty, and the pursuit of Happiness. –That to secure these rights, Governments are among Men, deriving their just powers from the consent of the governed."—Declaration of Independence, July 4, 1776

As discussed in previous chapters, we have come to an age where conservative political dominance, deregulation, financial bailouts, and declining rates of unionization drive our political debate and anti-government sentiments, and the American people are protesting to reclaim their democracy. Conservative right radicals are driving our discourse, feeding the fears and fostering the prejudices of ordinary Americans. The American democracy gives both conservative and progressive discourse public space, which gives America its unique character. However, the American people have recently experienced failures in the practice of democracy. A democratic government should reflect the will and choice of its people and provide encouragements that do not jeopardize their rights.[1] Given this assumption, many Americans have come to view political, philosophical, and legal contradictions in the way our democracy is currently practiced along race, class, gender, and sexual orientation lines.[2] Our economic crisis illustrates the way in which our political elite create a system that provokes cultural alienation among the populace, refusing to accept the changing demographics in this country that can change the face of politics.

The conservative right claims to embrace American "exceptionalism," and labels Obama as anti-American for his attempts to fix this nation's economic and social problems, but they go against the American Creed and for what the early colonists fought (fairness and egalitarianism). American exceptionalism is an ideology that "differs qualitatively from other developed nations, because of its unique origins, national credo, historical evolution, and distinctive political and religious institutions."[3] Seen by some as an imperfect creed, it has been misused by the conservative right to stir anti-Obama sentiment among the American electorate. The objective of this chapter is to define American exceptionalism, and discuss its roots (including the related concept of manifest destiny), limitations, and misperceptions. I provide some history on big government versus limited government, a major issue that is driving a wedge between the Obama administration and Congressional Republicans. Finally, I explain how Obama is committed, in spite of political rancor, to uphold those values of American exceptionalism that reflect the will of the people, thus serving to strengthen this nation's political, social, and economic landscape.

ROOTS OF AMERICAN EXCEPTIONALISM

Aristotle, the ancient Greek philosopher, chose democracy over other forms of government—oligarchy, monarchy, communism, totalitarianism, fascism, and so on. Aristotle asserted that democracy was derived from the people's will, and their power to tell the government how they wish to be served. It would be an understatement to say that America invented democracy, as America has given the ideals of freedom, justice, and liberty for all, and ensured that these ideals are realized by most Americans. In the democratic realm, representative government is America's proudest achievement. The United States has built its political system on democratic principles, and Americans have taken these principles for granted to guide their political, economic, social, and legal interests.[4] America derives its exceptional character from its foundations. In fact, being one of the first colonies to achieve independence, the nation defines its existence in terms of the American Revolution.[5] By revisiting the events of the revolution, we can understand the beginning of American exceptionalism.

Thomas Jefferson, John Adams, Benjamin Franklin, James Madison, and Alexander Hamilton, the first political intelligentsia and framers of the Declaration of Independence, created the landscape for a sovereign government. These framers fought for liberty and justice, devoting their entire lives to achieve freedom of religion, liberty, and equality for all (excluding Americans of color). They knew from personal experience that political and religious freedom was the bedrock of Republicanism, and they fought to free themselves from the tyranny of England under King George III. Rejecting the monarchial rule of Great Britain, the colonists, facing a new epoch, finally declared their independence on July 4, 1776, when the Declaration of Independence was signed, and declared the self-evident truth that all men are created equal.[6] Nonetheless, America's independence was only a step in a series of steps on an intricate and noteworthy journey that would later lead to its democratization and transcendent perfection.[7] The English who came to America from Great Britain were the criminals, oppressed, and downtrodden. When they came to America, they wanted to find a place where they could start afresh and create a political system that facilitated an individual freedom, unlike the experiences they had in Europe.

CANONICAL COMMITMENTS OF AMERICAN EXCEPTIONALISM

America's foundation was created on five ideal canons: liberty, egalitarianism, individualism, populism, and laissez-faire.[8] A key to understand the social, economic, and political trends throughout American history is to consider them in the context of this five-dimensional prism, the American Creed that makes the United States unique and exceptional in nature.[9] In 1917, William Tyler Page, author of the American Creed and descendent of the tenth president of the United States believed the American Creed to be a testing of individuals' patriotism in the faith of American politics. This Creed was accepted by the U.S. House of Representatives on April 3, 1918, on behalf of the American people. It is a doctrine for the American's belief in American exceptionalism, which states,

> [We] believe in the United States of America as a government of the people, by the people, for the people; whose just powers are derived from the consent of the governed, a democracy in a republic, a sovereign Nation of many sovereign States; a perfect union, one and inseparable; established upon those principles of freedom, equality, justice, and humanity for which American patriots sacrificed their lives and fortunes. [We] therefore believe it is [our] duty to [our] country to love it, to support its Constitution, to obey its laws, to respect its flag, and to defend it against all enemies.[10]

So what exactly does American exceptionalism mean? Do Americans understand what it is? To answer these questions we need to ask, from whose perspective is America exceptional, given our changing demographics? Is America exceptional from the perspectives of Americans of color and legal Mexican immigrants? Or is America exceptional from a white racial frame, based on social theorist Joe Feagin's work? Do all Americans believe Obama is anti-American, or is this a rhetorical strategy employed by his critics to play on the fears of a vulnerable American electorate?

AMERICAN EXCEPTIONALISM AND RACISM

The American Creed has not fully extended itself to African Americans, Native Americans, and other Americans of color. These racial groups have been denigrated to justify maltreatment and racial discrimination against them. As far back as the Declaration of Independence, the drafters edited the issue of slavery to appease the South that wanted to keep slavery as a justified living institution in favor of southern planters, Thomas Jefferson, and other power elite who contributed to the birth of American exceptionalism.[11] Although Thomas Jefferson believed all men were created equal, he embraced the institution of slavery, denigrated the intellect of enslaved blacks, politicized their bodies as inferior to whites, and fathered several children by his slave concubines. Asserting their legal right to rebel under the oppressive conditions of Great Britain, the colonial leaders were unwilling to bestow the same rights on African Americans and Native Americans to self-determine their lives and lives for their posterity.[12] The rationale of American's early leaders was that

> They emphasized the construct of civilization upon which Western law relied, depicting the indigenous peoples inhabiting the lands claimed by European and Euro-American colonizers as "heathen" and, increasingly "savage." Not being civilized—i.e., not having conquered nature—these Others made no "progress" in the Western scheme of development, and therefore have no prior history worth acknowledging. Once colonized people were defined as less than fully human, it was a short leap for justifying the appropriation of their "unsettled" lands for "productive" use and either eliminating the inhabitants or using them, much as domesticated animals, simply for their labor power.[13]

Consequently, the evolution of systemic racism embedded in America's institutions supported the ongoing racial discrimination against Americans of color.[14] Today, the rights of the elderly, Americans of color, women, and the poor have eroded, and there has been a curbing of government power to disenfranchise the few rights these groups have enjoyed under the tenure of the 112th Congress and State legislatures. Having said this, a number of Republican-controlled state houses have been suppressing the constitutional rights of the working class under the pretext of constitutional legitimacy to suppress their vote, as well as politicizing the bodies of women and interfering with their rights. As Obama observed, America was built on racism and created a stratified racialized system, while contemporary research of communication, political science, and sociology scholars have suggested that the economic successes and failures are based on one's racial background. Since America espouses a rugged individualist ideology of exceptionalism, individuals' successes and failures, in most cases, are their responsibility, regardless of the obstacles of race, class, and gender. On the other hand, for African

Americans, it is up to them to pull themselves up by illusory bootstraps, although inequality, as practiced in American institutions, has kept them impoverished from generation to generation.[15]

MANIFEST DESTINY

In addition to the analysis of racism and exceptionalism, social theorists have dealt with the subject of Manifest Destiny as well. From an external view, white Americans, in general, believe that God favors them over other nation-states. From an internal view, Americans believe that God favors whites over other ethnic groups existing within the American society.[16] In 1839, John L. O'Sullivan claimed that,

> The far-reaching, boundless future will be the era of American greatness. In its magnificent domain of space and time, the nation of many nations is destined to manifest to mankind the excellence of divine principles, to establish on earth the noblest temple ever dedicated to the worship of the Most High—the Sacred and the True. . . . Yes, we are the nation of progress, individual freedom, and universal enfranchisement. Equality of rights is the cynosure of our union of States, the grand exemplar of the correlative equality of individuals; and while truth sheds its effulgence, we cannot retrograde, without dissolving the one and subverting the other.[17]

According to Sullivan, America's destiny is tied to her divine birthright. He suggests that America was chosen in the womb of the American Revolution to lead the rest of the world. He further suggests that America is God's chosen vessel to demonstrate righteousness to all other nations, making America unique and favored by divine will. America has enabled the immigrants to install themselves in its bowels to practice religious freedom without fear of persecution. Moreover, it has used its military power to protect weaker nations that number among its lot, to use war to defeat and plunder other nations, and to help protect the innocent victims from despot leaders who denied them their divine rights.

However, Sullivan does not address the civil rights of African Americans, Native Americans, and other Americans of color. The rights the white colonists sought under George III's rule, are the same rights they have denied minorities. Based on Sullivan's analysis, has Providence trampled on the rights of Americans of color? Perhaps in the minds of Americans of color, it is not Providence that has trampled on their rights, but emperors, kings, and noble people of American society who have demonized Americans of color in art, literature, and science in the name of Providence and American exceptionalism.

Manifest Destiny is an ideological racial hierarchical model, which supports the role played by race in "the dominant narrative of racial difference."[18] Whites are at the top of the hierarchy, Asians are positioned in the middle, and blacks and Native Americans are located at the base. This ideological model significantly impacts whites' attitude towards Americans of color, and has gone unchallenged, as well as supported by the cultural institutions of U.S. society. This support helps the ruling elite maintain control over disenfranchised groups. Conservative black intellectuals support the power elite's handling of the masses of African Americans and other Americans of color, taking a critical posture towards Obama. They have given into a system that purports to favor them and have politically avoided anything that links them to a welfare state.

History has shown that disempowered whites are likely to engage in violent behavior towards African Americans and other Americans of color, scapegoating minorities for their inability to make it and directing their anger towards minorities for their (disempowered whites) failure to achieve the American dream.[19] Thus, it is understandable why the ruling elite counts on them to commit unimaginable violence against African Americans and other Americans of color, which they refuse to acknowledge, as the dominant hegemonic narrative[20] absolves them of all blame and cloaks them in the guise of a respectable history. Given disempowered white violent behavior, we can understand the sudden rage against the Obama administration, a rage over a once thriving economy that privileged them over Americans of color, and a rage that resents the fact that an African American occupies the White House.[21] Critical philosophers have argued that, "Domination has assumed a new form. It is exercised and established through the rule of consent and mediated through cultural institutions, such as schools, family, media, churches, and politics."[22]

Beyond this, average whites do not question the government's imperialistic practices or the imposition of power against other nation-states. Instead, they believe their government engages in benevolent practices, nonetheless benevolent hegemonic practices, towards less powerful countries. Countries that reject this government's interference are sanctioned and marginalized, and the media are used to politicize them. For example, the United States sanctioned Cuba under the pretext that Cuba abuses the human rights of its citizens, and refuses to have any formal diplomatic relation with Cuba or allow U.S. corporations to do business with them until this country practices democracy. However, American exceptionalism, like most American legal and social institutions, serves as a smoke screen to obscure America's continued abuse of its own citizens' human and civil rights, specifically Americans of color. Even though America believes in human rights abroad, it has failed to extend these same human rights to African Americans and other Americans of color.

VIEWS ON AMERICAN EXCEPTIONALISM

With respect to American exceptionalism, how would the framers respond to the state of affairs today? The following paragraphs provide an overview of what leading think tanks say about American exceptionalism, and how the roots of systemic racism have contributed to its development and limitations.

In the realm of foreign affairs, Michael Ignatieff, editor of *American Exceptionalism and Human Rights* and Director of the Carr Center of Human Rights Policy at the John F. Kennedy School of Government at Harvard University explains three main types of exceptionalism. The first type excludes America from adhering to bargains or agreements with other nation-states while simultaneously supporting them.[23] The second type is the double standard type where America chastises other nations that fail to adhere to treaties and international law.[24] The third type is legal isolationism where America tends to ignore other nation-state jurisdictions.[25] In distinguishing these three types of exceptionalism, America signs off on international human rights and humanitarian law conventions and treaties, but exempts itself from abiding by these treaties.[26] Consequently, America practices double standards and judges itself by a different set of standards than it does its enemies.[27] America supports international agreements, but demands that it and its citizens be exempted from adhering to any international principles.[28] For example, the Clinton administration negotiated with the International Criminal Courts (ICC), but wanted a guarantee that America's military, diplomats, and politicians would never go before that court.[29] Under the Bush administration, he reversed the agreement and signed it, but went on to make new agreements with allies that would guarantee they would never turn U.S. nationals over to ICC.[30] Given the way America practices its exceptionalism, it "may be out of step with globalization and with the convergence of state interests and practices in an interdependent world."[31]

In the realm of domestic affairs, Godfrey Hodgson has lived in America for many years and was "able to watch American politics from an unusually privileged vantage point."[32] Having observed America for the past quarter of a century, Hodgson notices something wrong in American public life. He has seen the rich take hold of politics and culture that once lay in the hands of ordinary Americans, observed corporations take power from the working class, and observed politics moving to the far-right from the earlier center-left position.[33] Hodgson argues that many historical realities, which made America exceptional, are now under attack, especially in the areas of poverty, inequality, and injustice. Even though he admires America and its good qualities, he does believe that the qualities that once made America exceptional are slowly disappearing. These exceptional qualities that the colonists fought for include, but are not limited to, economic advancement, mass political participa-

tion, reformation before revolution, education and educational opportunity, women's rights, respect for difference, and global stewardship.[34] He
claimed that America could do a better job by addressing its racial problems and ridding itself of the hegemonic attitude it is perceived to have
against other nation-states.[35] Hodgson also believes that America is not
known for the exceptionalism that made it great among all nations, but is
more known for its failure in health care, education, equality, human
rights, and even capitalism itself, as the financial meltdown of Wall Street
now makes American exceptionalism appear as a myth.[36]

Likewise, Seymour Martin Lipset views American exceptionalism as a
double-edged sword. When compared to other developed countries,
America falls short on the support it provides for the "poor through
welfare, housing, and medical care policies."[37] The Republicans oppose
the Affordable Care Act, better known as Obamacare, and wanted to
repeal it had Mitt Romney won the 2012 presidential election. Unlike
America, other countries have universal health care policies for the citizens who are unable to afford health insurance: Afghanistan and Iraq
(universal health coverage provided by United States war funding), Ar-
gentina, Austria, Australia, Brazil, Canada, Chile, China, Cuba, Costa
Rica, Cyprus, Denmark, France, Germany, the United Kingdom, and other countries.[38] Through empirical comparison with other countries, the
United States fails to provide many forms of government security such as
wage control legislation, job creation via shortened work weeks, funding
for projects that increase jobs, price control legislation, sufficient old age
pensions, and reduced income inequality.[39] America's perpetual myths
of equal opportunity, which fail to manifest into anything remotely re-
sembling true equality, are linked to crime, as the individuals unable to
reach their financial and material goals through hard work and self-disci-
pline are likely to be tempted to acquire what they desire through illegal
means. Furthermore, those who do reach their goals oppose paying taxes
to support those who are unable to pay them.[40]

America's uniqueness is rooted in her institutions, culture, and political structure.[41] From an institutional perspective, America is exceptional
concerning its impenetrable public institutions, which makes it difficult
over time to formulate institutional changes.[42] Once these institutions
and policies are in place, Americans are socialized to accept them even if
some of the features are not liked. It is also difficult to put social programs in place without them matriculating through multiple layers of
decision makers for approval or disapproval, unlike other countries.[43]
From a policy perspective, American citizens have the right to express
their disapproval for certain public activities and social programs
through the voting process.[44] Notwithstanding, some proponents of
American exceptionalism claim it will endure because of "America's
commitment to the ideal of republican self-rule born of a revolutionary
act of national self-creation."[45]

America with reference to her exceptionalism has her proponents and opponents. Nonetheless, America, unlike other states, is exceptional because of her Constitution (freedom of speech, press, and assembly; freedom to form opposition political parties and to run for office; commitment to the individual dignity and to equal opportunities for people to develop their full potential; checks and balances among the three government branches (executive, legislative, and judicial branches), federalism (which keeps the American people close to their government), her democratic nature, and her religious freedoms. America must also ask whether other nation-states still see it as exceptional and that it has not lost the qualities that made it exceptional. We know that America was endowed with exceptional qualities when she was first installed as the leader of the world. America, like other nation-states, is not perfect and is riddled with internal and external problems.

What great nation would not suffer problems? What great nation would not suffer decline? Despite these questions, Americans continue to assert America's superiority, relying on the evidence echoed in her history—from the Civil War to the women's rights movement, and through every president who has proudly declared "God Bless America."[46] Having looked at the roots of exceptionalism, as well as its modern-day implications and limitations, we now turn to an analysis of Obama and American exceptionalism.

OBAMA AND AMERICAN EXCEPTIONALISM

The Declaration of Independence states that the American government derives its powers from the consent of its people, without considering elitism. Given the language of this document, a small percentage of the American electorate and politicians may hold the belief that Obama is un-American and claim he is a statist and a socialist who does not respect the exceptional nature of America. If Obama is perceived as a statist and a socialist, perhaps he is experiencing the backlash of a racist ideology, which believes he ascended to the presidency to reform America's social institutions that have denied Americans of color the justice for which they continue to fight.

Obama is viewed as taking a socialist posture to resolve America's depressed economy by creating reform policies addressing the Wall Street financial, health care, educational, and housing crises. Conservative radio talk show host Rush Limbaugh has already stated that Obama's first stimulus package included reparations for African Americans, using the welfare state ideology to stir white hostility against African Americans. Similarly, Obama has been considered a political enemy for holding corporations like BP accountable. Could we consider conservative right-winger Joe Barton's position on the BP Oil crisis the opposite of what American exceptionalism is, fairness, justice, and the protection that supports the economic causes of working class Americans who cannot protect themselves against big corporate interests? Conservative politicians invoke Constitutionalism and use American exceptionalism against Obama, but they have overreached the rights and liberty of ordinary American citizens to support the plutocrats of this society. The conservative right also insists that Obama does not appreciate American exceptionalism as he apologizes for America's past hegemonic practices against other nation-states, particularly those states governed by people of color. Constructing Obama into a political enemy gives this spectacle the power to arouse individuals' passions and fears.

Amidst violent rhetoric, many Americans have been convinced that Obama is anti-American. Americans would presume that Obama is anti-American when elite politicians use this kind of rhetoric as a repeated talking point. For example, Jim DeMint (R-SC) calls the Obama administration as the most anti-business and anti-American administration compared to other presidential administrations.[47] Individuals, such as DeMint, who view Obama as socialist and anti-American, will certainly be motivated by their passions, fears, and discontentment to blame Obama for the ills of society. The backlash Obama has experienced, particularly from the conservative right, is no new phenomenon for Americans of color, specifically African Americans.

In direct contrast to this anti-American image created by the conservative right, Obama has repeatedly professed his belief in American exceptionalism. He proclaimed that "the true strength of our nation comes, not from the might of our arms or the scale of our wealth, but from the enduring power of our ideals; democracy, liberty, opportunity, and unyielding hope."[48] When Obama was elected president, he invoked one of the most common images of American exceptionalism: "The United States is the embodiment of freedom and democracy and, therefore, the light of hope for the rest of the planet."[49] While visiting Strasbourg and Prague, Obama stated that he subscribed to American exceptionalism and said,

> I believe in American exceptionalism, just as I suspect that the Brits believe in British exceptionalism and the Greeks believe in Greek exceptionalism. . . . We have a core set of values that are enshrined in our Constitution, in our body of law, in our democratic practices, in our belief in free speech and equality that though imperfect, are exceptional.

Despite Obama's words and actions, his belief is being challenged constantly, and the political and power elite have contaminated the public's perception of his policies and created the false image of Obama as anti-American. To understand Obama's views on exceptionalism and democracy, as well as the political reaction to his reforms, we need to revisit

Lipset's and Koh's description of American exceptionalism and work through each of the five tenets—liberty, egalitarianism, individualism, populism, and laissez-faire.

LIBERTY

Obama understands American democracy and knows that our democracy was founded on the ideals of *liberty*. Liberty is linked to the American people's pursuit of happiness and freedom. Individuals cannot be satisfied unless they are free to pursue their dreams without functioning under the tyranny of their government and/or hate groups.[50] We have "insisted throughout our history that certain freedoms should be expanded: voting rights, civil rights, and the freedoms afforded by expanded systems of public education, public health, highways, parks, libraries, and scientific research."[51] But the freedoms of the average American citizen are being rolled back by a group in Congress whose radical ideology is pushing the established Republican Party to the extreme far right. Today, many of the liberties and freedoms of the American people are disappearing in the name of corrupt banking, predatory lending, a fraudulent mortgage system, and corrupt deal making and governing that favors the elite, where "openness, economic opportunity, and compassion for the less fortunate"[52] are not important to the GOP.

Since liberty means freedom and political safeguard from arbitrary interference in one's pursuits by individuals or the government as guaranteed by the Bill of Rights and the Thirteenth, Fourteenth, and Fifteenth Amendments, the Obama administration appears to be at work recovering some of these freedoms, such as looking into the voter ID laws passed by several state houses. The Obama administration has also established a Making Home Affordable Program, which helps homeowners to refinance their homes for making affordable monthly payments, and has also signed a student loan reform bill. But the Republican Party wants Americans to believe the Obama administration is taking away people's liberties and freedoms by expanding the government to control people's daily lives. Specifically speaking, has the Obama administration interfered with the Fourteenth Amendment (adopted in 1868), which bars the application of any law that would abridge the privileges and immunities of U.S. citizens or deprive any person of life, liberty, or property without due process of law? Similar abridgement did occur under the political tenures of Senator James O. Eastland, George Wallace, and other southern governors. These men stood proudly before large audiences and openly communicated the overt violation of the rights of African Americans, as guaranteed by the Bill of Rights and the above-mentioned Amendments, and African Americans, Native Americans, and other

Americans of color were denied their liberty with the support of the local, state, and federal governments. Obama, in contrast, is trying to expand protection for the rights of the people.

When white Americans were affected by the major policy changes from governmental interference, they decried what concerned their interests. Franklin D. Roosevelt was called a socialist and communist for expanding the government to perform major economic changes for getting the country back on economic track. Now, Barack Obama is called a socialist and statist because he, like Roosevelt, is perceived as "barring a national revival of founding principles" and is expanding the government's role to effect economic reform.[53]

EGALITARIANISM

Second, Obama has an appreciation for American *egalitarianism*. Egalitarians view equality as fundamental to the goal of justice. It also means extending empathy to everyone.[54] Egalitarians also view equality of resources, responsibility, and advantage or opportunity as central to justice.[55] Egalitarians have the "deep compelling view that it is a bad thing, unjust and unfair, for some to be worse off than others through no fault of their own."[56] Unfairness "stifles freedom and opportunity, . . . and prosperity [requires] a certain base amount of material wealth [that] is necessary to lead a fulfilling life and pay for enough shelter, food, and health."[57] In short, the first colonists were concerned about the removal of inequalities among the people because this threat was seen as an infringement on their economic ability to achieve the American Dream. Therefore, the colonists wanted a government that would give them the individual right to achieve their dreams through egalitarianism. However, racial equality and egalitarianism have still not been realized by all American citizens.

Is Obama concerned about the equality of resources, equality of responsibility, and equality of advantage (opportunity) for all Americans? Obama's 2008 presidential campaign was about change and hope.[58] While Clinton and McCain constantly drew Obama into detailed policy debates, he addressed much deeper philosophical issues and used his knowledge of the Constitution to question his audiences on how our founding fathers would have approached a similar problem we face today. Emphasizing personal liberty, equality, and economic justice, Obama was able to describe a country in which economic opportunity would be available to all under an Obama administration.[59] We are "a nation of laws that are being written by corporate special interests. And we are a country founded on equality, liberty, justice, and opportunity for all that is slowly devolving into an unjust class society where life success is based more on inherited position and connections than individual effort and merit."[60] Nonetheless, Obama believes that a healthy economy is a bottom-up economy, and not a top-down economy dependent on trickle-down economics, where unfairness prevails.[61] Obama, with the support of top economists, such as Paul Krugman from Princeton University, notices that the middle-class play an important role in developing a strong economy. It is not the wealthy or what the conservative right call the "job creators" who contribute to a strong economy, but those Americans who stimulate the economy through spending. U.S. corporations control the government, and the average working American fails to see their dreams in an unjust economic system come to full fruition.[62] Obama's platform for change in the American infrastructure was his single most defining issue, economic justice for all.[63] He understands the U.S. Constitution and views it as the primary organizing principle of successful societies, governments, and economies because people wish to be treated fairly and judged on their own merits.[64]

As an example, the American school system is in disarray. High school students and seniors are graduating with poor math, writing, and communication skills, skills required for productive employment. A large percentage of students are unfamiliar with American and world history, and are as equally unknowledgeable about current events and the way the political system is diminishing their constitutional rights.[65] In organizing America for educational reform, the Obama administration is working out solutions to help single-headed household mothers to improve their educational status. These mothers are overburdened, and many have relied on state-supported organizations for public assistance. If these single mothers return to school and improve their educational background, they could help their children in turn. Obama said,

> At this defining moment in our history, preparing our children to compete in the global economy is one of the most urgent challenges we face. We need to stop paying lip service to public education, and start holding communities, administrators, teachers, parents and students accountable. We will prepare the next generation for success in college and in the workplace, ensuring that American children lead the world once again in creativity and achievement.[66]

Consequently, Obama introduced measures to help improve K-12 schooling, and said, "We will recruit an army of new teachers and develop innovative ways to reward the teachers who are doing a great job, and we will reform No Child Left Behind (NCLB) so that we support schools that need improvement, rather than punishing them."[67] Obama wanted to expand access to higher education and said, "After graduating high school, all Americans should be prepared to attend at least one year of job training or higher education to better equip our workforce for the 21st century economy. We will continue to make higher education more affordable by expanding Pell Grants and initiating new tax credits to make sure any young person who works hard and desires a college education can access it."[68] Obama further says that America must make sure our children are prepared for kindergarten, and said, "One of the most critical times to influence learning in a child's life is the period before he/she reaches kindergarten. We will invest in early childhood education, by dramatically expanding Head Start and other programs to ensure that all of our young children are ready to enter kindergarten."[69] The Obama administration recognizes that the only way children can compete in a global economy is to start with their mothers. If the mothers improve their economic status through education, they could help their children in their educational pursuit as well, and more children can overcome poverty.

When media and political analysts criticize Obama for focusing too much on education, not addressing the outsourcing of manufacturing jobs, they have overlooked an important fact that even factory jobs today rely on some degree of technology, and that technology means more education. In the 1980s, Lee Iacocca, former president and CEO for Chrysler Corporation, revived the automobile factory by retiring and laying off workers who did not want change. The copmany was forced to compete in a technological age and required workers to acquire training in technology.

Thus, given all of Obama's social initiatives, if the ruling elite, corporate elite, political elite, and Americans in general, did not believe that Obama embraced egalitarianism, perhaps the Obama administration has not been able to reach down far enough, due to GOP obstructionism, to bring economic justice, quality of life, and educational opportunities to the "have-nots."

INDIVIDUALISM

The third canonical commitment of American exceptionalism is *individualism*. Individualism arises "among persons whose experiences foster a belief in the freedom governmental constraints sense and their personal desires to achieve personal autonomy. For Americans, material acquisition contributes to one's individualism."[70] In an individualist society, such as the United States, expression of difference in opinion or lifestyle is important and societal members are seen as individualists who are separate from the societal group. These societies encourage citizens to pull themselves up by the "bootstrap" and make decisions based on their individual needs, desires, and interests in order to succeed.

As individualists, Americans tend to give priority to their own goals, needs, and interests, and define themselves in terms of their personal successes.[71] If one becomes successful, individualism posits that the individual should solely receive credit for his/her success, and no one else can share it. On the other hand, if one is unsuccessful, individualism posits that the individual should alone endure the blame and no one else can share the blame. However, as Obama writes in the *Audacity of Hope*, our nation's

> individualistic nature has always been bound by a set of communal values, the glue upon which every healthy society depends. We value the imperatives of family and the cross-generational obligations that family implies. We value community, the neighborliness that expresses itself in raising the barn or coaching the soccer team. We value patriotism and obligations of citizenship, a sense of duty and sacrifice on behalf of our nation. We value faith in something bigger than ourselves, whether that something expresses itself in formal religion or ethical precepts. And we value the constellation of behaviors that express our mutual regard for one another: honesty, fairness, humility, kindness, courtesy, and compassion.[72]

As such, Obama argues, cooperation is the key to sustaining America.[73] No one makes it alone.[74] But most importantly, it takes effective leadership to bring about the cooperation of both political parties and the American people to restore national community among the American people.[75]

POPULISM

The fourth commitment of American exceptionalism is *populism*. Populism is a political philosophy that champions economic causes of the average American citizen over the ruling and corporate elite. Populism urges change in the social and political systems to eliminate major disparities in the economic system,[76] and usually combines elements of the left and right, opposing large corporate and financial interests. However, today's conservative right, taken over by the Tea Party adamantine, is deliberately squeezing out the middle-class and leaning towards protecting the interests of the oligarchs and plutocrats. They are not interested in eliminating disparities in the economic system. To prevent the economy from flourishing in favor of the average working-class American, the conservative right has blocked Obama's every effort to grow the economy, then blames Obama for not fulfilling a promise that they themselves are blocking by using dog whistle politics to influence the American electorate against Obama's economic policies. With this deliberate obstructionist behavior and outright refusal to work with Obama, the conservative right uses political tactics to take back the White House and get control of the upper chamber of the House. Speaking to grassroots activists in 2003, Bill Moyer recalled the populist legacy. Moyer declared that "the social dislocations and the meanness of the 19th century" are being repeated by politicians who are strangling the spirit of the American

Revolution. Today, he calls on populists and progressives in the twenty-first century to restore the balance between wealth and commonwealth.[77]

Since U.S. presidents are elected by the people and *should* represent their economic interests, the Obama administration is taking a populist approach for solving America's economic problem. In his 2009 inaugural address, Obama proclaimed he would be the president for all Americans and will work on their behalf. He has worked towards the reformation of Wall Street to avoid future financial collapses and bailouts that favor the interest of the ruling and corporate elites. He used his "address in Manhattan to push back on Republican criticism that Democratic plans for financial reform are a ticket to endless bailouts and to ask Wall Street to join his efforts. He also insisted that the country would suffer from future financial collapses, just like the one that led to a devastating recession, if Wall Street reform is not approved by Congress."[78] Recently, the Securities and Exchange Commission charged Goldman Sachs with fraud, which further justified financial reform legislation.[79] Corporate financial fraud and Wall Street bailouts are a threat to America's prosperity, and average Americans have paid the price for them. Many of them have lost their jobs and homes, and students are graduating college with exorbitant school loan debts and no economic prospects to pay for these loans. Meanwhile, they see a recalcitrant Congress's refusal to work with Obama to introduce legislation for job creation and/or return jobs lost from outsourcing. Obama's job creation plan also seems to exemplify the populist themes of the New Deal era. In fact, "populist themes shaped the New Deal, and reemerged in the civil rights movement of the 1950s and 1960s, which stressed 'realization of democracy's promise.'"[80] However, its roots eroded quickly.[81]

Before Obama was elected the forty-fourth president, he made similar statements about other threats to America's prosperity. He believes the greatest threats to America's prosperity include, but are not limited to, world poverty, global warming, political corruption, human rights violations, uncontrolled growth and population, decline of education, international trade with China, weak energy policy, demise of workers' rights, prejudice, racism, tax policy and deficits, housing and financial crises, commercialization of the media, alcohol, drugs, crime, and prison, and of course, terrorism.[82] If we trace these threats to their root causes, corporate greed and the ruthlessness of today's politicians may play a major role in the problems faced by this country. However, it is the Americans who must decide on the course they want their government to take by electing politicians who best serve their interests.[83]

We now turn to the last canonical commitment of the American Creed, "laissez faire." In this context, I discuss the principles of limited government versus the principles of big government, and how the Republican Party is actually practicing the latter in the disguise of constitutional legitimacy.

LAISSEZ FAIRE: SMALL GOVERNMENT VERSUS BIG GOVERNMENT

The last commitment of American exceptionalism, *laissez faire*, posits that the best government is the one that remains small and unobtrusive: limited government versus big government. This principle also posits that the government's primary job is to maintain domestic peace and defend its people against external invasion. The notion of small government means to limit federal and state government power into the personal liberties of its people. This commitment flies in the face of the conservative right's interpretation of what limited government is.

The U.S. government was formed by the people and should, therefore, reflect their will. In the Preamble of the U.S. Constitution, it explicitly states "We the people . . . promote the general welfare, and secure the blessings of liberty to ourselves and our posterity, do ordain and establish this Constitution." The federal government's power is limited by the U.S. Constitution, and the state government's power is limited by each state's constitution. While all power rests with the people, Article I, Section 8, explicitly states that the people transfer power to Congress as the people's elected representatives. Some of the responsibilities of Congress are to collect taxes and duties, pay the nation's debts, borrow money on credit, and to regulate commerce with foreign countries. It is the responsibility of the President to see that the laws are well executed. He can also recommend needed legislation to Congress and ask senators and representatives to introduce these recommendations to Congress for consideration on behalf of the American people. However, the 112th Congress did not appear to be concerned about what is in the best interest of the average American citizen. Many Americans may not even realize that the government plays a significant role in their lives. If Americans listen to conservative right politicians, they will learn these politicians mislead the people to believe that the government should not play any role in their lives, which is a contradiction. After World War II, the government played a major role in building the middle class, giving us Social Security during FDR's years in office, giving us the GI or educational bill helping Americans go to college in order to improve their standard of living, and building the first highways during the Eisenhower years.

There are two major events in history, the Great Depression and the Recession of 2008, where the country found itself in a financial drought that shook the foundation of this nation's economic system and Americans had to bear the cost. With each circumstance, the Republican Party controlled the White House, the Senate, and the House of Representatives. In these times, the Republicans claim that they embrace limited government, while the Democratic Party uses government resources to help the neediest Americans in times of economic crises, such as extending unemployment benefits.[84] Although the Republican Party brands itself as the party of limited government, it has actually sought to roll back the liberties of the American people, extending the government's role into their lives. Republicans may also tout a small government libertarian conservative ideology, but they have adopted the authoritarian big government ideology.[85] Once the Party came into full power in Congress in 2010, they resolutely intruded into the lives of the American people, constricting their civil liberties and destroying their confidence and hope in the government. Instead of helping Obama restore the government to its position as an empire rather than a player in the economic game, the Party contradicted itself during the Bush years when it expanded the National Security Agency, thus giving the agency the ability to sift through citizens' private emails and wire-tap phone calls without a warrant, creating the Department of Homeland Security, and doubling the Defense Department budget between 2001 and 2008.

How does limited government work from a conservative perspective? The Republican Party has shown itself as anti-labor, and believes in free-trade deals that outsourced U.S. jobs overseas. The proposed GOP Road Map, authored by Republican Party nominee for vice president in the 2012 election and House Budget chairman Paul Ryan, was created with Wall Street, big corporations, and the wealthiest citizens in mind. Ryan proposed privatizing social security and cutting Medicare and Medicaid entitlements and services that benefit fixed-income citizens. The GOP's plan for limiting government was to cut entitlements and services that served the interest of ordinary citizens, but expand the government to lower taxes for the wealthy. Based on the GOP Road Map, Ryan proposed to balance the budget and lower the national debt without offering any plan to put pressure on Wall Street, major corporations, and the wealthiest Americans to pay a fair tax rate. It is also noteworthy that the national debt has continued to rise drastically under Republican administrations. According to the Office of Management and Budget, the national debt increased by 186 percent under the presidency of Ronald W. Reagan, 77.4 percent under George W. Bush, 53.8 percent under George H.W. Bush, 41.3 percent under Jimmy Carter, and 40.6 percent under Bill Clinton. The national debt did not grow as much during the Clinton and Carter administrations, but quadrupled under the Reagan and George W. Bush administrations.

Today, we see a parallel between our current situation and the Great Depression in terms of backlash against "big government." When the stock market crashed in 1929, Herbert Hoover, incumbent president from 1929 to 1933, argued that the American system of rugged individualism had brought untold prosperity and strength to the nation, and believed that socialism would lead to the destruction of self-government and undermine individual initiative and enterprise that made America exceptional.[86] In essence, Hoover rejected the notion that big government would become the master of people's lives, limiting their liberty and freedom.[87] Yet, Hoover contradicted himself. For political analysts, it seemed ironic that,

> Hoover should argue so vehemently against government intervention in the economic life of the nation. Since, as the chief architect of the Republican business program in the 1920s, Hoover had approved government aid to businesses that took not only the negative forms of stringent economies (usually in social services), huge tax reductions, the elimination of government competition with private industry, and the practical suspension of the anti-trust laws, but also the very positive form of subsidies and incredibly high tariffs.[88]

As Secretary of Commerce, Hoover ordered official sanctions on large-scale international private investment abroad in favor of his support for the vast domestic business community and a laissez-faire system.[89] Hoover's rugged individualist ideology became the ideology of America to reject Progressive reforms, refusing to summon full resources of the government to help the working class.

The popularity of the laissez-faire doctrine diminished in the late nineteenth century, when it lacked the capacity to deal with the social and economic problems. After the Great Depression and collapse of the stock market, the American people had had enough. Hoover was voted out of office, and the people elected Franklin Delano Roosevelt, a Democrat, affectionately known as FDR, to solve the economic depression caused by the Republicans. When FDR took office, he gave America the New Deal policies that privileged non-elite American citizens over the ruling and corporate elite. Roosevelt made a great impact on the economy. Although it was not a perfect solution, the New Deal marked a significant shift in the role of government in the economy and in the lives of American citizens. With this said,

> The New Deal did reflect a significant change in the nation's concept of the proper relationship between the State and the Individual, and to many Americans it seemed that the election of 1932, as Jefferson had written of his own election in 1800, was as real a revolution in the principles of our government as that [of the American Revolution] of 1776 was in its form. Government participation in the economic life of the country could no longer be considered an entirely novel response to the national crisis, but in the Roosevelt administration such activity became the *dominant* pattern, and the government assumed a broad and continuous new responsibility for the social and economic well-being of its people.[90]

Though politically risky, as some said that FDR would fail and alienate the Republican Party, FDR followed through with his plan of economically revitalizing the economy, and went on to win three more elections by a landslide.

THE OBAMA REVOLUTION

The triumphant election of Barack Hussein Obama marked one of the most "profound reaffirmation of America's continuing faith in the essential capacity of democracy to survive the crises of economic depression and instability."[91] Obama's election came on the heel of economic depression, war, a need for a massive banking financial reform, massive job loss, massive cases of personal bankruptcy by American citizens, inadequate healthcare for the poor, and one of the most tragic events in American history, the rise of terrorism in America. Revisiting Obama's 2009 inaugural speech, he said,

> Yet, ever so often the oath is taken amidst gathering clouds and raging storms. . . . That we are in the midst of a crisis is now well understood. Our nation is at war, against a far-reaching network of violence and hatred. Our economy is badly weakened, a consequence of greed and irresponsibility on the part of some, but also our collective failure to make hard choices and prepare the nation for a new age. Homes have been lost, jobs shed, businesses shuttered.

With a long history of discrimination, high rates of unemployment, homelessness, crime, poverty, and high number of under- or uneducated citizens, many Americans began to "question the efficacy of [our] democratic process" and the exceptional qualities of which we have always been proud.[92]

Given today's political climate, the Obama administration made significant accomplishments in the short time he was in office during his first term. His political orientation towards the State has become the persistent central theme of the Obama Revolution to guard the general welfare of the American people, although a majority of the Republican Congress has filibustered all of his reform bills.[93] In just six months, he accomplished more than many of his predecessors. FDR and LBJ have been heralded as two standard-bearers of presidential assessment and political and economic reform early in their presidencies. Like FDR and LBJ, Obama accomplished much early in his presidency. We must note that Obama's accomplishments were not done with a heavy-hand or top-down approach, but from a style that institutionalized his ability to reach across the aisle for which he has not received credit, encourage vigorous debate, and use town halls and panels of experts in the policy-making process. This process is good for democracy as our democratic processes have been battered and bruised over the last three decades.[94]

In the field of economics, Obama increased infrastructure spending for roads, bridges, and power plants, even though many Republican governors did not accept the stimulus funds. He authorized two GMAC rescue packages and saved thousands of jobs. He authorized the housing rescue plan and new FHA residential housing guarantees. He also authorized the federal government to make more loans available to small businesses, ordered lower rates for small business federal loans, signed a bill extending unemployment benefits that were set to expire in December 2010, and signed the HIRE Act to stimulate the economic recovery. The Senate also passed the Wall Street Reform bill that represents bold financial regulations since the aftermath of the Great Depression that includes the strongest consumer protections in history.[95]

Furthermore, Obama pushed for health care reform, The Affordable Care Act Bill, which provides uninsured Americans with affordable, quality health care. This bill would gradually reduce the increase in health care cost and thus create jobs.[96] The benefits of this Act include coverage despite pre-existing conditions; over 30 million people can be covered; it closes the "donut hole" in Medicare Part D; and would reduce the deficit by $100 billion over the next 10 years. Also in health care, Obama reversed some of the Bush-era restrictions that prevented Medicare from negotiating with pharmaceutical firms for cheaper drugs, allowing the government to undergo competitive bidding. It also should be noted that the GOP has wanted to repeal this Act from the very beginning because of the individual mandate that requires everyone to have insurance. The Affordable Care Act was upheld by the U.S. Supreme Court, thus becoming the law of the land. Obama has also accomplished initiatives in the areas of

- *human rights* (instituted enforcements for equal pay for women — the Lilly Ledbetter Bill, convened the White House Tribal Nations Conference, inviting representatives from 564 federally recognized Indian tribes, ordered the Justice Department and EEOC to enforce employment discrimination laws, and allowed the State Department to offer same-sex benefits to employees);
- *education* (increased student aid, increased funding for historical black colleges and universities, and in 2009 streamlined the federal student loan process to save $87 billion over the next 10 years);
- *ethics* (placed limits on White House aides working for lobbyists after their tenure in the administration, and reversed the Bush-era practice of politicizing Justice Department investigations and prosecutions against political opponents);
- *governance* (ended the Bush-era practice of having the White House staff rewrite the findings of scientific and environmental regulations and reports when they disagreed with the results);
- *national security* (cut the expensive Reagan-era missile defense program, saving $1.4 billion, and helped five nations completely clear out their stocks of highly enriched uranium as part of his plan for securing all weapons-usable materials worldwide [97]); and

- *military and veterans* (ordered the Pentagon to cover the expenses of families of fallen soldiers, if they wish to be on site when the body arrives back in the United States).[98]

Finally, Obama withdrew U.S. troops from Iraq in December 2011 and declared an end to one of the most divisive wars in American history. He also scored a major coup in the assassination of Osama Bin Laden. Adding to Obama's many accomplishments, a number of important bills were passed during the 2010 lame duck session: Matthew Shepard Hate Crimes Prevention Act, Children's Healthcare Expansion, Pentagon Waste Reduction, Troop drawdown in Iraq, START Treaty Ratification, Food Safety Bill, Modernization Act, 9/11 Health Bill, and the Korean Trade Agreement. These are just a few of the initiatives accomplished by Obama, for which he received little or no credit.

Although Obama's critics may carry a different message by calling him a statist, a socialist, and anti-American, conservatives and progressives alike do agree on one aspect of the Obama presidency: a lot was accomplished in his first term.[99] For the Obama administration, measures for relief, recovery, and reform were designed to ensure a free, democratic society against the ravages of poverty and insecurity. Obama is convinced that a democratic society is unsafe if its businesses and corporations fail to provide employment to Americans for sustaining an acceptable standard of living.

A POLITICAL BACKLASH

Despite his many accomplishments, no other president in recent history has endured the acrimony experienced by Obama. His revolutionary reforms have earned him a new title, the "Socialist President of the United States"—a statist, with a populist agenda, and the first welfare president. The extreme conservative right has labeled him as anti-American or claims that he does not understand American exceptionalism. Those who benefit from a system bestowing its financial blessings and over-the-rainbow good life upon the few privileged individuals are the ones who oppose any changes to these systems. Therefore, is it bad or just *unpopular* to summon the full resources of the government to provide relief for the disadvantaged, needy, poor, homeless, and jobless? Or has the American political system and national political agenda changed so much since the signing of the Declaration of Independence on July 4, 1776, that we only invoke American exceptionalism as a weapon against politicians who threaten the status quo? No doubt, Obama's reform policies may appear radical to the ruling and corporate elite, but for average working Americans, they provide hope and relief. Obama is not the first president to be labeled a socialist and a statist. FDR was knighted a socialist, communist, and statist by the conservative right, but the Republican Party of

the 1930s, despite their laissez-faire ideology, supported, with relu[
Roosevelt's New Deal for the sake of the American people.[100]

Although our founding founders were diverse in their persona[
opinions, education, and political differences, they always stood tog[
for the unity of their country, having penned the most august docum[
that no other nation-state could rival. Even though they were divid[
among party lines, history does not record any of these men publi[
disrespecting each other or disrespecting a sitting president on a nation[
or international level. With the recent political tension between the Dem[
ocratic and Republican Parties, the parties may need to revisit what mad[
us exceptional in the beginning. Instead, there is too much hostility and
tension, and the lack of honesty, fairness, humility, courtesy, and compassion is not helping America's exceptional image before the national
and international community. Americans understand that there will always be political dissension and polemical debates over various issues.
However, today, open uncivil and unconstructive tones of disagreement
have gone beyond the pale of dignity and respect.

CONCLUSION

Obama's critics may need to rethink how exceptional we are. We are no
longer first in education, technology, math, science, engineering, or research and development. America is no longer the strongest economy in
the world and has a weak dollar. We still struggle with racial, gender,
and income inequality, and millions have lost their jobs and homes. During his State of the Union address, Obama spoke to America's exceptional
nature and encouraged the American people that it will take reform in
areas of education, housing, and the financial sector, among others, for
America to genuinely reclaim its exceptionalism. For the critics who vig-
orously oppose Obama's reforms in the name of the Jeffersonian tradition
of limited government, the real threat to individual freedom lay not in
the expanding services of democratic government, but rather in the irresponsible power of concentrated wealth. Consequently, Americans' civil
"liberties are seriously endangered by a privileged, monopolistic economic power, and a limited Welfare State must supplant the Laissez-
Faire State of the nineteenth century."[101]

Political disagreements always blend to create a vitriol descending
from conflict.[102] Any president who suggests major change and reform in
the economic and political systems to save the economy and work for the
people by whom and for whom he was elected to serve will be labeled a
socialist with a populist agenda, who does not appreciate American exceptionalism. Obama, like FDR, LBJ, and JFK, dealt with extreme economic problems and political and social unrest. Obama will continue to
experience unabashed, open hostility over his reform policies and his

127

-class, while millions of Americans will continue
.e unemployment line. Like FDR, Obama is viewed
;ican exceptionalism. His legacy will be judged, not
.nt rhetoric, but by his American posterity—his politi-
the American people's general welfare and equality,
create policies that can put Americans back to work for

NOTES

.r Laqueur ed., *A Dictionary of Politics* (New York: The Free Press, 1971),

.1.

arold Hongju Koh, "America's Jekyll-and-Hyde Exceptionalism." In Michael
.f (Ed.), *American Exceptionalism and Human Rights*, (Princeton, NJ: Princeton
:rsity Press, 2005), 111–43.

. John Stewart, Ben Karlin, and David Javerbaum, "The Media: Democracy's Val-
. Vulgarians," in *America: A Citizen's Guide to Democracy Inaction*(New York: Warner
.oks, 2004), 1.

5. Ibid., 18.

6. John Stewart et al. *op cit.* (see reference 4), 19.

7. Ibid., 17.

8. Ibid.

9. Ibid.

10. John Landston, *American Doctrine* (Boston: Almar Publishing Company, 1942), 51.

11. Historical Documents. Resource Bank. Rough Draft of the Declaration of Independence 1776. http://www.pbs.org/wgbh/aia/part2/2h33.html (accessed November 19, 2012).

12. Natsu Taylor Saito. *Human Rights, American Exceptionalism, and the Stories We Tell, Vol. 23* (Atlanta, GA: *Emory International Law Review*, 2009), 49. See also http://www.law.emory.edu/fileadmin/journals/eilr/23/23.1/Saito.pdf (accessed January 1, 2013).

13. Ibid., 49–50.

14. Vincent N. Parrillo, *Understanding Race and Ethnic Relations* (Boston: Pearson, 2005), 73.

15. Joe R. Feagin, *Systemic Racism: A Theory of Oppre*ssion (New York: Routledge, Taylor & Francis Group, 2006), 7.

16. Mark P. Orbe and Tina M. Harris, *Interracial Communication: Theory Into Practice,* (Wadsworth Publishing: Florence, KY, 2001).

17. John L. O'Sullivan, "The Great Nation of Futurity (1839)," http://web.utk.edu/~mfitzge1/ docs/374/GNF1839.pdf (accessed January 1, 2013).

18. Mark P. Orbe and Tina M. Harris, op cit. (see reference 16). See also Ian Haney Lopez, *White by Law: The Legal Construction of Race* (New York, New York University Press, 1997).

19. Ibid.

20. Roxanne A. Dunbar, "Bloody Footprints: Reflections on Growing Up Poor White." In Matt Wray and Annalee Newitz, *White Trash: Race and Class in America* (New York: Routledge, 1997), 76.

21. Will Bunch, *The Backlash: Right-Wing Radicals, High-Def Hucksters, and Paranoid Politics in the Age of Obama* (New York: HarperCollins, 2010), 5.

22. Henry A. Giroux, *Pedagogy and the Politics of Hope: Theory, Culture, and Schooling* (Boulder, CO: Westview Press, 1997), 47–48.

23. Michael Ignatieff, *"American Exceptionalism and Human Rights*: Reviews: Book Reviews," http://press.princeton.edu/titles/8080.html (accessed September 3, 2012).

24. Ibid.

25. Ibid.

26. Michael Ignatieff, *op cit.* (see reference 22), 3.

27. Ibid.

28. Ibid.

29. Ibid.

30. Ibid.

31. Ibid., 21.

32. Godfrey Hodgson, *The Myth of American Exceptionalism* (News Haven, CT: Yale University Press, 2009), xi.

33. Ibid.

34. Ibid., 95.

35. Harold Hongju Koh, *op. cit.* (see reference 3).

36. Clive Crook, "Book Review: *The Myth of American Exceptionalism*," http://www. theatlantic.com/business/print/2009/03/book-review-the-myth-of-american-exceptionalism/9764/ (accessed October 17, 2012).

37. Martin Seymour Lipset, *American Exceptionalism: A Double-Edged Sword* (New York: W. W. Norton & Company, 1996), 75.

38. Justin Glow, "What Countries Have Universal Health Care?" http://www.gadling.com/2007/07/05/what-countries-have-universal-health-care/ (accessed July 3, 2012).

39. Ibid.

40. Martin Seymour Lipset, *op. cit.* (see reference 36).

41. Charles Lockhart, *The Roots of American Exceptionalism: Institutions, Culture, and Policies* (New York: Palgrave MacMillan, 2003), IX.

42. Ibid., 7.

43. Ibid.

44. Ibid., 22.

45. Michael Ignatieff, *American Exceptionalism and Human Rights* (Princeton, NJ: Princeton University Press and Princeton and Oxford, 2005), 21.

46. Unknown author.

47. Jed Lewison, "Jim DeMint Calls Obama the Most Anti-American President of his Lifetime." http://www.dailykos.com/story/2011/08/11/1005785/-Jim-DeMint-calls-Obama-the-most-anti-American-president-of-his-lifetime (accessed September 23, 2012).

48. Natsu Taylor Saito, *op. cit.* (see reference 12), 44.

49. Ibid.

50. George Lakoff and the RockRidge Institute, *Thinking Points: Communicating Our American Values and Vision* (New York: Farrar, Straus and Giroux, 2006), 53.

51. Ibid., 87.

52. Ibid.

53. David M. Berman, "Obama Wins—Liberty Loses." http://newhampshirefreepress.com/node/261 (accessed December 12, 2012).

54. George Lakoff, *The Political Mind: Why You Can't Understand 21st-Century American Politics with an 18th-Century Brain* (New York: Penguin Group, 2008), 53.

55. Ibid.

56. Larry S. Temkin, "Inequality." *Philosophy and Public Affairs* 15, no. 2 (1986): 99-121.

57. George Lakoff, *op. cit.* (see reference 54), 53.

58. John R. Talbott, *Obamanomics: How Bottom-Up Economic Prosperity Will Replace Trickle-Down Economics* (New York: A Seven Stories Press, 2008), 18.

59. Ibid.

60. Ibid.

61. Ibid., 18–19.

62. Ibid.

63. Ibid., 31.

64. Ibid.

65. Ibid., 15.

66. "Barack Obama on Education." http://www.barackobama.com/issues/education/ (accessed June 4, 2012).

67. Ibid.

68. Ibid.

69. Ibid.

70. Charles Lockhart, *op. cit.* (see reference 41), 180.

71. Ibid.

72. Barack Obama, *The Audacity of Hope: Thoughts on Reclaiming the American Dream*, (New York: Three Rivers Press, 2006), 55.

73. Ibid.

74. George Lakoff, *op. cit.* (see reference 53).

75. Barack Obama, *op. cit.* (see reference 71), 55.

76. Harold Hungju Koh, "America's Jekyll-and-Hyde Exceptionalism." In Michael Ignatieff (Ed.), *American Exceptionalism and Human Rights* (Princeton, NJ: Princeton University Press, 2005), 111–43.

77. Harry C. Boyte, *Everyday Politics: Reconnecting Citizens and Public Life* (Philadelphia: University of Pennsylvania Press, 2004), 17–18.

78. Sam Youngman, "Obama on Wall Street: A Vote for Reform is a Vote to Stop Tax-Payer Bailouts," http://thehill.com/homenews/administration/93773-obama-a-vote-for-reform-is-a-vote-to-stop-bailouts (accessed May 2012).

79. Ibid. (accessed January 1, 2012).

80. Ibid.

81. Harry C. Boyte, *op. cit.* (see reference 76), 21.

82. John R. Talbott, *op. cit.* (see reference 58), 178.

83. Ibid., 179.

84. Richard D. Heffner, *A Documentary History of the United States: An Expanded and Updated Seventh Edition* (New York: A Signet Book, Penguin Putnam, Inc., 2002), 307.

85. Jason Easley, "Rachel Maddow Calls Out the Republicans on Their Big Government Agenda" http://www.politicususa.com/en/rachel-maddow-gop-agenda (accessed August 25, 2011).

86. Ibid., 306.

87. Ibid.

88. Ibid.

89. Ibid.

90. Richard D. Heffner, *op. cit.* (see reference 84), 317.

91. Ibid., 316.

92. Ibid.

93. Heffner, *op. cit.* (see reference 84), 317.

94. Ibid.

95. "Congress Passes Wall Street Reform," http://my.barackobama.com/page/content/ WSRVictory?source=20100715_MS_act&keycode= (accessed February 2, 2012).

96. H. R. 3962. Passed by the 111th Congress, 1st Session. http://docs. house.gov/rules/ health/111_ahcaa.pdf

97. Douglas Birch, "US says 5 nations clear out weapons-grade uranium," http://articles.boston.com/2012-03-22/news/31225898_1_weapons-grade-uranium-low-enriched-uranium-nuclear-material.Associated Press (accessed March 24, 2012).

98. The PCTC Blog, "Updated and Expanded List of 212 Obama Accomplishments with Citations," http://pleasecutthecrap.typepad.com/main/what-has-obama-done-since-january-20-2009.html (accessed on March 23, 2012).

99. Sam Stein, "Obama's First 100 Days: 10 Achievements You Didn't Know About," http://www.huffingtonpost.com/2009/04/29/obamas-first-100-days-10_n_192603.html (accessed April 3, 2012).

100. Seymour Martin Lipset, *American Exceptionalism: A Double-Edged Sword* (New York: W. W. Norton, 1996), 37–38.

101. Richard D. Heffner, *op. cit.* (see reference 84), 320.

102. Harry C. Boyte, *op. cit.* (see reference 77), 34.

FIVE

The Re-Election of Barack Obama

"The People Spoke"

"Change will not come if we wait for some other person or some other time. We are the ones we've been waiting for. We are the change that we seek." —President Barak Obama

"Our lives begin to end the day we become silent about things that matter." —Martin Luther King, Jr.

THE IMPACT OF CHANGING DEMOGRAPHICS ON PRESIDENTIAL ELECTIONS

The previous chapters laid the foundation of how systemic racism, racialized rhetoric, GOP obstructionism and ideological warfare, a backlash of radicalism, white retribution, biased conservative media, and conservative voices of extremism constrained Obama's political agenda in his first term. Overcoming GOP myths of gutting welfare, raiding Medicare, government creating jobs, failure of the stimulus, and operating out of his league contributed to the re-election of Barack Obama, in spite of a 7.9 percent national unemployment rate. No president, according to political pundits and political scientists, racism or no racism, has won a resounding victory for re-election with an unemployment rate over 6 percent. Even though Obama accomplished much in his first term, an NBC Poll asked Americans what they believed were President Obama's greatest achievements: ending the Iraq War, killing Osama bin Laden, preventing middle-class tax hikes, and ending the Bush era tax cuts were Obama's chief accomplishments at the end of his historic first term.[1] Politically, Obama winning re-election can be added to these greatest achievements because his first term could have been easily dismissed as an election in reaction to Americans' dissatisfaction with the Bush years or an anomaly rather than Americans wanting to see real change. Obama's opponent, the conservative right, and the Tea Party adamantine should receive credit for Obama's re-election, thus making their contribution to American politics, African American history, and American history. Also in the tradition of Speaker John Boehner, when Congressional Republicans were swept into power and took back the House, he said he did not know what the Democrats did not hear during the 2010 election — "the American people spoke pretty loudly." Given Boehner's political stance since Obama won re-election, he did not hear that the people spoke pretty loudly when they kept Obama in the White House.

Obama's opponent, former Governor Mitt Romney, contributed to his resounding ability to win a second term due mainly to Romney's policies and Romney's "47 percent" remarks. Beyond this, Romney continued to wordsmith Obama's words by taking them out of context, such as "You didn't build that," but Obama actually said, "If you were successful, somebody along the line gave you some help. There was a great teacher somewhere in your life. Somebody helped to create this unbelievable American system that we have that allowed you to thrive. Somebody invested in roads and bridges. If you've got a business, you didn't build that. Somebody else made that happen." Romney went on to accuse Obama of apologizing for America as other conservatives have done throughout his first term, but there is no evidence to support this fact. Furthermore, Romney charged the Obama administration with creating anti-Israeli policies, and the Israeli government denied these false assertions. In fact, Obama was awarded the Israeli Medal of Distinction "for his unique and significant contribution to strengthening Israel and the security of its citizens" during his visit to Israel on March 21, 2013.[2] Obama is the first sitting U.S. President to receive such a distinction at a state dinner from an Israeli president. At the moment Obama was receiving this high civilian honor, Fox News was running a sound bite accusing Obama of being an enemy of the State of Israel. This is what Fox News was telling its low information conservative audience. Another example of Romney helping Obama to win re-election was when he kept running a false ad accusing Obama of eliminating the welfare work requirement, a political ideology ad that would anger Romney's white working class base, specifically against African Americans. Though Romney was warned that the ad was false, he did not pull it from airing over the network. Obama did not eliminate the work requirement for welfare recipients, but signed an executive order giving certain Republican governors the authority to improve the system to put more people to work who received state assistance. These are just a few false assertions Romney made against Obama, but there are many more false assertions, such as the jeep moving to China, that struck fear in an already fragile electorate by politicizing these falsehoods against Obama because he knew his white base would accept them at face value. Nonetheless, Romney was a man with an early twentieth-century mentality and "Even though his quest for the presidency was unsuccessful, his ideas about foreign policy, taxation, wealth inequality, and women's rights typified the year of 1912 as no one else has," writes Andy Borowitz of *The New Yorker*.[3]

While the GOP was declaring culture wars on the electorate, politicizing women's bodies, creating voter ID laws some say were "functionally equivalent to a poll tax,"[4] gerrymandering the electoral boundaries to gain more seats in national elections and re-elections, manufacturing crises, making political noise to divert the American electorate's attention away from the accuracy of Obama's achievements, becoming "a lagging indicator of public opinion,"[5] dismissing the impact of changing demographics on presidential and other national elections, losing political dividends, and limiting their political vision as once being touted as the party of the poor, African Americans, and the working and middle-classes during the nineteenth and early-twentieth centuries, these factors demonstrate a confluence of political subversion. With this said, the GOP no longer functions as a viable party willing to engage in honest intellectual debates or is able to draw Americans of color to the ideals of conservatism. In essence, the GOP has become a party of political and religious heretics and will excommunicate any of its members who are willing to work with or praise President Obama. On the other hand, Obama expanded his political vision and took advantage of the changing demographics and social media and had conservative political pundits and commentators scratching their heads when he took a lion's share of the electoral votes. They were left paralyzed in their tracks because they believed Mitt Romney would win the presidency. Consequently, Romney had prepared a victory speech, knowing he would clinch the victory. When Ohio, a critical swing state, gave Obama the necessary electoral votes to win re-election, Romney initially wanted a recount but reneged minutes later and Karl Rove did not know for about twenty minutes that Obama had won Ohio and re-election. Former Bush speechwriter David Frumm writes that the Republican Party is politically "isolated and [has] estranged itself from modern America."[6] Frumm goes on to say on MSNBC's *Morning Joe* a few days after the election that the GOP had been "fleeced, exploited, and lied to by a conservative entertainment complex." Simply put, the party is out of touch with electoral politics and the needs of modern America.

Historically, Obama has joined the exclusive list of three other presidents — Franklin D. Roosevelt, Dwight Eisenhower, and Ronald Reagan — by winning two terms with over 300 electoral votes and more than 50 percent of the popular vote for both terms.[7] The Obama team relied on the changing demographics to seek re-election while the GOP relied heavily on the old-order post-Reconstruction conservative party ideology to woo older whites, white males, and southern states, where some still believe in the ideology of the Confederacy and General Robert E. Lee, a post-war icon, who commanded the Confederate Army in the American Civil War to preserve the institution of slavery. Consequently, Obama won re-election largely with the help of African Americans, Latinos, Asian Americans, and women, but single women posed the most serious threat to the GOP. They are the fastest growing demographic, and a large number of women are graduating college, postponing marriage, entering the workforce in droves after college, and have issues and interests that the GOP refuses to address, making women a viable demographic and cultural force with which the party must contend. Women also have become political and cultural weak spots for the GOP. Even evangelical Christians helped the GOP to impart more cultural damage on women and Americans of color rather than egalitarian concerns, an American exceptionalism creed, which darkened their political vision, causing the party to embrace a plutocratic mentality that abhors individuals along the lines of race, class, gender, and sexual orientation. Evangelical Christians dismissed the concept of separation of state and church, went on a rampage pushing their form of Christian morality on to the electorate, and rhetorically condemning those who did not agree with their ideological practices.

Obama did not receive a majority white vote. America is a racialized country and views social phenomenon through a white racial frame, as suggested by social theorist Joe Feagin. Perhaps Obama received fewer white votes compared to the ethnic groups and women who voted for him because contemporary research indicates that many average Americans vote against themselves and their interests. Or perhaps white voters were motivated by racism and did not want an African American president occupying the White House. Nonetheless, the majority of these voters lived in southern states where the legacy of slavery and the Confederate ideals still exist.

The politics of obstructionism affected Obama's ability to bring about economic and social change that left the American people disillusioned. The GOP's radical vision to win the White House did not see the importance of changing demographics and the role it plays in the election process nor did it see the importance of meeting the average American's needs. Since Obama's initial platform of change was obstructed in his first term, he seized the opportunity to put forth a "forward" platform for re-election that relied heavily on the changing demographics of this country, which was partly the GOP's political waterloo. E. J. Dionne, a political commentator and Fellow at the Brookings Institution said this about the GOP's attitude toward Obama and Latino voters, who are part of the changing demographics in America:

> [The GOP] attempts to demonize President Obama and undercut him by obstructing his agenda didn't work. Their assumption that the conservative side would vote in larger numbers than Democrats was wrong. . . . Blocking immigration reform and standing by silently while nativist voices offered nasty thoughts about newcomers were bad ideas. Latino voters heard it all and drew the sensible electoral conclusion.[8]

People are naturally subjected to the dominating powers of the power elite and must fight to emancipate themselves from political-ideological colonization. The worldview of the conservative right today did not take into account the tenets of American exceptionalism, such as liberty, justice, and egalitarianism with respect to working Americans.[9] Nor did it take into account the changing demographics of this country. The party of obstruction had become too inclusive and divisive and began warring against the American electorate, although 48 percent of the electorate engaged in blind partisanship to vote against their own social, economic, and political interests during the 2012 election. Nonetheless, "the people spoke" at the ballot box and made a decision to re-elect Barack Obama for a second term, despite the GOP's efforts to make him a one-term president. Now that the election is over, a few younger GOP elected officials, specifically those of color, are speaking on the issue of party expansion, given the changing demographics and the voices of those who are demanding to be part of the national conversation. Sole reliance on an older white and male electorate will not win the White House for the old-order GOP in the presidential election. Even though the GOP did well during the mid-term elections and won sweeping victories from state houses to congress largely by white older voters, the party feels that this is not enough.

No one knows better than Barack Obama that systemic racism and inequality are consummate cruelties in American society and obstacles to real change. And no one knows better than Obama that the GOP, the corrupting influence of money, big corporations, and banks tried to rig the game to defeat him and other top Democrats, such as Elizabeth Warren, from winning their elections. From a critical communication perspective, ideology tells us what is possible, what changes to public policy can or cannot be made and what constrains our political and social reality. A change in America's institutions means to socially and politically set free those Americans who are affected by draconian policies because of their race, class, and gender if true democracy and the legitimacy of American exceptionalism are to prevail. In this final chapter, I conclude that Obama and his ground troops relied on the changing demographics phenomenon and the politics of the future to get him re-elected. I also argue that it was through the collective action of "We the People" who understood that the U.S. ideals of freedom, liberty, and justice for all must be protected for all.

OBAMA'S VISION FOR MOVING "FORWARD": HOPE AFTER RE-ELECTION

Obama was clear about his vision for this country in his 2009 inaugural address when he said, "The time has come to reaffirm our enduring spirit; to choose our better history; to carry forward that precious gift, that noble idea, passed on from generation to generation: the God-given promise that all are equal, all are free, and all deserve a chance to pursue their full measure of happiness." In the words of Martin Luther King, Obama has not been "silent about things that matter." King fought for change, hope, and the possibility for the day when an African American or other Americans of color could ascend to the highest office of this land. King believed that it would take a new person with clean politics to bring about change in the national and international communities. If King were alive today, I believe he would describe Obama as one who is endowed with certain inalienable abilities, willing to take risks and stand up for what he believes is just with courage and conviction, has a new sense of dignity and destiny and self-respect, and is diplomatic and polite with a growing honesty.[10] Obama is well aware of the American traditions of justice and liberty. As a constitutional scholar and politician, he knows the importance of being treated as a full member of society, irrespective of race, class, and gender, with access to the same rights and privileges that the power elite enjoy and take for granted.

Obama's vision of hope and epochal change for moving America forward led him to run for the presidential office, which ultimately gave him victory for a second term. His vision for change focuses our attention on the fundamental values of fairness, justice, freedom, equality, integrity, security, and shared responsibility. He ran on a platform as a reformer, a transformer, and a nonpartisan politician whose desire was to pave the way for all Americans to have the opportunity to pursue their dreams and goals, as promised in the Declaration of Independence. Here, we are talking about opportunity made available to all Americans, whether or not some Americans take advantage of the opportunity to succeed. When Obama took the oath of office in January 2009, he stepped into the rubbish of a depressed economy and had to fight ideological warfares with Congressional Republicans, who from the beginning wanted to make him a one-term president. If the Congressional Republicans had not obstructed Obama from moving in the right direction in his first term, perhaps Obama would have been one of the most successful presidents in modern times because he wanted to be the president for all the people, especially for the working poor and middle class. A survey conducted by Stanford University in collaboration with *The Associated Press* and *Yahoo* suggests that support for Obama in his first term would have been six percentage points higher had he been white.[11] As a man of African ancestry, Obama understands the struggles of the working class, what Karl Marx refers to as the proletariat of society. With high unemployment overshadowing the mythical American dream, Obama knows that race, class, and gender discrimination; injustice, inequality, and sexual orientation have always been a problem in American society. But power, money, and a broken political system have put America on a path of destruction and the power derived of and by the people has been lost on elected officials.

REWRITING OBAMA'S POLITICAL SAGA: "WE THE PEOPLE"

Can Obama rewrite his political saga in his second term? What are the responsibilities of the American people to help him write this saga and fight for an electorate that gave him the political capital to fight unfairness, discrimination, and the radical politics that keep them divided? Obama's pragmatic ability to relate to and pursue the full humanity of the oppressed and form a "perfect union" between the oppressed and oppressor would require fellowship, shared responsibility, and solidarity between the two. However, Congressional Republicans have shown a willful lack of interest to compromise with Obama during his first term and tried to force a political waterloo upon him in order to win the White House. Towards the end of his first term, Obama began rewriting his political saga by communicating his policies and appealing directly to the people. A pragmatic, decisive, and astute Obama found his niche and communicated his accomplishments and "forward" vision to the electorate in the tail end of his first term.

In spite of Republican obstructionism, Obama made progress in many areas, as discussed in chapter 4. These areas include the economy, health care, human rights, education, governance, national security, military, veteran's affairs, foreign policy, energy and environment, disaster response, etc. Beyond this, Obama often put polite disagreement and pragmatism ahead of partisan politics and craftily operated within a hostile conservative political environment to achieve his progressive goals.[12] Obama also ranked number one on Forbes' most powerful list, among the world's most powerful and influential leaders.[13] Zbigniew Brzezinski, a political scientist and statesman, who served in the Carter administration, informs us that opinion polls show that most nation states view America more positively as a whole because of Obama's image and rhetoric of shared sacrifice.[14] Obama's background, perceived cosmopolitan outlook, and living in other parts of the world have given him a better grasp on cultural, religious, and educational differences in a world where demographics are changing.[15] Thus, he understands American exceptionalism in a much broader context, more than the credit he has been given by the conservative right. In fact, it appears that the conservative right does not fully understand American exceptionalism and has used it as a political talking point against Obama.

In spite of the racialized rhetoric, the American electorate listened to Obama. For example, during the debt-ceiling crisis in July 2011, Obama appealed to the people to contact their Congressional representatives to raise the debt ceiling and the people responded overwhelmingly. This was Obama's best option for rewriting his political saga, given the radical, partisan, and divisive politics of an extreme right ideology that took over the old-order Republican Party that tried to destroy his first term. Even in his second term, Obama can now feel free to appeal to the people should the conservative right try to block his political agenda. It was *We the People* who spoke and re-elected him, and it will be the people who can help him recapture his "forward" vision in his second term.

THE EMANCIPATORY GOALS: LIBERATING THE ELECTORATE

The lives of many working class Americans are destroyed because they are not armed with sufficient political knowledge to understand the economic crisis and the strident political discourse that has influenced them negatively. This obscures the true culprit of their problems: a radical conservative right. We can see that at least 50 percent of the American electorate emancipated themselves from partisan political ideology that helped them make more informed decisions in the voting booth. As a nation, the electorate may need to focus on three emancipatory goals: understanding and insight, critique, and education. When Americans are armed with sufficient political knowledge, they can link the power of judgment to urge social, economic, and political change given the changing demographics, independent of race, class, and gender. When radical politics and malefic rhetoric overshadow critical thought, the American people's political and social construction of reality dissolves into a world where tensions, conflicts, and contradictions are heightened.[16]

UNDERSTANDING AND INSIGHT

Understanding and insight are a type of "practical knowing, [and] seeing what is important."[17] Insight refers to Americans' ability to closely analyze the systems of relations that make political meaning possible such as individuals' gaining insight into how capitalism and the free market work for or against their interests.[18] Without insight, it would be impossible for working Americans to understand the workings of capitalism and how the power elite manipulate them in the name of "free market." Americans are powerless because the "impasse in which the nation finds itself stems directly from the American people's limited access to power—and their equally limited access to responsible sources of information about how the American economy works."[19] Jürgen Habermas argues that it is the "role of social and critical theorists to expose the interests behind knowledge and the knowledge that exists behind the interests."[20] American citizens have a Constitutional responsibility to acquire an understanding of our national polity and to execute the ideological power delegated to them by the U.S. Constitution.

The American electorate's political, economic, and social experiences are essential for understanding how the decisions of presidents, congressional members, the media, and the national polity affect their everyday lives. For working Americans, understanding, in this case, also means creating "insight" into the way the media distort and slant news stories in favor of the power elite and special interest groups over their own interests (see chapter 3). Even though the American electorate accepts these apparatuses, many of them minimally interrogate them intellectually. Perhaps Americans accept these apparatuses based on the assumption that the media, elected officials, and the power elite will automatically do what is in their best interests since they believe the media will engage in the objective reportage of news. *We the People* elected politicians to represent their interests. Instead, some elected officials, swayed by the corrupting influence of money and power, allow the power elite to tell people what is good for them, what is bad for them, and what is possible for them to have. In sum, working Americans have given in to biased media ideologies and their Congressional representatives have been given the green light to socially and politically construct a reality that benefits the power elite, a reality that shapes the attitudes of working Americans by manipulating their belief and value system to make them believe their elected officials have their best interests at the forefront. As discussed in chapter 3, the media have focused more attention on Obama's critics who level negative, coded racialized discourse against his ability to lead this country than on his achievements. The problem with this picture is that the media, especially the right-wing media, such as Fox News and Rush Limbaugh, have helped Obama's critics influence the electorate, playing on their fears and giving them the impression that Obama's economic policies are doing more harm than good.

A prime example of this impression is the state of the economy and the public's perception of blame, where Obama inherited a disastrous economy from the Republicans and had to shoulder the blame. As a side note, this is no new phenomenon. During slavery, when slave owners' children or other white citizens committed an infraction, the blame was put on the slave. This practice has become part of the experiences of African Americans and other Americans of color. During the Jim Crow era, African Americans were blamed and punished for white infractions. Historically speaking, the Rosewood Massacre and Tulsa Race Riot are examples of entire black communities being decimated because of false accusations by whites, even when white officials knew the truth. However, the economic crisis that Obama inherited was directly caused by the policies of Republican deregulation, which were put in place during the Clinton and Bush administrations.[21] Yet, Clinton has been heralded as producing millions of jobs and leaving the country in good economic shape, and the information about his cooperation with Congressional Republicans to deregulate and pass legislation that hurt the most vulnerable citizens received no attention. Unlike Clinton, Obama would not deregulate and was harshly punished by the conservative right with visceral racialized rhetoric, and at times, denounced in un-phallus ways to attack his manhood and leadership ability. On the other hand, it was Clinton's speech at the Democratic National Convention that informed millions of viewers that the economy Obama inherited could not have been turned around by him or any of his predecessors in the short time that Obama had been in office. Clinton went on to say that when he was president, those were different economic times. In fact, he said the old economy is gone, and Americans need to prepare themselves for a new economy that requires a different set of skills. Although the Clinton administration was beset with anti-government sentiments, he was not a president of color whose birth certificate, religious faith, and domestic and foreign policies were under constant scrutiny, called a socialist and un-American, and maliciously threatened with a political waterloo.

Consequently, it is up to the American people and political historians to judge Obama's legacy. To do this, the people need to gain critical understanding and insight into our political and social institutions. Working knowledge requires an immense amount of political and media facts to be investigated. For citizens to have this kind of knowledge, they would need to redouble their efforts to think about the values and aims they pursue, given these depressed political and economic times. First, the American people would need to acquire objective information about what the president is doing, why he is doing it, and judge his decisions based on the evidence and proposed outcome of his policies without relying on false analyses of his opponents. For example, Obama has ordered the White House to provide a website on all economic stimulus projects and spending.[22] This authorization was not done on this scale during previous administrations, but Obama wanted his administration to be transparent to the people. By doing so, this initiative on the part of Obama can empower the people to know how they are affected by the information revealed to them rather than relying on certain media outlets to provide them distorted information. Furthermore, the President could extend this process by giving monthly televised speeches from the oval office about what he is achieving on behalf of the American people. Reagan and Clinton used this strategy quite effectively. Second, Americans need to tune in to the president's messages and exercise their autonomous judgment, rather than putting their trust in the conservative right, specifically to interpret Obama's messages. For example, during the debt ceiling debate, Obama appealed directly to the people through a televised address to cut through the right-wing rhetoric and the people over-whelmingly responded to his message. Last, if Americans do not agree with the president, they can always send a collective message expressing their disapproval. Open communication would strengthen the democra-cy over the partisan politics, which dismisses either side without critical thought or reflection.

Gaining understanding and insight can also help working Americans influence their state and congressional representatives to make informed decisions about this country, their state, and the importance of interna-tional relations with other nation-states. Americans also need to acquire understanding and insight into the national polity, if they want to be informed about political issues that affect their livelihood. That is to say, they need to demand communication with their Congressional represen-tatives and senators. If their representatives are nonresponsive to their requests but only listen to big donors, then the American electorate can take action in the voting booth. For example, the whole nation saw a demonstration of Ohioans taking action against the radical policies of their governor who failed to listen to their concerns when they wanted to discuss Senate Bill 5 (SB 5), a piece of draconian legislation the Ohio State Assembly passed to dismantle unions. When the governor refused to listen, *We are Ohio*, union leaders, and Ohioans repealed the notorious SB 5 and the governor admitted that political officials should listen to the people.

If American citizens acquire emancipatory knowledge that is appro-priate for taking collective action against elected officials, this knowledge would lead to a transformed consciousness and political emancipation. Equipped with emancipatory knowledge, working class Americans, re-gardless of race, class, and gender could find ways to change the political and economic systems that render them invisible. As a start, they could set aside their differences, become more enlightened about politics, espe-cially when political decisions go against their interests, and will see how divisive partisan politics, systemic racism, sexism, and classism obstruct equality and justice for all.

CRITIQUE

Communication and political science scholars have stressed the impor-tance of marginalized society gaining voice and agency in the political arena.[23] Critique is one way to gain voice and agency. Critique simply involves holding the taken-for-granted social, political, and media cul-ture up for careful scrutiny to determine whose interests are being served or blocked in favor of the power elite. Political and economic forces result in the blockage of people's interests, repressions, and distorted communication.[24] Meaning structures are filled with the privileged interest of the power elite, and working class Americans are politically and economically oppressed by structures of power and domination.[25] From what Americans have recently experienced, they can see that their political and economic interests have been blocked, and they are constantly bombarded with sound bites of distorted communication. For example, when natural disasters such as wild fires, tornadoes, and oil spills destroyed lives and livelihoods, some Republican governors turned down federal support from the Obama administration, with only a few accepting the help, as victims looked on helplessly. As previously mentioned, the conservative right has expressed its disdain on Obama holding major corporations accountable for disastrous oil spills that destroyed the livelihood of working Americans living in the gulf region, and the conservative right apologized to BP. We can understand the conservative right's apologia and their reason to protect the interests of large corporations because some of these elected officials rely on campaign funds from large corporations and big banks to protect their interests of deregulation. This is the kind of critique the American people should engage. They should not take it for granted that their elected officials are concerned about their political and economic interests.

Another example is when former presidential candidate John McCain (R-Arizona) made it clear that he would do nothing to help homeowners save their homes and has consistently voted against mortgage protections and other steps to help consumers fight unfair credit terms.[26] McCain also voted against protections to curtail predatory lending practices, voted against a bill to overhaul mortgage lending practices of FHA, and voted against the Predatory Lending Consumer Protection and Truth in Lending Act.[27] During the 2012 primaries, former Governor Mitt Romney articulated a similar sentiment. If average working Americans were on the brink of losing their homes, Romney believed that the housing market should "bottom out to repair itself." Whether these economic problems originated in the financial irresponsibility of American citizens or in the pathologies of political and social institutions, the American people can learn to critique the actions and words of their representatives and hold them accountable for working against their interests.[28] After all, they are the people's representatives. The question over whose interests are served and whose interests are blocked catalyze political action and rational courses of action.[29]

As we have seen, the American electorate is beginning to take a more active role in critiquing the actions of elected officials. Those who fail or refuse to critique the actions of their elected officials are perhaps too loyal to their political party because they follow the traditions of previous generations. It is time for the American people to put a stop to the vitriolic racist, sexist, and classist rhetoric and prevailing ideologies, and take a hard look at what their elected officials are actually doing for them. If the

American people's interests are to reclaim the democratic ideals on which this country was founded, there needs to be a link between their collective thought, experiences, struggles, and voice. To this end, constructive critique of existing political regimes is necessary for the American people's continued political, social, and economic existence. The American electorate will have to act to initiate effective lines of communication for productive national conversation with their Congressional representatives. If the political process fails to work or if their representatives refuse to listen to them or take action, as evidenced by Occupy Washington D.C., the use of protests to reopen lines of communication may be the only option, which may result in the arrests of protesters to have their voices heard, if they are serious about changing the status quo.

EDUCATION

Education is very much a natural counterpart of understanding, insight, and critique and produces ways of seeing, thinking, and contexts for action. The majority of working Americans have yet to educate themselves on the relationship between capitalism and domination that comes in the guise of free market, which prevents moderate progressive and transformative change for the people.[30] There needs to be a major push for change among those in public service to educate the electorate. But the "corrupting influence of money" and radical politics hinder such a push.[31] Some Americans allow whatever little democracy they experience to elude them, producing in them lethargy about the economic, political, and social problems or the feeling that this is the natural order of things and nothing can be done. As Paulo Freire argues:

> Ignorance and lethargy are the direct product of the whole situation of economic, social, and political domination—and of the paternalism. Rather than being encouraged and equipped to know and respond to the concrete realities of their world, [individuals are] kept "submerged" in a situation in which such critical awareness and response [are] practically impossible. And it [becomes] clear . . . that the whole [political, economic, social], and educational system [are] . . . major instruments for the maintenance of a culture of silence.[32]

Education involves politicians, scholars, and educators forming new ways of helping average citizens "engage in productive and constructive conflict and participative decision-making" in the area of politics.[33] It can help citizens become active agents of their own political education rather than inactive spectators. Individuals who are educated in political understandings are persons who can act upon a situation rather than being acted upon. With proper education in politics, ordinary citizens can equip themselves with liberating knowledge and learn how ideological hegemony and power operate through the media, national polity, and distorted discourse. Education can liberate the electorate from deceptive political language that would negatively skew Obama's efforts, deny them access to voice, and constrain their voices from speaking in ways to be heard and understood.[34] When citizens take the time to understand their national polity and how the media and politicians influence them, we can say we have politically educated citizens.

If working Americans were challenged about their political knowledge, would they be able to communicate the way politics affects their lives and in what form? Would they be able to communicate who currently owns the political space? What is a citizen's role in sustaining democracy? Are citizens well versed in civic affairs and do they have the will to engage in civic action, if necessary? Does the average American citizen know the contents of the Declaration of Independence and the U.S. Constitution? We articulate a litany of questions about the kind of knowledge Americans need to effectively exercise their rights as citizens, but what is most important is that they need to take the role of *actor* rather than *spectator*. Working Americans must take action against the mechanisms of oppression. By doing so, they can give Obama a second chance to push their interests and to rewrite his political saga.

A NEW CIVIL RIGHTS MOVEMENT AND CHANGING DEMOGRAPHICS

The struggle for liberation does not come without sacrifice. Like the early colonists who fought for their freedom, today's working class Americans will have to constantly raise their voices in protest against an oppressive political system that is trying to ideologically enslave their minds with authoritarian conservatism that wants to maintain and reproduce the status quo. Since Obama was overwhelmingly elected for a second term, he has earned the political capital to protect the interests of those who elected him because the vulnerable sections of society are more important than a political party or its ideology that may act against the interests of the vulnerable.

Today, we can see Americans act in collective communal ways, much like those who participated in the civil rights movement of the 1960s, when oppressed groups fought for the freedom that dominant group members took for granted. One example of this new civil rights movement is when women spoke out against the policies of the conservative right at both the national and state levels to politicize their bodies. Many women argued that their bodies should not be legislated by a body of governing men and their rights trampled upon. Women's rights are a civil right for which they fought and won, and they were determined to retain power over that right. According to *MoveOn.org*, the GOP wanted to reduce women's access to abortions and redefine rape should a woman become impregnated, as a result of that rape. After a major backlash, Republicans wanted to change the legal term for victims of rape, stalking, and domestic violence to "accuser." But victims of other less gendered crimes, like burglary, would remain "victims." In some states, GOP proposed bills that would make it legal to murder doctors who provided abortion services. Consequently, Congressional Republicans passed HR 358, the "Protect Life Act" or "Let Women Die" bill that would permit hospitals to let a woman die rather than perform the necessary abortion to save her life.[35] Furthermore, Congressional Republicans voted for an amendment to cut all federal funding from Planned Parenthood health centers, one of the most trusted providers of basic health care and family planning. As single women fought for their rights to make their own health decisions, with Obama's support, they helped him rewrite his political saga. It portrayed him as the reasonable president whose concerns for the working poor, the middle class, racial minorities, and women were/are at the center of his agenda.[36]

As we have seen across the nation, the American electorate is beginning to repossess the political arena, learning the skills of political work in cooperation with others who are politically, economically, and socially unlike themselves.[37] Occupy Wall Street, Occupy College Campuses, Occupy the Capitol, union protests, and women on the move are fighting the good fight of political faith to retain their Constitutional rights, which is the beginning of another civil rights movement where Americans have joined forces on the political battlefield along race, class, and gender lines to exercise not only their God-given rights, but also the ideological power given to them by the U.S. Constitution. This is the beginning of a new civil rights movement because the voting rights of Americans of color, health decisions of single women, and labor rights, according to the Universal Declaration of Human Rights, Article 23,[38] of the 99 percent are being rolled back in the name of radical conservatism.

CONCLUSION

Obama's vision and audacity of hope to make "equality" change in the American system has been met with Republican obstructionism, ideological warfare, and biased media reporting that has contaminated the perceptions of an ill-informed and misinformed electorate. Had the Republicans and some Democrats cooperated with Obama to work on behalf of the American people to fix the economy, perhaps the Great Recession would not have affected a great number of America's working class. There is no doubt that systemic racism, sexism, and classism will continue to dominate and consume the lives of both the oppressed and oppressor if the status quo prevails. As Martin Luther King and his followers believed, the oppressed can no longer wait for the Establishment to create

a more egalitarian society, where social, economic, and political institutions should support the "U.S. ideals of freedom, liberty, and justice for
all." The burden will rest on the shoulders of African Americans, women,
and other Americans of color to stand up and say "no more" in the
fashion of the civil rights movement "to force large-scale changes in systems of oppression."[39] But systemic racism, sexism, classism, conservatism radicalism, and a broken political system cannot be addressed until
all working class American citizens understand that their interests are at
stake. The American electorate that live in "red" states have not fully
understood that they continue to vote against their own political and
economic interests and are unaware that they are in complicit with their
own oppression.

Understanding and insight, critique, and education are emancipatory
goals that every American should embrace to fight destructive ideological hegemony, systemic racism, sexism, classism, and economic domination by enabling them to critique the meaning structures that enslave
them. Going forward means that the American electorate should help
Obama achieve his vision of equality of opportunity. They can do this by
insisting that our national and state governments invest in its people,
infrastructure, job skills, education, public transportation, and basic research and development. With this said, the American people will not be
able to compete in the global economy that now requires a new set of
economic skills. The American electorate should also demand that both
political parties start thinking about the greater good of America and find
ways to resolve the nation's systemic problems to enable this country to
thrive again. These problems cannot be solved if our leaders see politics
as a contest for domination of the White House, the Senate, and the
Congress, and are less responsive to the needs of the people. Lawrence
Lessig, Professor of Law at Harvard University and author of *Republic
Lost*, informs us that Congress has "lost their focus on the job of governing so they can pursue their passion of beating the other party and to get
back into power. . . . What we have to do is begin to put pressure on
people inside of Washington to make it that they are responsive to all of
us and not to a tiny slice of us."[40]

People on both sides of the political aisle would like to move beyond
the partisanship of both parties. Early in Obama's first term, former First
Lady Laura Bush went against her own party and praised Obama's performance on *CNN's Live with Larry King*. She told King that Obama was
doing a good job under tough circumstances. Bush also indicated that she
did not think it was fair for Obama to be labeled a socialist and expressed
her disappointment with the intensely polarized nature of contemporary
American politics.[41] Building on Bush's sentiment, it is only through the
collective, nonpartisan action of our elected officials that the political
faith of the American electorate can be renewed in public life. This requires new politics in which the electorate can act together to reclaim

ownership of polite politics. And this is what Obama communicated to the American people. Obama has continued to argue that all Americans are in it together, should look out for each other, should be one another's keeper, should share a common purpose for everyone's good, and should work together. This political statement supports the new civil rights movement that speaks about changing the demographics of this country. As Obama reminded us in his State of the Union address:

> Our destiny is stitched together like those fifty stars and those thirteen stripes. No one built this country on their own. This nation is great because we built it together. This nation is great because we worked as a team. . . . As long as we're joined in common purpose, as long as we maintain our common resolve, our journey moves forward, and our future is hopeful, and the state of our union will always be strong.[42]

Only when the American people arm themselves with emancipatory knowledge and everyone in our democracy—the president, Congress, and the electorate—work together for change, we can reclaim our politics of hope for a more perfect union. With the re-election of Barack Obama, "We the People" have given him the opportunity to recapture his vision of hope to move the nation forward. "Americans who want to replace polarization with balance, extremism with moderation, obstruction with problem-solving, and blind partisanship with compromise needed Obama to win again. An Obama defeat would have empowered those whose go-for-broke approach to policies was largely responsible for the distemper of our public life and the dysfunction in Washington."[43]

NOTES

1. Hart/McInturff, "Study #13018: NBC News/Wall Street Journal Survey," http://msnbcmedia.msn.com/i/MSNBC/Sections/A_Politics/_Today_Stories_Teases/13018_JANUARY_NBC-WSJ.pdf (accessed February 1, 2013).

2. Yori Yalon and The Associated Press, "Israel to award Obama prestigious medal during visit," http://www.israelhayom.com/site/newsletter_article.php?id=7429 (accessed February 20, 2013).

3. Andy Borowitz, "Time Names Mitt Romney Man of the Year 1912," http://www.newyorker.com/online/blogs/borowitzreport (accessed December 20, 2012).

4. Ta-Nehisi Coates, "The Emancipation of Barack Obama: Why Reelection of the First Black President Matters Even More Than His Election," http://www.theatlantic.com/magazine/ archive/2013/03/the-emancipation-of-barack-obama/309237/ (accessed February 26, 2013).

5. Julian Epstein's interview with MSNBC Martin Bashir on March 1, 2013.

6. David Frumm, *Why Mitt Romney Lost and What the GOP Can Do About It* (New York: A *Newsweek* ebook, 2012), Electronic Kindle Edition, Paragraph 1, Location 61 of 705.

7. The Last Word with Lawrence O'Donnell, "Presidents Who Won with 50% of the Vote Twice" http://www.msnbc.msn.com/id/45755883/#49973743 (accessed November 26, 2012).

8. E. J. Dionne, Jr. "The inconvenient truths about 2012," http://www. washingtonpost.com/ opinions/ej-dionne-jr-the-inconvenient-truths-of-2012/2012/11/ 14/c3c1d452-2e96-11e2-beb2-4b4cf5087636_story.html (accessed November 22, 2012).

9. George Lakoff, *Moral Politics: How Liberals and Conservatives Think* (Chicago: The University of Chicago Press, 2002), 367.

10. "Open Mind with Dr. Martin Luther King, Jr., who shares his insights on The New Negro during a televised panel discussion." Black History, Volume 3, Disk 3. *Black History, Civil Rights Movement: From Civil War Through Today.*

11. Nichloas D. Kristof, "Racism Without Racists," http://www.nytimes.com/2008/ 10/05/opinion/05kristof.html (accessed March 25, 2012).

12. David Corn, *Showdown: The Inside Story of How Obama Fought Back Against Boehner, Cantor, and the Tea Party* (New York: William Morrow Publisher, 2012).

13. "Obama Tops Forbes' 'Most Powerful' List," http://www.newsmax.com/ Newsfront/obama-most-powerful-forbes/2012/12/05/id/466603. (accessed December 8, 2012).

14. Zbigniew Brzezinski, *Strategic Vision: America and the Crisis of Global Power* (New York: Basic Books, 2012), Kindle Electronic Edition, Paragraph 2, Location 1752 of 3355.

15. Ibid.

16. Henry A. Giroux, *Politics After Hope: Obama and the Crisis of Youth, Race, and Democracy* (Boulder, CO: Paradigm Publishers, 2010), 15.

17. Ibid.

18. Ibid., 82-88.

19. James T. Kloppenberg, *Reading Obama: Dreams, Hope, and the American Political Tradition* (Princeton, NJ: Princeton University Press, 2010), Kindle Electronic Edition, Paragraph 1, Location 50 of 3768.

20. Jürgen Habermas, *Stanford Encyclopedia of Philosophy* (2007), http://plato. stanford.edu/entries/habermas (accessed March 24, 2012).

21. James T. Kloppenberg, *op. cit.* (see reference 15).

22. "Jobs and The Economy: Putting America Back To Work," http:// www.whitehouse.gov/economy (accessed August 12, 2012).

23. Douglass Kellner, "Toward a Critical Theory of Education," http://www.gseis. ucla.edu/ faculty/kelllner/p. 7 (accessed July 7, 2011).

24. Stanley Deetz, *Democracy in an Age of Corporate Colonization: Developments in Communication and the Politics of Everyday Life* (Albany, NY: State University of New York Press, 1992), 86.

25. Ibid.

26. McCain's Record of Denying Assistance to Homeowners. http://wonk-room.thinkprogress.org/2008/03/25/mccain-housing-speech/ (accessed July 1, 2011).

27. Ibid.

28. Murray Edelman, *Constructing the Political Spectacle* (Chicago: University of Chicago Press, 1988), 3.

29. Ibid.

30. Stanley Deetz, *op. cit.* (see reference 20), 90.

31. George Lakoff and the Rockridge Institute, *Thinking Points (A Progressive's Handbook): Communicating Our American Values and Vision* (New York: Farrar, Straus and Giroux, 2006), 108.

32. Paulo Freire, *Pedagogy of the Oppressed* (New York: Continuum, 1997), 12.

33. Ibid.

34. Murray Edelman, *op. cit.* (see reference 24), 129.

35. "House Passes 'Let Women Die' Bill After Extremely Depressing Debate," http:/ /jezebel.com/5849839/house-passes-let-women-die-bill-after-extremely-depressing-debate (accessed May 18, 2012).

36. "US election: Barack Obama urges women to fight for their right to contraception," http://www.telegraph.co.uk/news/worldnews/barackobama/9265740/US-elec-

tion-Barack-Obama-urges-women-to-fight-for-their-right-to-contraception.html   (accessed May 19, 2012).

37. Harry C. Boyte, *Everyday Politics: Reconnecting Citizens and Public Life* (Philadelphia: University of Pennsylvania Press, 2004), 13.

38. The Universal Declaration of Human Rights, Article 23, http://www.un.org/en/documents/udhr/index.shtml#a23 (accessed May 9, 2012).

39. Joe R. Feagin, *Systemic Racism: A Theory of Oppression* (New York: Routledge, 2006), 323.

40. Lawrence Lessig, "Corruption Going On Behind Closed Doors?" http://www.aol.com/video/youve-got-lawrence-lessig/517320465/?icid=maing-grid7%7Cmain5%7Cvideo-module%7Csec3_lnk1%7C148042 (accessed May 31, 2012).

41. Zain Verjee, "Laura Bush Praises Obama, Bemoans Excessive Partisanship," http://www.cnn.com/2009/POLITICS/09/07/laura.bush/ (accessed July 23, 2011).

42. http://www.washingtonpost.com/politics/state-of-the-union-2012-obama-speech-excerpts/2012/01/24/gIQA9D3QOQ_story_4.html (accessed July 1, 2012).

43. E. J. Dionne, Jr., "The Case for Barack Obama," http://swampland.time.com/2012/11/01/the-case-for-barack-obama/ (accessed November 9, 2012).

Bibliography

Adesioye, Lola. "Why So Serious about Obama as Joker?" www.guardian.co.uk/ comments free/cifamerica/2009. Retrieved August 5, 2009.

Alexander, Michelle. *The New Jim Crow: Mass Incarceration in the Age of Colorblindness.* New York: The New Press, 2010. Kindle Electronic Edition, Paragraph 2, Location 115, 2847.

Allport, Gordon W. *The Nature of Prejudice.* Reading, MA: Addison-Wesley Publishing Company, 1979.

Alvarez, Alex. "Ann Coulter On Debate: Obama Looked Depressed, Could See 'Michelle Wanted To Go Home With Mitt.'" www.mediaite.com/tv/ann-coulter-on-debate-obamalooked-depressed-could-see-michelle-wanted-to-go-home-with-mitt/ . Retrieved 1/23/2013.

Austin, D. Andrew. "The Debt Limit: History and Recent Increases." fpc.state.gov/ documents/organization/105193.pdf. Retrieved 8/25/2012.

Babington, Charles. "Obama Wants Big 2012 Campaign Map, GOP Wants Small." *Huffington Post.* June 20, 2011. http://www.huffingtonpost.com/2011/06/20/obama-wants-big-2012camp_n_880205.html. Retrieved 7/8/2012.

Balkin, Jack M. "How Mass Media Simulate Political Transparency." www.yale.edu/ lawweb/jbalkin/articles/media01.htm. Retrieved 7/24/2011.

Barker, David C. *Rushed to Judgment.* New York: Columbia University Press, 2002.

Benen, Steve. "Embarrassingly Unpatriotic." *AlterNet.* February 14, 2009. www. alternet.org/blogs/workplace/126984/embarrassingly_unpatriotic:_conservatives_ who_wantthe_u.s._to_fail. Retrieved 6/26/2012.

Berman, David M. "Obama Wins—Liberty Loses." http://new hampshirefree-press.com/node/261. Retrieved 12/12/2012.

Bilotta, James D. *Race and the Rise of the Republican Party, 1848–1865.* Philadelphia: Xlibris, 2002.

Birch, Douglas. "US says 5 nations clear out weapons-grade uranium." articles.boston. com/201203-22/news/31225898_1_weapons-grade-uranium-low-enriched-uranium-nuclearmaterial.Associated Press. Retrieved 3/24/2012.

Blackistone, Kevin. "As Vanity Fair Cashes In, Tiger's Image Gets Tossed Into the Gutter." www.aolnews.com/2010/01/06/as-vanity-fair-cashes-in-tigers-image-crawls-into-the-gutter. Retrieved 1/12/2012.

Borowitz, Andy. "Time Names Mitt Romney Man of the Year 1912." http:// www.newyorker.com/online/blogs/borowitzreport/2012/12/time-names-mitt-rom-ney-man-of-the-year-1912.html. Retrieved 12/20/2112.

Boyte, Harry C. *Everyday Politics: Reconnecting Citizens and Public Life.* Philadelphia: University of Pennsylvania Press, 2004.

Bristor, Julia M., Renee Gravois Lee, and Michelle R. Hunt. Race and Ideology: African American Images in Television Advertising. *Journal of Public Policy & Marketing* 14, no. 1 (1995), 48–59.

Brittain, Becky. "Congressman Calls Obama a 'Tar Baby.'" www.blogs.cnn.com/2011/ 08/01/congressman-calls-obama-a-tar-baby. Retrieved July 5, 2012.

Brock, David. *The Republican Noise Machine: Right-wing Media and How It Corrupts Democracy.* New York: Crown Publishers, 2004.

Brooks, Roy L. *Racial Justice in the Age of Obama.* Princeton, NJ: Princeton University Press.

Broughton, Kris. "President Obama Chumps Donald Trump and the Birthers." http://bigthink.com/ideas/38111. Retrieved 9/11/2011.

Brown, Erica. "Congress Honors Slaves Who Built United States Capitol." www.thecincinnatiherald.com/news/2011-02-12/News/Congress_honors_slaves_who_built_United_States_Cap.html. Erica Brown is an NNPA Special Correspondent in Washington, D.C. See also 111th Congress 1st Session, S. CON. RES. 24. www.gpo.gov/fdsys/pkg/BILLS-111sconres24is/pdf/BILLS-111sconres24is.pdf. Retrieved 4/11/2012.

Brown, Gwen. "'A More Perfect Union': Barack Obama's Failed Apologia and Successful Use of Identity Politics." In Robert E. Denton, Jr., ed., *Studies of Identity in the 2008 Presidential Campaign*. Lanham, MD: Lexington Books, 2010.

Brzezinski, Zbigniew. *Strategic Vision: America and the Crisis of Global Power*. New York: Basic Books, 2012.

Buchanan, Patrick J. *Where the Right Went Wrong* (New York: Thomas Dunne Books: St. Martin's Griffin, 2005), 160.

Bunch, Will. *The Backlash: Right-wing Radicals, High-Def Hucksters, and Paranoid Politics in the Age of Obama*. New York: HarperCollins, 2010.

Byrd, Robert C. *Losing America: Confronting a Reckless and Arrogant Presidency*. New York: W. W. Norton & Company, Inc., 2004.

Burris, Val. "Reification: A Marxist Perspective," *California Sociologist* 10, no. 1 (1988): 22–43. www.uoregon.edu/~vburris/reification.pdf. Retrieved 11/16/2011.

Cannon, Carl M. "The Top 15 Winners and Losers of 2009," www.politicsdaily.com/2009/12/30/the-top-15-winners-and-losers-of-2009. Retrieved 1/4/2012.

Clifton, Jon. "Worldwide Approval of U.S. Leadership Tops Major Powers: U.S. also remains top desired destination for potential migrants." www.gallup.com/poll/146771/Worldwide Approval-Leadership-Tops-Major-Powers.aspx. Retrieved 4/5/2012.

Coates, Ta-Nehisi. "The Emancipation of Barack Obama: Why Reelection of the First Black President Matters Even More Than His Election." www.theatlantic.com/magazine/ archive/2013/03/the-emancipation-of-barack-obama/309237. Retrieved 2/26/2013.

"Congress—Job Rating." http://www.pollingreport.com/CongJob.htm. Retrieved February 12, 2012.

"Congress Passes Wall Street Reform." my.barackobama.com/page/content/WSRVictory?source=20100715_MS_act&keycode. Retrieved 2/2/2012.

Corn, David. *Showdown: The Inside Story of How Obama Fought Back Against Boehner, Cantor, and the Tea Party*. New York: William Morrow Publisher, 2012.

Covert, Tawnya Adkins and Philo C. Washburn. "Information Sources and the Coverage of Social Issues in Partisan Publications: A Content Analysis of 25 Years of Progressive and the National Review." *Mass Communication & Society* 10, no. 1 (2007): 67–94.

CNN's *Black in America* documentary. Aired in July 2008. See "Fox Attacks: Black America." Retrieved 8/3/2011.

Critical Assessments of Joel Augustus Rogers. www.africawithin.com/ bios/joel_rogers.htm. Retrieved 7/12/2011.

Crook, Clive. *The Myth of American Exceptionalism*. www.theatlantic.com/ business/print/2009/03/book-review-the-myth-of-american-exceptionalism/9764/. Retrieved 10/17/2012.

Daily Mail Reporter. "Tea Party takes on pro-union protesters as 70,000 demonstrators descend on Wisconsin Capitol in biggest rally yet." http://www.dailymail.co.uk/news/article-1358675/Wisconsin-Capitol-protests-Tea-Party-takes-70-000-pro-union-demonstators.html. Retrieved February 27, 2012.

Deetz, Stanley. *Democracy in an Age of Corporate Colonization: Developments in Communication and the Politics of Everyday Life*. Albany, NY: State University of New York Press, 1992.

Delgado, Richard. "Words That Wound: A Tort Action for Racial Insults, Epithets, and Name Calling," *Critical Race Theory: The Cutting Edge*. Philadelphia: Temple University Press, 1995.

Delgado, Richard, and John Stefancic. "Images of the Outsider in American Law and Culture: Can Free Expression Remedy Systemic Social Ills?" In R. Delgado (Ed.), *Critical Race Theory: The Cutting Edge*. Philadelphia: Temple University Press, 1995.

DellaVigna, Stefano, and Ethan Kaplan. "The Fox News Effect: Media Bias and Voting." *Quarterly Journal of Economics* 122 (August 2007): 1187–1234.

Dennis, Everette E. and Melvin L. DeFleur. *Understanding Media in the Digital Age*. New York: Allyn & Bacon, 2010.

Denton, Jr., Robert E., Jr. "Identity Politics in the 2008 Presidential Campaign: An Overview." In Robert E. Denton, Jr. ed., *Studies of Identity in the 2008 Presidential Campaign*. Lanham, MD: Lexington Books, 2010.

Devos, Thierry, and Mahzarin R. Banaji, "American = White," *Journal of Personality and Social Psychology* 88, no. 3 (March 2005): 447–66.

DiMaggio, Anthony. *When Media Goes to War: Hegemonic Discourse, Public Opinion, and the Limits of Dissent*. New York: Monthly Review Press, 2009.

Dionne, E. J., Jr., "The Case for Barack Obama." swampland.time.com/2012/11/01/thecase-for-barack-obama.Retrieved 11/9/2012.

———. "The inconvenient truths about 2012." washingtonpost.com/ opinions/ejdionne-jr-the-inconvenient-truths-of-2012/2012/11/14/c3c1d452-2e96-11e2-beb4b4cf5087636_story.html. Retrieved 11/22/2012.

Dowd, Maureen. "Tempest in a Tea Party." www.nytimes.com/2011/07/31/opinion/sunday/dowd-tempest-in-a-tea-party.html?_r=1&emc=eta1. Retrieved 1/5/2012.

———. "Not O.K. at the O.K. Corral." www.nytimes.com/2011/07/27/ opinion/27dowd.html?emc=eta1. Retrieved 7/21/2012.

Draper, Robert. *Do Not Ask What Good We Do: Inside the House of Representatives*. New York: Free Press, 2012.

Dubois, W.E.B. *The Souls of Black Folk*. College Station, PA: The Pennsylvania State University Press, 2006.

Duffy, Jim. "Mother Knows Best." *Johns Hopkins Magazine* (April 2005) . www.jhu.edu/jhumag /0405web/steele.html. Retrieved 9/29/2011.

Dunbar, Roxanne A. "Bloody Footprints: Reflections on Growing Up Poor White." In Matt Wray and Annalee Newitz, *White Trash: Race and Class in America*. New York: Routledge, 1997.

Dwyer, Devin. "GOP Gets More Positive Press Than Obama, Pew Study Finds," abcnews.go.com/blogs/politics/2011/10/gop-gets-more-positive-press-than-obama-pew studyfinds. Retrieved 12/18/2012.

Dyson, Michael Eric. "Barack Obama." *Nation* 285, no. 17 (2007): 22–23.

Easley, Jason. "Rachel Maddow Calls out the Republicans on Their Big Government Agenda." www.politicususa.com/en/rachel-maddow-gop-agenda. Retrieved 8/25/2011.

Economic Policy Institute: US Debt Deal Will Cost 1.8 Million Jobs. www.economy watch.com/in-the-news/economic-policy-institute-us-debt-deal-will-cost-1-8-million-jobs.0308.html. Retrieved 9/5/2011.

Edelman, Murray. *Constructing the Political Spectacle*. Chicago: University of Chicago, 1995.

———. *The Politics of Misinformation*. Cambridge, UK: Cambridge University Press, 2001.

Editorial, "Short Take: Wisconsin Recall Effort," *Wisconsin State Journal*. www.startribune.com/opinion/141237603.html. Retrieved 3/5/2012.

Elwell, Craig K. "Foreign Outsourcing: Economic Implications and Policy Responses." Congressional Research Service, The Library of Congress. fpc.state.gov/documents/organization/50272.pdf. Retrieved 1/23/2012.

Eskow, Richard (RJ). "Insanity: After the Big Crash, The GOP Wants to Deregulate … Again," ourfuture.org/blog-entry/2010083426/insanity-after-big-crash-gop-wants-deregulate-again. Retrieved 10/28/2012.

Fanon, Frantz. *Black Skin, White Masks*. New York: Grove Press, 1967.

———. "The Fact of Blackness." In David Theo Goldberg ed., *Anatomy of Racism*. University of Minneapolis: Minnesota Press, 1990.

Farber, Daniel A. and Suzanna Sherry. "Telling Stories Out of School: An Essay on Legal Narratives." In Richard Delgado ed., *Critical Race Theory: The Cutting Edge*. Philadelphia: Temple University, 1995.

Feagin, Joe R., Hernan Vera, and Pinar Batur. *White Racism: The Basics*, 2nd ed. New York: Routledge, 2001.

Feagin, Joe and Eileen O'Brien. *White Men on Race: Power, Privilege, and the Shaping of Cultural Consciousness*. Boston: Beacon Press, 2003.

Feagin, Joe R. *Systemic Racism: A Theory of Oppression*. New York: Routledge, Taylor & Francis Group, 2006.

———. *The White Racial Frame: Centuries of Racial Framing and Counter-Framing*. New York: Routledge, 2010.

Fears, Lillie M. "Colorism of Black Women in News Editorial Photos," *The Western Journal of Black Studies* 22, no. 1 (1998): 30–36.

First Confiscation Act of 1861. June 24, 2011. www.teachingamerican history.org/library/index.asp?document=557. Retrieved 2/4/2012.

Foner, Eric. *Reconstruction: America's Unfinished Revolution, 1863-1877*, New American Nation Series. New York: HarperCollins, 1988.

"Fox News Viewers Know Less Than People Who Don't Watch Any News: Study." http://www.huffingtonpost.com/2011/11/21/fox-news-viewers-less-informed-people-fairleighdickinson_n_1106305.html. Retrieved December 18, 2012.

Freire, Paulo. *Pedagogy of the Oppressed*. New York: Continuum, 1997.

Frumm, David. *Why Mitt Romney Lost and What the GOP Can Do About It*. New York: A *Newsweek* ebook, 2012.

Gane-McCalla, Casey. "Top 5 Fox News Uncle Toms." www.newsone.com/ nation/casey-ganemccalla/top-5-fox-news-uncle-toms. Retrieved 3/13/2013.

Giroux, Henry A. *Pedagogy and the Politics of Hope: Theory, Culture, and Schooling: A Critical Reader*. Boulder, CO: Westview Press, 1997.

Giroux, Henry A. *Politics After Hope: Obama and the Crisis of Youth, Race and Democracy*. Boulder, CO: Paradigm Publishers, 2010.

Glow, Justin. "What Countries Have Universal Health Care?" www.gadling.com/ 2007/07/05/what-countries-have-universal-health-care. Retrieved 7/3/2012.

Goff, Phillip A., Jennifer L. Eberhardt, Melissa J. Williams, and Matthew Christian Jackson. "Not Yet Human: Implicit Knowledge, Historical Dehumanization, and Contemporary Consequences." *Journal of Personality and Social Psychology* 94 (2008): 292–306.

Goldberg, David Theo. *Racist Culture: Philosophy and the Politics of Meaning*. Oxford: Blackwell, 1993.

Goodwin, Doris Kearns. *Team of Rivals: The Political Genius of Abraham Lincoln*. New York: Simon & Schuster, 2005.

Gramsci, Antonio. *Selections from the Prison Notebooks*. New York: International Publishers, 1971.

Griffin, Paul. *Seeds of Racism in the Soul of America*. Naperville, IL: Sourcebooks, Inc., 2001.

Gutmann, Amy and Dennis Thompson, *The Spirit of Compromise: Why Governing Demands It and Campaigning Undermines It*. Princeton, NJ: Princeton University Press, 2012.

Habermas, Jurgen. "Stanford Encyclopedia of Philosophy." http://plato.stanford.edu/ plato.stanford.edu/entries/habermas. Retrieved 8/3/2012.

Halperin, Mark, and John Heilemann. *Game Change: Obama and the Clintons, McCain and Palin, and the Race of a Lifetime*. New York: HarperPerennial, 2010.

Hamburger, Tom and Peter Wallsten. *One Party Country: The Republican Plan for Dominance in the 21ˢᵗ Century*. Hoboken, NJ: John Wiley & Sons, 2006.

Harms, John and Douglas Kellner. "Toward a Critical Theory of Advertising," *Illuminations*. http://www.uta.edu/huma/illuminations/kell6.htm.

Harris, Angela P. Introduction: Economies of Color. In Evelyn N. Glenn ed., *Shades of Difference: Why Skin Color Matters*. Stanford, CA: Stanford University Press, 2009.

Hart/McInturff. "Study #13018: NBC News/Wall Street Journal Survey." http://msnbcmedia.msn.com/i/MSNBC/Sections/A_Politics/_Today_Stories_Teases/13018_JANUARY_NBC-WSJ.pdf. Retrieved February 1, 2013.

Haymes, Stephen N. *Race, Culture, and the City: A Pedagogy for Black Urban Struggle*. Albany, NY: State University of New York Press, 1995.

Heffner, Richard D. *A Documentary History of the United States. An expanded and updated Seventh Edition*. New York: A Signet Book, Penguin Putnam, 2002.

Herman, Edward S. *Triumph of the Market: Essays on Economics, Politics, and the Media*. Cambridge, MA: South End Press, 1995.

Hersh, Adam, Michael Ettlinger, and Kalen Pruss. "The Consequences of Conservative Economic Policies." *Center for American Progress*. www.americanprogress.org/issues/2010/10/conservative_economics.html. Retrieved 6/26/2012.

"High Stakes Histrionics." seekingalpha.com/article/283896-high-stakes-histrionics retrieved 8/12/2011.

Hill, Shirley A. *Black Intimacies: A Gender Perspective on Families and Relationships*. Lanham, MD: AltaMira Press, The Gender Lens Series, 2006.

Historical Documents. Resource Bank. Rough Draft of the Declaration of Independence 1776. www.pbs.org/wgbh/aia/part2/2h33.html. Retrieved 11/19/2012.

Hodgson, Godfrey. *The Myth of American Exceptionalism*. New Haven, CT: Yale University Press, 2009.

hooks, bell. *Postmodern Blackness*. New York: Columbia University Press, 1994.

———. "Postmodern Blackness." In Patrick Williams and Laura Chrisman (eds.), *Colonial Discourse and Post-Colonial Theory: A Reader*. New York: Columbia University Press, printed in Great Britain, 1996.

———. "Straightening Our Hair." In Lester Faigley and Jack Selzer, eds., *Good Reasons with Contemporary Arguments*. Needham Heights, MA: Allyn & Bacon, 2001.

Hunter, Margaret L. *Race, Gender, and the Politics of Skin Tone*. New York: Routledge, 2005.

———. "The Persistent Problem of Colorism: Skin Tone, Status and Inequality." www.muse.jhu.edu.www.mills.edu/academics/faculty/soc/mhunterThePersistentProblemofColorism.pdf. Retrieved 4/4/2012.

"House Passes 'Let Women Die' Bill After Extremely Depressing Debate." http://jezebel.com/5849839/house-passes-let-women-die-bill-after-extremely-depressing-debate. Retrieved May 18, 2012.

Hunter, Tera W. "Putting an Antebellum Myth to Rest." www.nytimes.com/2011/08/02/opinion/putting-an-antebellum-myth-about-slave-families-to-rest.html. Retrieved 8/2/2011.

Huston, Warner Todd. "AP Confuses Criticism of Obama with 'Racial Slurs'" www.redstate.com/warner_todd_huston/2009/04/01/ap-confuses-criticism-of-obama-withracial-slurs/. Retrieved 3/30/2012.

Hutchinson, Earl Ofari. "Why So Many Whites Vote Against Themselves, www.huffingtonpost.com/earl-ofari-hutchinson/why-so-many-whites-vote-a_b_1342425.html. Retrieved 5/25/2012.

Ignatieff, Michael. *American Exceptionalism and Human Rights*. Princeton, NJ: Princeton University Press, 2005.

Ikemoto, Lisa C. "Story of African/Korean American Conflict." In Richard Delgado, ed., *Critical Race Theory: The Cutting Edge*. Philadelphia: Temple University Press, 1994.

Jefferson Monticello, "Thomas Jefferson and Sally Hemings: A Brief Account," www.monticello.org/site/plantation-and-slavery/thomas-jefferson-and-sally-hemings-briefaccount. Retrieved 11/16/2012.

Johnson, Jason. "Was News Anchor Rhonda Lee Fired Over Her Short Natural Hair? Not Likely." http://politic365.com/2012/12/12/was-news-anchor-rhonda-lee-fired-over-her-short-natural-hair-not-likely. Retrieved 12/13/2012.

Johnson, Sheri L. "Black Innocence and the White Jury." In Richard Delgado ed., *Critical Race Theory: The Cutting Edge*. Philadelphia: Temple University Press, 1995.

Keith, Verna M. "A Colorstruck World." In Evelyn N. Glenn ed., *Shades of Difference: Why Skin Color* Matters. Stanford, CA: Stanford University Press, 2009.

Kellner, Douglass. "Toward a Critical Theory of Education." gseis.ucla.edu/faculty/kelllner/p7. Retrieved July 7, 2011.

Kennedy, Helen. "Tea Party Express leader Mark Williams kicked out over 'Colored People' letter." http://www.nydailynews.com/news/politics/2010/07/18/2010-07 18_tea_party_express_leader_mark_williams_expelled_over_colored_people_letter. html. Retrieved 7/5/2012.

Kenski, Kate, Bruce Hardy, and Kathleen Hall Jamieson. *The Obama Victory: How Media, Money, and Message Shaped the 2008 Election*. New York: Oxford University Press, 2010.

Kloppenberg, James T. *Reading Obama: Dreams, Hope and the American Political Tradition*. Princeton, NJ: Princeton University Press, 2010.

Koh, Harold Hongju. "America's Jekyll-and-Hyde Exceptionalism." In Michael Ignatieff (Ed.), *American Exceptionalism and Human Rights*. Princeton, NJ: Princeton University Press, 2005.

Kornblut, A. E., and Krissah Thompson. "Race Issue Deflected, Now as in Campaign" September 17, 2009, p. 1, www.washingtonpost.com/wp-dyn. Retrieved 6/2/2012.

Kristof, Nicholas D. "Racism Without Racists." nytimes.com/2008/10/05/opinion/05kristof.html. Retrieved 3/25/2012.

Kuttner, Robert. *Obama's Challenge: America's Economic Crisis and the Power of a Transformative Presidency*. White River Junction, VT: Chelsea Green Publishing Company, 2008.

Lakoff, George. *Moral Politics: How Liberals and Conservatives Think*. Chicago: The University of Chicago Press, 2002.

———. *The Political Mind: Why You can't Understand 21st-Century American Politics with an 18th-Century Brain*. New York: Viking, 2008.

Lakoff, George, and the Rockridge Institute. *Thinking Points (A Progressive's Handbook): Communicating Our American Values and Vision*. New York: Farrar, Straus and Giroux, 2006.

Landston, John. *American Doctrine*. Boston: Almar Publishing Company, 1942.

Laquer, Walter ed. *A Dictionary of Politics*. New York: The Free Press, 1971.

The Last Word with Lawrence O'Donnell. "Presidents Who Won with 50% of the Vote Twice." http://www.msnbc.msn.com/id/45755883/#49973743. Retrieved November 26, 2012.

Lemelle, Jr., Anthony J. *Black Male Deviance*. Westport, CT: Praeger Publishers, 1997.

Lennard, Natasha. "The Real Problem With Buchanan Calling Obama 'Boy.'" www.salon.com/news/politics/war_room/2011/08/03/pat_buchanan_boy_comment. Retrieved3/30/2012.

Lessig, Lawrence . "Corruption Going On Behind Closed Doors?" aol.com/video/youve-got lawrence-lessig/517320465/?icid=maing-grid7%7Cmain57Cvideo-module7Csec3_ lnk17C148042. Retrieved 5/31/2012.

Lewison, Jed. "Jim DeMint Calls Obama the Most Anti-American President of His Lifetime." www.dailykos.com/story/2011/08/11/1005785/-Jim-DeMint-calls-Obama-the-most-anti American-president-of-his-lifetime. Retrieved 9/23/2012.

Lipset, Martin Seymour. *American Exceptionalism: A Double-Edged Sword*. New York: W. W. Norton & Company, 1996.

Locke, Alain. *The New Negro: An Interpretation*. New York: Arno Press, 1968.

Lockhart, Charles. *The Roots of American Exceptionalism: Institutions, Culture, and Policies*. New York: Palgrave MacMillan, 2003.

Lopez, Ian Haney. *White By Law: The Legal Construction of Race*, 10th Anniversary Ed. New York: New York University Press, 2006.

Lukas, Georg. "History and Class Consciousness: Reification and the Consciousness of the Proletariat." www.marxists.org/archive/lukacs/works/history/hcc05.htm. Retrieved 5/10/2011.

Luntz, Frank I. *What Americans Really Want . . . Really: The Truth About Our Hopes, Dreams, and Fears*. New York: Hyperion Publishers, 2009.

Lusane, Clarence. "Why Herman Cain Will Not Become President." www. progressive.org/mplusane062911.html. Retrieved 5/4/2012.

Marable, Manning. *How Capitalism Underdeveloped Black America*. Boston: South End Press, 1983.

Mass Media & Politics: "An Analysis of Influence." www.progressiveliving.org/mass_media_ and_politics.htm. Retrieved 1/26/2012.

Mauer, Marc. "The Crisis of the Young African American Male and the Criminal Justice System," prepared for the U.S. Commission on Civil Rights, April 15-16, 1999. www.sentencingproject.org/doc/publications/rd_crisisoftheyoung.pdf. Retrieved 3/25/2012.

Mays, Jeff. "How Racist Are You?" www.bvblackspin.com/2009/10/28/racist-test. Retrieved 6/5/2012.

McAuliff, Michael. "Darrell Issa: Obama's Government Most Corrupt in History." http://www.huffingtonpost.com/2012/04/24/darrell-issa-obama-corrupt-government_n_1449521.html. Retrieved 5/12/2012.

McChesney, Robert W. and John Nichols, *Our Media Not Theirs: The Democratic Struggle Against Corporate Media*. New York: Seven Media Stories, 2002.

McInturff, Hart. "Study #13018: NBC News/Wall Street Journal Survey." msnbcmedia.msn.com/i/MSNBC/Sections/A_Politics/_Today_Stories_Teases/13018_JANUARY_NBC WSJ.pdf. Retrieved 2/1/2013.

McMahon, Kevin J. *Reconsidering Roosevelt on Race: How the Presidency Paved the Road to Brown*. Chicago: University of Chicago Press, 2003.

Mendacity Index. "Cadillac Queens." www.washingtonmonthly. com/features/2003/0309. mendacity-index.html. Retrieved 1/4/2012.

Milton, Meltzer. *Thaddeus Stevens and the Fight for Negro Rights*. New York: T.Y. Crowell Co, 1967.

Mumby, Dennis K. *Narrative and Social Control: Critical Perspectives*. Newbury Park, CA: Sage, 1993.

Murray, Edelman. *The Politics of Misinformation*. Cambridge: Cambridge University Press, 2001.

Neiwert, David. *The Eliminationists: How Hate Talk Radicalized the American Right* (Sausalito, CA: PolitiPointPress, 2009), 12.

Netter, Sarah. "Racism in Obama's America One Year Later." www.abcnews. go.com/WN/Obama/racism-obamas-america-year/story?id=9638178. Retrieved 1/3/2013.

Neubeck, Kenneth, and Joel A. Cazenave, *Welfare Racism: Playing the Race Card Against America's Poor*. New York: Routledge, 2001.

Newton-Small, Jay. "The Weak Speaker: How a Failed Debt Vote Disarmed the Nation's Top Republican." news.yahoo.com/weak-speaker-failed-debt-vote-disarmed-nations-top111905041.html. Retrieved 6/28/2012.

Nocera, Joe. "Tea Party's War on America." www.nytimes.com/2011/08/02/ opinion/the-tea partys-war-on-america.html?emc=eta1. Retrieved 9/12/2011.

Novak, Tim. "Mass Media and the Concept of Ideology," Media and Social New School for Social Research, http://timnovak.org/uploads/Ideology_proofed.pdf. Retrieved 3/12/2012.

Obama, Barack Hussein. *The Audacity of Hope: Thoughts on Reclaiming the American Dream*. New York: Three Rivers Press, 2006.

————. *Dreams from My Father: A Story of Race and Inheritance*. New York: Crown Publishers, 1995, 2004.

————. "Text of Obama's Inauguration Speech." *Associated Press*. www2. hickoryrecord.com/content/2009/jan/20/text-obamas-inauguration-speech.   Retrieved3/19/2012.

"Obama State of the Union Address." washingtonpost.com/politics/state-of-the-union-2012obamaspeech-excerpts/2012/01/24/gIQA9D3QOQ_story_4.html.   Retrieved 7/1/2012.

"Obama Tops Forbes' 'Most Powerful' List." www.newsmax.com/Newsfront/obama-mostpowerful-forbes/2012/12/05/id/466603. Retrieved 12/8/2012.

"Obama, Barack, on Education." http://www.barackobama.com/issues/education, retrieve 6/4/2012.

"Older White People' Are Bigots, Says NBC News' Matthews." nation.foxnews.com/ chris   matthews/2011/01/17/older-white-people-are-bigots-says-nbc-news-matthews. Retrieved 2/23/2012.

Olorunda, Tolu. "FOX News Finds Another Way To Attack Black People." www.opednews.com/articles/FOX-News-Finds-Another-Way-by-Tolu-Olorunda-090309-876.html. Retrieved 12/20/2012.

————. "Fox News Is Using the Obamas to Perfect Its Racist Attacks on Black America."   www.alternet.org/story/123574/ fox_news_is_using_the_obamas_to_perfect_its_racist_attacks_on_black_America. Retrieved 1/19/2012.

Orbe, Mark P., and Tina M. Harris. *Interracial Communication: Theory Into Practice*. Florence, KY: Wadsworth Publishing, 2001.

O'Reilly, Bill. *Pinheads and Patriots: Where You Stand in the Age of Obama*. New York: HarperCollins, 2010.

O'Sullivan, John L. "The Great Nation of Futurity (1839)." web.utk.edu/~mfitzge1/ docs/374/GNF1839.pdf. Retrieved 1/1/2013.

Parrillo, Vincent N. *Understanding Race and Ethnic Relations*. Boston: Pearson, 2005.

PCTC Blog. "Updated and Expanded List of 212 Obama Accomplishments with Citations." pleasecutthecrap.typepad.com/main/what-has-obama-done-since-january-20-2009.html. Retrieved 3/23/2012.

Politicalticker. "www.politicalticker.blogs.cnn.com/2011/07/03/clinton-to-obama-dont-blink-ondebt-ceiling-showdown. Retrieved 10/3/2011.

Pollard, D. T. *Obama Guilty of Being President While Black*. Grand Praire, TX: Book Express, 2009.

Press, Bill. *The Obama Hate Machine: The Lies, Distortions, and Personal Attacks on the President—and Who Is Behind Them*. New York: Thomas Dunne Books, St. Martin's Press, 2012.

Price, Frederick K.C. *Race, Religion & Racism*, Volume 1. Los Angeles: Faith One Publishing, 1999.

Procter, David E., and Kurt Ritter. "Inaugurating the Clinton Presidency: Regenerative Rhetoric and the American Community." In Robert E. Denton, Jr., and Rachel L. Holloway (Eds.), *The Clinton Presidency: Images, Issues, and Communication Strategies*. Westport, CT: Praeger Series in Political Communication, 1996.

Ramazanoglu, Caroline, and Janet Holland. *Feminist Methodology: Challenges and Choices*. Thousand Oaks, CA: Sage, 2002.

Reed, Ismael. *Barack Obama and the Jim Crow Media: The Return of the Nigger Breakers*. Canada: Baraka Books, 2010.

Rep. Joe Wilson Yells Out "You Lie!" During Obama Health Care Speech (video). http:// www.huffingtonpost.com/2009/09/09/gop-rep-wilson-yells-out_n_281480.html. Retrieved 9/16/2012.

Ritter, Karl and Matt Moore. "Obama Wins Nobel Peace Prize." www. huffingtonpost. com/2009/10/09/obama-wins-nobel-peace-pr_n_314907.html. Retrieved 1/12/2012.

Rockler-Gladen, Naomi. "Antonio Gramsci's Theory of the Hegemonic Media," Hegemony and Media Studies. http://medialiteracy.suite101.com/article.cfm/hegemony_and_ media_studies. Retrieved 4/28/2012.

Rogers, Joel A. *Race and Sex*. St. Petersburg, FL: Helga Rogers, 1968.

Rothman, Noah. "Andrea Mitchell Visibly Shocked After Sununu Calls Obama 'Lazy,' Asks Him If He Would Take It Back," http://www.mediaite.com/tv/andrea-mitchell-visibly-shocked-after-sununu-calls-obama-lazy-asks-him-if-he-would-take-it-back/. Retrieved January 26, 2013.

Roy, Morris, Jr. *Fraud of the Century: Rutherford B. Hayes, Samuel Tilden, and the Stolen Election of 1876*. New York: Simon & Schuster, 2004.

Sage, Jud. "The Mississippi Black Code." http://chnm.gmu.edu/courses/122/recon/code.html. Retrieved 6/21/2012.

Saito, Natsu Taylor. *Human Rights, American Exceptionalism, and the Stories We Tell, Vol. 23*. (Atlanta, GA: *Emory International Law Review*, 2009), 49. See also http://www.law.emory.edu/ fileadmin/journals/eilr/23/23.1/Saito.pdf. Retrieved 1/1/2013.

Schechter, Patricia A. "The Anti-Lynching Pamphlets of Ida B. Wells, 1892-1920," dig.lib.niu.edu/gildedage/idabwells/pamphlets.html. Retrieved 3/18/2013.

Scott, Lilly. "Whose Economic Problem Is It?" www.americanprogress.org/issues/2009/07/whose_problem.html. Retrieved 5/14/2011.

Sessions, David. "Democrats Sense Racism Is Driving Obama Critics." www.politicsdaily.com/2009/09/14/democrats. Retrieved 9/16/2011.

Sherman, Jake, John Bresnahan, and Kenneth Vogel. "Sheldon Adelson Met with John Boehner,Eric Cantor." www.politico.com/story/2012/12/sheldon-adelson-met-with-john-boehner-ericcantor-84692.html. Retrieved 12/27/2012.

Shkury, Shimon. "Wage Differences between White Men and Black Men in the United States ofAmerica" (master's thesis, University of Pennsylvania, 2001), 22–23. www.lauder.wharton.upenn.edu/pages/pdf/ SimonShkury_Thesis.pdf. Retrieved 2/2/2012.

Steele, Shelby. "Why Black Messiah Obama Won't Win." aalbc.com/ reviews/shelby_steele.htm. Retrieved 9/27/2011.

Stein, Sam. "Obama's First 100 Days: 10 Achievements You Didn't Know About." www.huffingtonpost.com/2009/04/29/obamas-first-100-days-10_n_192603.html. Retrieved 4/3/2012.

Steinhauser, Paul. "CNN Poll: Which Candidate Cares More About You?" www.politicalticker.blogs.cnn.com/2012/08/26/cnn-poll-which-candidate-cares-more-about you. Retrieved 10/23/2012.

"Stereotypes of African Americans: Essays and Images." www.authentichistory.com/diversity/african/chickenwatermelon/index.html. Retrieved 2/8/2012.

Stewart, Jon, Ben Karlin, and David Javerbaum. *America: A Citizen's Guide to Democracy Inaction*. New York: Warner Books, 2004.

"STFU with the eliminationist rhetoric." 2politicaljunkies.blogspot.com/2011/01/stfu-witheliminationist-rhetoric.html. Retrieved 8/23/2012.

Sugrue, Thomas J. *Not Even Past: Barack Obama and the Burden of Race*. Princeton, NJ: Princeton University Press, 2009.

Sullivan, Lena. "'Now You Know Why There's No Birth Certificate' Jokes Tea Party Member in Racist Email Showing Obama and Parents as Chimps, www.allmetronews.com/politics/65356-now-you-know-why-there-s-no-birth-certificate-jokes-tea-party-member-inracist-email-showing-obama-and-parents-as-chimps.html#ixzz1MlR4Nl8w. Retrieved 10/3/2011.

Takaki, Ronald. *Iron Cages: Race and Culture in 19th Century America*. New York: Oxford University Press, 1990.

———. "A Different Mirror: A History of Multicultural America." *Revisiting America: Readings in Race, Culture, and Conflict*. Edited by Susan Wyle. Upper Saddle River, NJ: Pearson/Prentice Hall, 2004.

Talbott, John R. *Obamanomics: How Bottom-Up Economic Prosperity Will Replace Trickle Down Economics*. New York, NY: Seven Stories Press, 2008.

Tau, Byron. "Sununu Calls Obama Lazy, Disengaged and Incompetent." www.politico.com/politico 44/2012/10/sununu-calls-obama-lazy-disengaged-and-incompetent-137529.html. Retrieved 1/26/2013.

Temkin, Larry S. "Inequality." *Philosophy and Public Affairs* 15, no. 2 (1986): 99–121.

Thomas, Velma M. *Lest We Forget: The Passage from Africa to Slavery and Emancipation.* New York: Crown Publishing Group, 1997.

Tucker, Cynthia. "Herman Cain's Bigotry." blogs.ajc.com/cynthia-tucker/ 2011/ 07/22/ hermancains-bigotry/?cp=6. Retrieved 7/24/2011.

United Press International. "Clergy Arrested in Capitol Budget Protest." www. readersupportednews.org/news-section2/320-80/6811-clergy-arrested-in-capitolbudget-protest. Retrieved 4/5/2012.

Universal Declaration of Human Rights, Article 23. www.un.org/en/documents/udhr/ index.shtml#a23. Retrieved 5/9/2012.

"U.S. election: Barack Obama urges women to fight for their right to contraception," www.telegraph.co.uk/news/worldnews/barackobama/9265740/US-election-Barack-Obamaurges-women-to-fight-for-their-right-to-contraception.html. Retrieved 5/19/ 2012.

"U.S. House Speaker Boehner urges Senate to act on 'fiscal cliff.'" www.reuters.com/ article/2012/12/26usa-fiscal-boehner-idUSL1E8NQ7TJ20121226. Retrieved 12/27/ 2012.

Vigna, Stefano Della and Ethan Kaplan. "The Fox News Effect: Media Bias and Voting." *Quarterly Journal of Economics* 122 (August 2007): 1187–1234.

Walker, Alvin Wyman. "The Conundrum of Clarence Thomas: An Attempt at a Psychodynamic Understanding." http://www.raceandhistory.com/historicalviews/ clarencethomas.htm. Retrieved 5/13/2011.

Walsh, Eileen T. "Representations of Race and Gender in Mainstream Media Coverage of the 2008 Democratic Primary." *Journal of African American Studies* 13 (2009), 1210130. DOI 10.1007/s12111-008-9081-2.

Watson, Robert P. "Obama's Accomplishments to Date." Email, September 2011. See also http://curmilus.wordpress.com/2010/03/02/what-has-president-obama-accomplished-by-robert-p-watson-ph-d/. Retrieved April 12, 2010.

Weaver, David H., Doris A. Graber, Maxwell E. McCombs, and Chaim H. Eyal. *Media Agenda Setting in a Presidential Election: Issues, Images, and Interest.* New York: Praeger, 1981.

West, Cornel. *Race Matters.* New York: Vintage Books, 1994.

Wharton, Billy. "Obama's No Socialist. I Should Know." *The Washington Post*, March 15, 2009.

Wingfield, Aidia Harvey, and Joe R. Feagin. *Yes We Can? White Racial Framing and the 2008 Presidential Campaign.* New York: Routledge, 2009.

Woodson, Carter G. *The Mis-Education of the Negro.* Blacksburg, VA: Wilder Publications, 2008.

Worcester, Donald E. *Forked Tongues and Broken Treaties.* New York: Caxton Printers, 1975.

Yalon, Yori. "Israel to award Obama prestigious medal during visit." israelhayom. com/site/newsletter_article.php?id=7429. Retrieved 2/20/2013.

Youngman, Sam. "Obama on Wall Street: A vote for reform is a vote to stop tax-payer bailouts." thehill.com/homenews/administration/93773-obama-a-vote-for-reform-is-a-vote-to-stopbailouts. Retrieved 5/12/2012.

Zachary, Roth. "Conservative Activist Forwards Racist Pic Showing Obama As Witch Doctor." www.tpmmuckraker.talkingpointsmemo.com/2009/07/conservative_ activist_forwards_racist_pic_showing.php. Retrieved 10/2/2011.

Zain Verjee. "Laura Bush Praises Obama, Bemoans Excessive Partisanship." cnn.com/ 2009/POLITICS/09/07/laura.bush/. Retrieved 7/23/2011.

Zeitlin, Irving M. *Ideology and the development of Sociological Theory*, 6th Edition. Upper Saddle River, NJ: Prentice Hall, 1997.

Zeleny, Jeff. "Reid Apologizes for Remarks on Obama's Color and 'Dialect.'" www.nytimes.com/2010/01/10/us/politics/10reidweb.html. Retrieved 7/15/2012.

Zengerle, Patricia. "Analysis: Race Issues Beset Obama's 'Post-racial' Presidency." Retrieved 7/5/2012.

Zernike, Kate. "That Monolithic Tea Party Just Wasn't There." www.nytimes.com/2011/08/02/us/politics/02teaparty.html?_r=1&emc=eta1. Retrieved 9/12/2011.

Index

abortion, 146

accommodation, of Obama, xiv

accomplishments, of Obama, 124–126, 133

Adelson, Sheldon, 33

advertising: before election, 96; reelection and, 134; reification and, 95–96

affirmative action, 27

Affordable Care Act Bill, 56, 65, 112, 125

African Americans: after Civil War, 4; colorism among, 19–21; as colorism victims, 25; as conservatives, 67–70, 90, 93; disempowerment of, 8; economic prosperity of, 5; expectations for, 1; GOP related to, 6–7; hostility against, 5, 9; marriage for, 15, 17; as scapegoat, 141; welfare queens as, 10–11; white comparisons with, 9; white mobs against, 5

Ahmed, Akbar S., 79

Alexander, Michelle, 13

America: as demonstration, 109; polls on, 81, 82

American creed, 107, 108

American exceptionalism, 127; canonical commitments of, 107; change in, 111–112; conservatives and, 114; description of, 105; economic crisis and, 105; egalitarianism and, 116–118; endurance of, 112–113; failures of, 111–112; Hodgson on, 111; hypocrisy of, 111; individualism and, 108, 118–119; liberty and, 115–116; Lipset on, 112; Obama and, 113–114, 139; perspective for, 107; populism and, 119–120; Providence

and, 109; racism and, 108; roots of, 106; types of, 111; views on, 111–113

American Exceptionalism and Human Rights, 111

American Revolution, 106

Angles, Sharron, 88

appointments, 58

Aristotle, 106

Asians, 9, 24, 27, 109

attacks, on Obama, xiv, 34, 39

Audacity of Hope (Obama), 48, 119

Bachmann, Michelle, 17, 65, 83, 88, 89

backlash, political, 126–127

Balkin, Jack, 81

Barbour, Haley, 91

bargaining, collective, 99

beauty, colorism and, 19–20

Bernadotte, Jean Baptiste, 23

big government, xvii

Bin Laden, Osama, 55, 126

birther movement, 35–36

black church, 14; Wright from, 34, 70–71

black families, 12, 14; Bachmann on, 17; children of, 15, 17, 21; norms in, 15–18; slavery and, 17, 21; violence in, 14

Black in America, 93

black males: crime by, 11–12; employment for, 11–12; as fathers, 11; patriarchy of, 14–15; role models for, 11

blackness, 28, 32, 36, 69, 94

Black Skin White Masks (Fanon), 21

black stereotyping: colorism and, 23–24; Obama related to, 11, 34, 37, 67; welfare queen as, 10–11

black women: beauty for, 19–20; jobs for, 12; sexuality of, 21; in slavery,

18, 21, 28; as welfare queens, 10–11
Boehner, John, 33, 52, 59, 134
Boortz, Neal, 84
Borowitz, Andy, 135
Brewer, Jan, 36
Brock, David, 94
Broken, Stephen, 89
Brooks, Roy L., 15–16
Brown-Simpson, Nicole, 25
Brownstein, Ron, 89
Brzezinski, Zbigniew, 139
Buchanan, Pat, 34, 51
Bush, George W., 39, 48, 49, 122;
    administration of, 50–51, 51–52; tax
    cuts from, 59; working class under,
    97
Bush, Laura, 148

Cain, Herman, 69
Cantor, Eric, 2
Carter, Jimmy, 34, 122
Cebull, Richard, 39
change, 133; in American
    exceptionalism, 111–112; media as
    agent for, 97–99
changing demographics, 137, 147–149;
    critique in, 143–144; education in,
    145–146; GOP estrangement from,
    135; hope from, 138; insight in,
    140–143; Latinos in, 136–137; new
    civil rights movement from,
    146–147; obstructionism and,
    136–137; participation in, 140, 143;
    Romney related to, 134–135;
    understanding in, 140–143; women
    in, 136; working class in, 140
Charlotte of Mecklenburg-Strelitz, 22
Christianity, 136; slavery related to, 3
citizens, 140, 143
citizenship, 34, 35–36
Civil Rights Act (1964), 6
Civil Rights Movement, xvi;
    constraints and, 49–50; new civil
    rights movement, 146–147; Parks in,
    6; segregation and, 5
Civil War, 4
Clinton, Bill, 122; economic crisis
    related to, 49, 142; Obama
    compared to, 142; racism of, 34

Clinton, Hillary, 71
collective bargaining, 99
colorism, xvi; among African
    Americans, 19–21; beauty and,
    19–20; black stereotyping and,
    23–24; divisiveness of, 2; Obama
    related to, 19, 36–38; roots of, 18–21;
    in slavery, 21; systemic racism from,
    18; victims of, 25
communication, 142–143. *See also*
    media
community, 119
compromises, 50, 52, 55, 65; democracy
    as, 57; Republican Congress against,
    31, 139
Confiscation Act (1861), 4
conservative media. *See* media
conservatives, 100; African Americans
    as, 67–70, 90, 93; American
    exceptionalism and, 114; political
    discourse of, 90–92; rhetoric from,
    48; against working class, 52
Constitution, U.S., 59, 65, 73;
    egalitarianism and, 116; working
    class and, 108
constraints, xiv, xv, xvi; Civil Rights
    Movement and, 49–50; systemic
    racism related to, 63–65
corporations, 86, 120; GOP and, 51–52,
    51, 53; Obama on, 116; tax rates for,
    51–52, 51, 53, 54
corruption, 14, 33, 54, 66; liberty related
    to, 115; of Murdoch, 93
criminal justice system, 11–12; ICC,
    111; prison terms in, 12, 13; whites
    in, 12–13
critics, 87, 126, 126–127. *See also* media;
    Republican Party; *specific critics*
critique, 143–144
Cuba, 110
cultural deformation, 18

Dahler, Don, 93
debt ceiling, 96; appeal to citizens
    about, 140, 143; Tea Party and,
    60–61, 61
Declaration of Independence, 105, 106,
    113; indigenous peoples and, 108
definitions, xv–xvi

Delgado, Richard, 38
DeMint, Jim, 114
democracy: Aristotle for, 106; as compromises, 57; contradictions in, 105; liberty in, 115–116
Democratic Party, 6, 31; media against, 82. *See also specific Democrats*
demographics: presidential election and, 133–137; segregation and, 5. *See also* changing demographics
demonization, 4, 62, 66, 70, 74
Dionne, E. J., 136–137
discrimination: reification of, 19; as systemic racism, 4; terminology of, 9, 24, 28
Dodd, Maureen, 37
Dreams of My Father (Obama), 48
Dred Scott, 35
DuBois, W. E. B., xiii, 27
Dunham, Stanley Ann, 29

Eastwood, Clint, 81
economic crisis, 49, 52, 57; American exceptionalism and, 105; blame for, 141; Clinton, B., related to, 49, 142; debt ceiling in, 58–61, 61, 96, 140, 143; eliminationist and racialized rhetoric in, 80; obstructionism in, 73, 73–74; socialism and, 113; stimulus package for, xvii. *See also* Wall Street
economics, 124; from Jim Crow, 16; poverty in, 56, 59, 64; prosperity in, 5, 7, 120
Edelman, Murray, 86
education, 15, 125; accountability of, 117; in changing demographics, 145–146; for egalitarianism, 117; kindergarten, 118; of mothers, 117, 118; about politics, 142–143; technology and, 118
egalitarianism: for American Dream, 116; American exceptionalism and, 116–118; education for, 117; middle class and, 117; obstructionism and, 118; U.S. Constitution and, 116
election, 124, 138; advertising before, 96; presidential, demographics and, 133–137. *See also* reelection
eliminationist, 52

eliminationist and racialized rhetoric, xvi, 80, 100
eliminationist rhetoric, 87, 88–89, 89
Elizabeth II (queen), 22
employment. *See* jobs
Erickson, Erick, 89
ethics, 125
Europeans, 22–23
exploitation: by power elite, 66, 67, 76n63; of working class, 62

false consciousness, 86. *See also* reification
Fanon, Franz, 21, 25, 26
Feagin, Joe, 9, 71, 136
Fears, Lillian, 20
filibusters, 62
Fineman, Howard, 67
"Food Stamp President", 7, 11, 62
Forrest, Nathan Bedford, 91
Fourteenth Amendment, 4, 7, 59, 115
Fox News, 2, 13, 81; bias from, 93–94; divisiveness of, 94; on protests, 91; terminology of, 91. *See also specific commentators*
free blacks, 4
Freire, Paulo, 145
Frumm, David, 135

Game Change (Halperin and Heilemann), 38
Gingrich, Newt, 8, 11, 62
Goff, Phillip A., 24
GOP. *See* Republican Party
governance, 125; big government, xvii. *See also* laissez faire; *specific leaders*
Gramsci, Antonio, 70
Griffin, Paul, 92

Habermas, Jürgen, 85, 141
Haley, Alex, 28–29, 39
Halperin, Mark, 38
Hayes, Rutherford B., 7
health issues: generations of, 14; Obamacare, 56, 65, 112, 125
hegemony, 70–73; definition of, 92; media racialized discourse and, 92
Heilemann, John, 38
Herman, Edward, 100

history, 3–6
Hodgson, Godfrey, 111
hostility, 5, 9
housing, 124; critique related to, 144
Huffington Post, 67
human rights, 110, 125; Universal
    Declaration of Human Rights, 147.
    See also racism; slavery
Hunter, Tea, 18
Hunter, Tera W., 43n69

Iacocca, Lee, 118
ICC. *See* International Criminal Courts
Ignatieff, Michael, 111
inaugural speech, 55, 124
indigenous peoples, 108. *See also*
    Native Americans
individualism: American
    exceptionalism and, 108, 118–119;
    community within, 119; cooperation
    for, 119; differences in, 118; success
    in, 118
insourcing, 54
intermarriage, 4
International Criminal Courts (ICC),
    111
interracial marriage, 25
Iowa Straw Poll (2011), 82
Israel, 134
Issa, Darrell, 14

Jackson, Michael, 26
Jefferson, Thomas, 18, 21, 108
Jews, 4, 23; sexual abuse of, 22
Jim Crow, 4, 11, 38; basis of, 8;
    economics from, 16
jobs, 57, 65; for black women, 12; GOP
    and, 52–53, 95; insourcing, 54;
    outsourcing, 51, 53; reification
    related to, 95; unemployment,
    51–52, 51, 133
Johnson, Lyndon B., 124
Johnson, Sherri, 12–13

Kasich, John, 99
King, Larry, 148
King, Martin Luther, Jr., 32, 64, 133,
    138, 147
Krugman, Paul, 117

Ku Klux Klan, 38, 71, 91

laissez faire, 121–123; New Deal and,
    123
lame duck session, 57, 126
land division, 7
Latinos, 136–137
leadership, 58; challenges to, 14; in
    polls, 81, 139
Lee, Rhonda, 20
Lemelle, Anthony, 8
Lessig, Lawrence, 148
liberty, 115–116
Limbaugh, Rush, 72, 83, 85, 113
Lincoln, Abraham, 31, 37–38
Lipset, Seymour Martin, 112
Livingston, Michael, 56
Locke, Alain, 32
Lopez, Ian Haney, 15, 23

Maher, Bill, 64
Manifest Destiny, 109, 110; hierarchy
    of, 109; O'Sullivan on, 109;
    Providence and, 109
marriage: for African Americans, 15,
    17; interracial, 25. *See also* black
    families
Marx, Karl, 86
Matthew, Chris, 81
Matthews, Chris, 88
McCain, John, 89, 144
McConnell, Mitch, 53, 60
media, xvii, 31, 79; acceptance of, 141;
    as agent for change, 97–99;
    democratic, 100; against Democratic
    Party, 82; divisiveness of, 83–84;
    false information from, 82–83; as
    Fourth Estate, 80; influence of,
    80–82, 82; power elite related to, 85,
    97–99; racialized discourse and
    hegemony by, 92; racialized rhetoric
    and, 82–85; role of, 97–98, 100;
    slavery in, 28–29; working class for,
    86–87, 97. *See also* polls; *specific
    journalists; specific media*
military, 126
Minnick, Walt, 38
miscegenation: of Europeans, 22–23;
    hypocrisy of, 23

Mississippi Black Code (1865), 4
Mitchell, Andrea, 84
moral mission, 97
"A More Perfect Union" speech
    (Obama), 1
Morning Joe, 135
MoveOn.org, 146
Moyer, Bill, 119
Mumby, Dennis, 18
Murdoch, Rupert, 93
Muslims, 35, 37, 49; respect for, 54–55,
    69

national identity, 6, 13
National Journal, 89
national security, 125
Native Americans, 29, 108
Nazi Germany, 4, 23, 63; sexual abuse
    in, 22
Neiwert, David, xvi
New Deal, 123
News of the World, 93
New Yorker, 37, 135
New York Times, 2, 52, 69
Nobel Peace Prize, 32

Obama, Barack Hussein. *See specific
    topics*
Obama, Barack Hussein, Sr., 29
Obamacare, 56, 65, 112, 125
obstructionism, xvi, 2, 33, 52–53, 82;
    changing demographics and,
    136–137; in economic crisis, 73,
    73–74; egalitarianism and, 118;
    against populism, 119–120; progress
    despite, 139
Occupy Wall Street, 79, 98, 120, 147
Occupy Washington D.C., 145
Ohio protests, 99, 143
"one-drop rule", 21, 28; as systemic
    racism, 4
O'Reilly, Bill, 13, 62, 89
O'Sullivan, John L., 109
outsourcing, 51, 53

Page, William Tyler, 107
Palin, Sarah, 65, 88, 89
Parks, Rosa, 6
patriarchy, 14–15

Pike, James Shepard, 35
Planned Parenthood, 62, 91, 147
Plessy v. Ferguson (1896), 5
poker game allegory, 16–17
political backlash, 126–127
political discourse, 90–92
politics, 148; backlash in, 126–127;
    disrespect in, 127; education about,
    142–143; empathy related to, 96–97;
    racism in, 71; reification and, 65–67;
    traditional, 55
polls, 31, 52, 57, 138; on America, 61,
    81; on budget cuts, 60–61, 61;
    leadership in, 81, 139; on Obama, 80,
    133, 139
populism: American exceptionalism
    and, 119–120; definition of, 119;
    Moyer on, 119; obstructionism
    against, 119–120; prosperity and,
    120
poverty, 56, 59, 64
power elite, 38, 47, 50, 59, 65, 110;
    allegory on, 16–17; critique of,
    143–144; exploitation by, 66, 67,
    76n63; media related to, 85, 97–99;
    special interests and, 85–87. *See also*
    corporations
pragmatism, 30, 54–55
privatization, 97
progressives, 96; for working class,
    96–97. *See also specific progressives*
proletariat, 56
prosperity: in economics, 5, 7, 120;
    populism and, 120
*The Prostrate State: South Carolina Under
    Negro Government* (Pike), 35
protection, by government, 96–97, 115
protests: Fox News on, 91; in Ohio, 99,
    143; against union busting, xvii, 99,
    143; in Wisconsin, 99
Providence, 109

Quayle, Ben, 14

race, 23
racism, xiii, 47; American
    exceptionalism and, 108; of Clinton,
    B., 34; generations of, 17; ideology
    hegemony and, 70–73; intellectuals

for, 92; in politics, 71; redemption
from, 2; rise of, xiii; working class
related to, 92. *See also* systemic
racism
radicalism, xiv, xv
rape, 21–22, 28, 146
Reagan, Ronald, 10–11, 73, 122
Reconstruction Act: land division in, 7;
passage of, 7
Reed, Ishmael, 2
reelection, xiii, xvii, 1, 133, 149;
advertising and, 134; hope after,
138; white votes in, 136
regenerative rhetoric, 54
Reid, Harry, 38, 60
reification: advertising and, 95–96; of
discrimination, 19; jobs related to,
95; politics and, 65–67; working
class and, 95
religion: Christianity, 3, 136; clergy
from, 56; Jews, 4, 22, 23; Muslims,
35, 37, 49, 54–55, 69; Wright in, 34,
70–71
repatriation. *See* tax rates
Republican Congress: approval ratings
of, 57; against compromises, 31, 139;
corporations and, 51–52, 51, 53;
filibusters by, 62; goals of, 53, 63;
jobs and, 51–52, 51, 52–53. *See also*
Tea Party
Republican Party (GOP), 49, 67, 90;
abandonment of, 7; African
Americans related to, 6–7;
corporations and, 51–52, 51, 53;
estrangement from, 135; jobs and,
52–53, 95; white vote for, 137. *See
also* media; *specific Republicans*
Republic Lost (Lessig), 148
responsibility: of government, 97; of
individuals, 108
retribution, xvi
Rogers, Joel Augustus, 22–23
Romney, Mitt, 33, 134–135; on housing,
144
Roosevelt, Franklin, 8, 48, 116, 124, 126;
New Deal from, 123
Roots: The First Generation, 28–29, 39
Rove, Karl, 81, 135
Ryan, Paul, 122

Santorum, Rick, 10
segregation, 18, 35; Civil Rights
Movement and, 5; demographics
and, 5; as systemic racism, 5
Senate Bill 5, 99
Sessions, David, 39
sexual abuse, 21–22, 28, 146
sexuality: of black women, 21;
miscegenation in, 22–23
Simpson, O. J., 25
slavery: black families and, 17, 21;
black women in, 18, 21, 28; blame in,
141; Christianity related to, 3;
colorism in, 21; contributions from,
3; free blacks after, 4; Jefferson
related to, 18, 21, 108; justification
for, 3; in media, 28–29; systemic
racism from, 3
small government, xvii
socialism, 127; definition of, 62;
economic crisis and, 113; filibusters
and, 62; Obama related to, 113–114,
126; social spending and, 62–63
Southern states, 6, 7
Sowell, Thomas, 16
Spitzer, Eliot, 93
State of the Union address, 57, 100, 127;
destiny in, 149; on technology, 52
Steele, Michael, 68
Steele, Shelby, 16, 31, 55, 69–70
Stevens, Thaddeus, 7
stimulus package, xvii
Sununu, John, 84
survey, 138. *See also* polls
systemic racism, 38; aggression
against, 63, 64; black males' crimes
from, 11–12; colorism from, 18;
constraints related to, 63–65;
definition of, xv; discrimination as,
4; as external factor, 16; focus on,
xiv; foundation of, 3; history of, 3–6;
in infrastructure, 8; land division in,
7; misinformation in, 9; modern-day
implications of, 8–9; "one-drop rule"
as, 4; rationale for, 108; segregation
as, 5; from slavery, 3

Taney, Roger, 35

tax rates, 59, 64–65; for corporations, 51–52, 51, 53, 54; working class and, 64

Tea Party, xiv, 37, 38, 48, 53; debt ceiling and, 60–61, 61; goals of, 66

technology, 52

terminology, xv–xvi; of discrimination, 9, 24, 28; of Obama, 96

Thernstrom, Abigail, 16

Thernstrom, Stephan, 16

Thomas, Clarence, 26, 67–68

Tilden, Samuel, 7

traditional politics, 55

transparency, 81, 142

Trump, Donald, 35

Tucker, Cynthia, 69

unemployment, 51–52, 51, 133

union busting protests, xvii, 99, 143

Universal Declaration of Human Rights, 147

Vanity Fair, 28

vilification, 66, 88

violence, xvi, 88–89, 89; in black families, 14; disempowerment for, 110; rape as, 21–22, 146

Walker, Alvin Wyman, 26

Walker, C. J., 20

Walker, Scott, 99

Wall Street, 98, 113, 120

Washington, Booker T., 68

Washington Post, 62

welfare, 14, 17; work requirement for, 134

welfare queen, 10–11

Wells-Barnett, Ida B., 22

West, Allen, 68

Wharton, Billy, 62

white mobs, 5

white radicalism, xv

whites: African Americans comparisons with, 9; in criminal justice system, 12–13; disempowerment of, 110; national identity as, 6, 13; sexual abuse by, 21–22, 28

white supremacy: basis of, 3; Confiscation Act as, 4; Ku Klux Klan, 38, 71, 91

white women, 22

Williams, Mark, 37–38

Wilson, Joe, 34

Wingfield, Aidia Harvey, 71

Wisconsin protests, 99

women: abortion for, 146; rape of, 21–22, 28, 146; as voters, 136; white, 22. *See also* black women

Woods, Tiger, 27–28, 72

Woodson, Carter G., 68

working class: under Bush, G. W., 97; changing demographics in, 140; conservatives against, 52; exploitation of, 11, 62; for media, 86–87, 97; political emancipation of, 140; progressives for, 96–97; racism related to, 92; reification and, 95; tax rates and, 64; U.S. Constitution and, 108. *See also* jobs

Wright, Jeremiah, 34, 70–71

Zoeller, Fuzzy, 27

About the Author

Mary L. Rucker is professor of communication at Wright State University. She is also division chair of the Communication Studies degree program. Rucker teaches organizational communication courses and research methods and conducts research in the areas of political communication and ideology, intercultural communication, and race, class, and gender. She has published widely in communication and interdisciplinary journals at the national and international levels. This book is among her most recent publications on politics and ideology.